Battle Atlas
of the
Falklands War 1982

by Land, Sea and Air

Battle Atlas of the Falklands War 1982
by Land, Sea and Air

Gordon Smith

Naval-History.Net

To my son Nick, from Britain, his wife Victoria,
from Argentina and their daughter Mica

May our two countries never fight again

First published by Ian Allan Ltd as "Battles of the Falklands War", 1989

Revised edition 2006

ISBN 978-1-84753-950-2

© Gordon Smith 2006

Published by Naval-History.Net, Penarth, UK
www.naval-history.net
naval-history@ntlworld.com

Cover illustrations: Sea Harrier on board HMS Hermes, courtesy, MOD, Navy
Jacket cover from "Battles of the Falklands War"

CONTENTS

Page

Introduction & Notes
I. Original Introduction & Note to this Edition ... 7
II. Reading Notes & Abbreviations ... 9

Argentine Invasion & British Response
1. Falkland Islands ... 11
2. Argentina ... 12
3. History of Falklands Dispute ... 13
4. South Georgia Invasion ... 14
5. Falkland Islands Invasion ... 17
6. Early Diplomatic Events ... 19

Argentine & British Units Taking Part
7. Argentine Armed Forces ... 22
8. British Task Force Build-up ... 24
9. Royal Navy Warships ... 27
10. Fleet Air Arm Squadrons ... 28
11. Royal Fleet Auxiliary Ships ... 29
12. Merchant Navy Ships ... 31
13. 3 Commando Brigade Royal Marines ... 33
14. 5th Infantry Brigade ... 34
15. Royal Air Force ... 35
16. Argentine Defences on Falklands ... 37

Early British Task Force Movements
17. Advanced Group Sails South ... 39
18. Carrier Battle Group Follows ... 40
19. Ascension Island ... 43

Preliminary British Operations
20. 3 Commando Brigade Approaches Ascension ... 46
21. Carrier Battle & Advanced Groups Join up ... 48
22. South Georgia Retaken ... 50
23. Amphibious Group Exercises at Ascension ... 52
24. ARA General Belgrano Sunk ... 55
25. Task Force in Action ... 57
26. HMS Sheffield Sunk ... 60
27. 5th Infantry Brigade Sails on QE2 ... 62
28. Pebble Island Raid by SAS ... 64
29. Amphibious Task Group Joins Task Force ... 66
30. Sea King-to-Chile Incident ... 68

Summary of Losses Inflicted and Sustained
31. Argentine Aircraft and Their Sucesses against British Ships ... 71
32. British Successes against Argentine Ships and Aircraft ... 72

Page

San Carlos Landings and Consolidation
33. Landings at San Carlos Water	75
34. Air Battles of 21st May 1982	77
35. Initial Moves Out of San Carlos	80
36. 5th Infantry Brigade Reaches South Georgia	82
37. "Coventry" & "Atlantic Conveyor" Sunk	85
38. 2 Para's Approach to and Battle for Darwin and Goose Green	87
39. 3 Commando "Yomps/Tabs" from San Carlos	90
40. 5th Infantry Brigade Lands at San Carlos	92

Approach to and Battle for Stanley
41. 3 Commando Reaches Stanley Defences	95
42. Final Task Force Moves	97
43. "Sir Galahad" & "Sir Tristram" Bombed	100
44. 3 Para's Approach to and Battle for Mount Longdon	103
45. 45 Commando's Approach to and Battle for Two Sisters	105
46. 42 Commando's Approach to and Battle for Mount Harriet	106
47. 2 Para's Approach to and Battle for Wireless Ridge	108
48. 2nd Scots Guards Approach to and Battle for Tumbledown Mountain	110
49. 1/7th Gurkhas Approach to Mount William	111

Victory, Surrender, Part of the Price Paid
50. Falkland's Surrender and Aftermath	112
51. Main British Task Force Returns Home	114
52. British Ships Lost & Damaged	117
53. British Aircraft Lost	119
54. Argentine Aircraft Lost	121
55. British Gallantry Awards	125
Bibliography	128

Index
People, Places and Events	130
Argentine and British Air, Land and Sea forces	136

I. ORIGINAL INTRODUCTION & NOTE TO THIS EDITION

ORIGINAL INTRODUCTION

The definitive battlefield atlas of the Falklands War will have to wait some years or even decades for the release of full British information and the publication and analysis of much more from Argentina. In the meantime, this one pulls together much of the data published in the U.K., not so much in greater detail, but as an accurate-as-possible, step-by-step picture of how the war progressed from incident to Argentine invasion and on to British response and victory.

Like many human events, the Falklands War can best be treated like a jigsaw puzzle, but one neither so big that most of the ships, land forces and aircraft squadrons taking part and British gallantry awards earned, cannot be included, nor so specialised that it cannot be treated as a total war of the conventional variety. In telling the story in the battlefield atlas form, the build-up is slow as the British Task force progresses south, but as the great logistics success the South Atlantic campaign was, it perhaps deserves to be told in this way. And like any jigsaw, a lot of pieces have to be sorted, so that first the border can be established before a small group is collected together here, and another there, until a fuller picture emerges.

Appendices - The appendices are included more for the sake of completeness, and thought was given to an additional one listing the British war dead by date and action. However many families and servicemen will not want to see their men and comrades listed yet again. So even though the dead and the wounded are a major part of the price paid for the liberation of the Falklands, it was decided to omit this information. However it should be remembered that what to many readers may be a fascinating military and logistics story, is, to more than 250 families in Britain (and over a thousand in Argentina) still a cause for mourning.

Information Sources - An early decision was taken to rely as far as possible on existing publications, and those used are listed in the Bibliography, but for some, a special word of appreciation is due.

Books - For the most comprehensive accounts of the war, "The Battle for the Falklands" by Max Hastings and Simon Jenkins and the later "Task Force" by Martin Middlebrook can not be bettered. "No Picnic" by Brigadier Julian Thompson covers the land campaign with both depth and feeling at all levels. "The Forces Postal History of the Falklands Islands and the Task Force" by John Davies, perhaps not surprisingly when it is realised that most participants received letters, is a real mine of information, and the more recently published "The Royal Navy and the Falklands War" by David Brown was most timely and helpful. But the all-round accolade for basic information on the air and to a slightly lesser extent, the sea and some land actions, and for its scholarship and helpfulness must go to "Falklands: The Air War" by members of the British Aviation Research Group. These include Rodney Burden, Michael Draper, Douglas Rough, Colin Smith and David Wilton. To them I am particularly grateful.

Other Publications - Some of the publications used as well as other sources of information were supplied by a number of people who I would like to thank, including Bill Burkett, Mr A L Carter, BP Shipping Ltd, Bosun R Cartwright RFA, Captain S J Crowsley, Gurkha Rifles, Colonel W T Dennison RE, Mardie Esterkin, P & O Group, Philip Forbes, Major (Retd) J I Grant, Scots Guards, Brigadier R J Lewendon (Retd) RA, John Miller, Captain A G Newing RM and Chris Newman.

Photographs - And for the photographs and permission to use them, Mr F R Andrews, Royal Fleet Auxiliary Service, Lieutenant Commander C W Beattie RN, RNAS Yeovilton, Matthew Little, Royal Marines Museum, Major (Retd) G Norton, Airborne Forces Museum, Alison Pickard, United Towing Ltd., Brigadier J F Rickett, Welsh Guards, Commander T J K Sloane RN, MOD (Navy), Group Captain G Thorburn RAF (Retd), MOD (RAF) and Major D R d'A Willis, 7th Duke of Edinburgh's Own Gurkha Rifles.

Special Thanks - Most importantly, my sincere thanks to Nicholas Smith, Michael Smith, Alex and Jane Welby, and David and Betty Chapman. Without their support at crucial stages, the book would not have been completed.

NOTE TO THIS EDITION

I am grateful to Ian Allan Ltd, London for originally commissioning and then publishing "Battles of the Falklands War" in 1989, which later became one of the foundations of www.naval-history.net, and thus made available to a far wider audience. It seems appropriate, now that nearly 25 years has elapsed since this sad breakdown in international relations, that a revised version should be issued.

No further research has been carried out on the original edition. Ideally the facts and figures and events should be cross-checked against more recent British publications and even more importantly, Argentine sources that are now available. However the following reviews may reassure the reader:

> "contributed tremendously to my knowledge of the war" - Francois Heisbourg, Director, The International Institute for Strategic Studies, London, November 1989

> "a concise and meticulous handbook describing the strategy, tactics and logistics....." - "Navy News", June 1989

> "may prove to be a most useful source.... maps are well presented.... (there are no) inconsistencies between text and maps - additional corroboration of the general accuracy and thoroughness of the author's research and collation..... So far as.... the Official Secrets Act permits - the detail is remarkably accurate" - Commander James McCoy RN, "Naval Review"

in 1999

..... from a British born journalist/researcher/writer in Argentina who has specialised in the Falklands Conflict, was recently editor of the English-language "Buenos Aires Herald", and was writing a PhD thesis on the diplomatic side of the war:

> "since 1982 I have visited the Falkland Islands over 15 times and on every occasion your book has been in my rucksack and has become something of my bible on the war. Over the years of research I have also had numerous opportunities to crosscheck the information there contained against the Argentine versions of the same events and have usually found that is stands up as a fair appraisal of the war even 17 years later."

and **in 2000**

"Battle of the Falkland's War" headed the list of recommended British-published books, described as "a very useful and detailed guide to the day-by-day development of the war", Argentine Army journal "Soldados", April 2000

Gordon Smith, 2006

II. READING NOTES and ABBREVIATIONS

Reading Notes

Distances - All distances are statute miles, unless stated otherwise.

Times - All times are local. The British forces operated on Greenwich Mean Time or "Zulu" time, 3 or 4 hours ahead of the Falklands and Argentina. Few books are consistent or clear on the subject, and there will no doubt be discrepancies in this one. However, the aim has been to use a local time equal to "Zulu" minus three hours for the Falklands.

Abbreviations

[a.] - Argentine (Argentine aircraft lost)
AA - anti-aircraft
AAC - Army Air Corps
AAM - air-to-air missile
AB - Able Seaman
ADC - Aide-de-Camp
AEM(L, M or R) - Air Engineering Mechanic (Electrical, Mechanical or Radio)
AFC - Air Force Cross
ammo - ammunition
ARA - Armada Republica Argentina (Argentine Navy)
Arty Bty - Artillery Battery
Asst - Assistant
ASW - anti-submarine warfare
[b.] - British (British aircraft lost)
BAS - British Antarctic Survey
Bde - Brigade
Bdr - Bombardier
BEM - British Empire Medal
Brig - Brigadier
Bty, bty - Battery, battery
c - circa
CAB - Battalion de Aviacion de Combate (Combat Aviation Battalion of Argentine Army)
CANA - Comando Aviacion Naval Argentina (Argentine Naval Aviation Command)
CAP - combat air patrol
Capt - Captain
casevac - casualty evacuation
CB - Companion of the Bath
CBAS - Commando Brigade Air Squadron
CBE - Commander of Order of British Empire
CBU - cluster bomb unit
Cdo - Commando
Cdo Bde - Commando Brigade (British 3rd)
Cdo Regt - Commando Regiment
Cdr - Commander
Cdre - Commodore
CGM - Conspicuous Gallantry Medal
Ch - chartered
CO, co - commanding officer

Coy, coy - Company, company
Cpl - Corporal
CPO - Chief Petty Officer
CV - aircraft carrier
CVBG - Carrier Battle Group
DCM - Distinguished Conduct Medal
DD - destroyer
DFC - Distinguished Flying Cross
DFM - Distinguished Flying Medal
DSC - Distinguished Service Cross
DSM - Distinguished Service Medal
DSO - Companion of Distinguished Service Order
ECM - electronic counter-measures
EEC - European Economic Community
Eng Off - Engineering Officer
EOD - Explosive Ordnance Disposal
Esc - Escuadrilla (CANA squadron)
EW - Electronic Warfare
F - Fighter
FAA - Fleet Air Arm (Royal Navy)
FAA - Fuerza Aerea Argentina (Argentine Air Force)
Flt - Flight
Flt Lt - Flight Lieutenant
FOB - forward operating base
FR - frigate
FSB - forward support base
GBE - Knight Grand Cross of British Empire
Gdsm - Guardsman
GM - George Medal
GPMG - general purpose machine gun (7.62mm)
grt - gross registered tonnage
H – helicopter or helipad
HAS. - anti-submarine helicopters (primary role)
HC. - assault helicopters (primary role)
HMS - Her Majesty's Ship
HQ - headquarters
HU. - assault/utility helicopters (primary role)
Ind Cdo Sqdn - Independent Commando Squadron
Inf Bde - Infantry Brigade (British 5th)

Inf Regt - Infantry Regiment
IPV - ice patrol vessel (HMS Endurance)
KBE - Knight Commander of Order of British Empire
KCB - Knight Commander of Order of the Bath
LAW - light anti-armour weapon (66mm)
L/Cpl - Lance Corporal
LCU - landing craft, utility
LCVP - landing craft, vehicle and personnel
Ldg - Leading
LS - Leading Seaman
L/Sgt - Lance Sergeant
LSL - landing ship, logistic
LST - landing ship, tank
Lt - Lieutenant
Lt Cdr - Lieutenant Commander
Lt Col - Lieutenant Colonel
LVTP - landing vehicle, tracked, personnel
Maj - Major
M & AW Cadre - Mountain and Arctic Warfare Cadre (Royal Marines)
MAW - medium anti-armour weapon (84mm Carl Gustav)
MBE - Member of British Empire Order
MC - Military Cross
MCMS - Mine Countermeasures Squadron
MEA(M or P) - Marine Engineering Artificer (Mechanical or Propulsion)
MEM(L or M) - Marine Engineering Mechanic (Electrical or Mechanical)
MEZ - maritime exclusion zone (excluded Argentine naval vessels from zone 200 nautical miles in radius from Falkland Islands as from 12th April 1982)
MID - Mention in Despatches
MM - Military Medal
Mne - Marine
MR - maritime reconnaissance
MVO - Member of Royal Victorian Order
NAS - Naval Air Squadron
NATO - North Atlantic Treaty Organisation
NCO - non-commissioned officer
NGFO - Naval Gunfire Forward Observer
NP - Naval Party
OAS - Organisation of American States
OBE - Officer of British Empire Order
Off - Officer
Para - Parachute Battalion
paras - paratroopers
PNA - Prefectura Naval Argentina (Argentine Coastguard)
PO - Petty Officer
post - posthumous
POW - prisoner-of-war
Pte - Private
PTI - Physical Training Instructor
QGM - Queen's Gallantry Medal
RA - Royal Artillery

RAF - Royal Air Force
RAOC - Royal Army Ordnance Corps
RAPC - Royal Army Pay Corps
RAS - replenishment-at-sea
RCB - Red Cross Box (to north of Falklands)
RCT - Royal Corps of Transport
RE - Royal Engineers
Recon - Reconnaissance
Regt, regt - Regiment, regiment
REME - Royal Electrical and Mechanical Engineers
Req - requisitioned
RFA - Royal Fleet Auxiliary
RM - Royal Marine(s)
RMAS - Royal Maritime Auxiliary Service
RMP - Royal Military Police
RN - Royal Navy
RO-RO - roll-on, roll-off
RO(W) - Radio Operator (Warfare)
SAM - surface-to-air missile
SAR - search and rescue
SAS - Special Air Service
SBS - Special Boat Service
SC - Satcom (satellite communication)
Sgt - Sergeant
SN - Satnav (satellite navigation)
Sqdn, sqdn - Squadron, squadron
Sqdn Ldr - Squadron Leader
SS – submarine, conventionally-powered
SSM - surface-to-surface missile
SSN – submarine, nuclear-powered
Stuft – ships(s) taken up from trade
STWS - ships torpedo weapon system
Sub Lt - Sub Lieutenant
TB - Torpedo Bomber
TEZ - total exclusion zone (excluded all Argentine vessels and aircraft from zone 200 nautical miles in radius from the Falkland Islands as from 30th April 1982; and outside 12 nautical mile zone from Argentine coast from 7th May)
TF - Task Force
TG - Task Group
TRALA - Tug, Repair and Logistic Area (to east of Falklands)
UK - United Kingdom
UN - United Nations
US - United States
UXB - unexploded bomb
vertrep - vertical replenishment (by helicopter)
VC - Victoria Cross
WEA(-/App) - Weapon Engineering Artificer (including Apprentice)
WEM(O or R) - Weapon Engineering Mechanic (Ordnance or Radio)
Wing Cdr - Wing Commander
WO1/2 - Warrant Officer Class I/II

Argentine Invasion & British Response
(Parts 1-6)

Part 1. FALKLAND ISLANDS

Some 8,000 miles from Britain (7,000 nautical miles), nearly two-thirds the size of Wales and often compared with the western isles of Scotland, the Falklands are the only major island group in the South Atlantic and lay 300 miles to the east of the Strait of Magellan.

Geography and Climate - The main islands of West and East Falkland and more than 100 smaller ones total over 4,700 square miles. They are chiefly moorland, treeless and the highest point is Mount Usborne on East Falkland. The climate is cool, damp and often windy with mean monthly temperatures varying between 49F in January (summer) and 36F in July (winter). Air temperature rarely exceeds 70F or falls below 12F.

Population and Economy - Total population at the 1980 census was 1,813 with just over 1,000 living in Stanley on the east coast of East Falkland, the capital and only town in the colony. The reminder lived outside in 'the Camp' where there were no roads, although some of the settlements had an airstrip. Most of the people are of British extraction and mainly engaged in farming the 600,000 sheep which occupy much of the land. In 1980, exports to Britain of wool and hides totalled £2.8 million and imports including food, manufactured goods, timber and machinery, £2 million.

Government - The Governor, (later Sir) Rex Hunt was president of the mainly nominated and advisory Executive Council and also of the partly elected Legislative Council which included six people's representatives. The Government balanced public revenue and expenditure at around £2.4 million in 1981/82. The Government also administered two dependencies:

South Georgia - 900 miles east-south-east of the Falklands, the 100 mile long island is completely mountainous, covered with glaciers and is likened to a partly submerged stretch of the Swiss Alps. With an area of 1,450 square miles, conditions are near Antarctic, and its only regular population was the 20 or so staff of the British Antarctic Survey based at King Edward Point near the old whaling station of Grytviken.

South Sandwich Islands - 350 miles further on is the start of this 150 mile long island chain which continues down to Southern Thule. Normally uninhabited and actively volcanic, the islands are totally Antarctic in climate.

Part 2. ARGENTINA

This huge country occupies most of the southern part of South America, and stretches a total of 2,300 miles from Bolivia in the north to near Cape Horn far away to the south. Just smaller than India and the eighth largest country in the world, Argentina totals 1,080,000 square miles. To the west, bordering the length of Chile are the Andes Mountains and to the east, down to the Atlantic are the great plains and pampas. Climate ranges from sub-tropical to cold temperate.

Population and Economy - Out of a 1980 population of 27,900,000, nearly 10 million lived in and around the seaport capital of Buenos Aires on the River Plate estuary. The great majority of the people are of European origin, mainly from Spain and Italy and the native Indian population is small. Language is Spanish, the main religion Roman Catholic and much of the country's culture is European Mediterranean in character.

Agriculture and livestock have long been an important part of the country's economy, and the meat-packing and food processing industries reflected this. Apart from oil and mineral production, there had been a considerable growth in recent years in the textile, plastics, machine tool, car and steel product industries. Exports to Britain in 1980 were worth £144 million, and imports £173 million. Communications by rail, road and airline, and through the medium of television and radio were well developed, and education compulsory from 6 to 13, with secondary education up to 17 plus in most of the big cities and towns. Literature flourished, and around 450 newspapers were published throughout the country.

History - The Spanish first went ashore in what was to become Argentina in 1515. Following three centuries of colonisation, a six year long struggle led by General Jose de San Martin brought independence in 1816. Then a long period of dictatorship by Juan de Rosas was ended in 1852, Buenos Aires became the seat of federal government, and the country developed rapidly. The military took over in 1930, Juan Peron was later elected president in 1945 with the strong support of his wife Evita who died in 1952, and he was then ousted three years later. Political and economic instability over the next eighteen years led to Peron being recalled from exile and becoming president again in 1973, but he died within a year.

Further difficulties brought about a bloodless military coup in 1976 along with repressive and often brutal government by a junta composed of the commanders of the armed forces. Lieutenant General Videla served as the first president for the five years until 1981, but after a few months, his successor Viola was moved out and replaced in December by Army General Leopoldo Galtieri, with the support of the other members, Air Force Brigadier General Basilio Lami Dozo and the Navy's Admiral Jorge Anaya.

As the 150th anniversary of British control over the Falkland Islands neared, the junta gave priority to the recovery of the Islas Malvinas, if necessary by force. Argentina would thus resolve what to them was a major and long-standing territorial dispute, but to Britain a distant and almost forgotten remnant of empire.

Part 3. HISTORY OF FALKLANDS DISPUTE

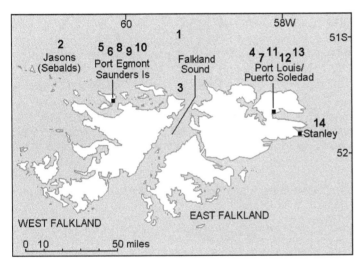

Summary of Early Falklands History

1. 1592 - British sighting by Capt Davis
2. 1600 - Plotted by Dutchman Sebald de Weert
3. 1690 - British landing by Capt Strong
4. 1764 - First French settlement by de Bougainville
5. 1765 - British landing by Capt Byron
6. 1766 - British settlement by Capt MacBride
7. 1767 - French settlement handed over to Spanish control
8. 1770 - Spain expelled British colonists
9. 1771 - Britain allowed to return, but Spain reserved right to sovereignty
10. 1774 - British colony abandoned
11. 1820 - Recently-independent Argentina took possession
12. 1831 - US declared the island "free of government"
13. 1833 - Britain took possession from Argentina
14. 1842 - Britain declared colonial administration

Argentina - continued to claim Falklands/Malvinas

First European Sightings and Landings - Claims for the first sightings of these uninhabited islands included the Italian Amerigo Vespucci in 1502 and the expedition of Portuguese-born Ferdinand Magellan in 1520. Thereafter three firsts are generally accepted - Capt John Davis made the first British sighting in 1592, Dutchman Sebald de Weert first accurately plotted the westerly Jason Islands in 1600, and the first British landing was made in 1690 on the north coast by Capt John Strong. He named Falkland Sound after Lord Falkland of the Admiralty.

Spanish Control - The 1713 Treaty of Utrecht confirmed Spain's continued control of her traditional territories in the Americas, including the offshore islands, but by now the French, many from St. Malo were visiting the islands from which they received the name Les Iles Malouines, subsequently the Spanish Islas Malvinas. In the 1740's, Admiral Lord Anson, back from his voyage around the world recommended them as a naval base because of their strategic position near Cape Horn.

French and British Settlement - The first settlement was established in 1764 at Port Louis in Berkeley Sound by the French under Antoine de Bougainville, who claimed the colony in the name of the King of France, a step which brought strong protests from allied Spain. Next year British Captain John Byron arrived to survey the north coast, went ashore on Saunders Island off West Falkland and in turn claimed the islands for Britain, naming Port Egmont before sailing away. Captain John McBride followed him there in 1766 to set up a permanent colony, and that same year tried to eject the French from Port Louis, but unknown to both of them, de Bougainville had already sold out to Spain.

Spanish Colony - De Bougainville formally handed over the French colony in 1767 and Port Louis was renamed Puerto Soledad. A Spanish governor was appointed under the Captain-General of mainland Buenos Aires, but both the British on West Falkland and Spanish on East Falkland carried on until 1769 when each tried to get the other to leave. In 1770, on orders from Buenos Aires, five Spanish ships with 1,400 troops arrived and the small marine garrison at Port Egmont was forced to leave in a move which nearly led to war between the two countries. After intensive negotiations Spain agreed in 1771 to Britain returning to Port Egmont, but reserved the right to sovereignty. She also claimed Britain had secretly agreed to pull out and indeed the settlement was abandoned three years later in 1774. Until the early 19th century, the Falklands remained the Spanish colony of Islas Malvinas.

Argentine Claim and Possession - Following independence from Spain in 1816, the future state of Argentina laid claim to the previous colonial territories, and in 1820 sent a frigate to take possession of the Falklands. In 1826, Louis Vernet of French origin established himself and a number of colonists at Puerto Soledad to develop fishing, farming and trade, and as governor from 1828 attempted to control the widespread sealing. Waking up to developments, Britain's consul general in Buenos Aires protested in 1829 against the appointment of a governor and re-asserted old claims to sovereignty.

United States and British Involvement - In 1831, after arresting American sealers accused of poaching, Louis Vernet sailed in one of them for Buenos Aires where the captain was to stand trial. In reprisal, the US warship "Lexington" arrived off Puerto Soledad, destroyed the fortifications, arrested some of the people and declared the islands free of government before sailing away. Argentina and the United States argued furiously over each other's high-handed behaviour, and next year a new governor was appointed but then murdered by rebellious colonists. As Argentine forces attempted to restore order, Royal Navy warships "Clio" and "Tyne" under the command of Captain Onslow arrived in early 1833, forced them to leave and claimed the Falklands for Britain.

Argentina protested strongly, but the British Government maintained that all rights to sovereignty were retained during the 1770 negotiations with Spain.

British Colonisation - Britain later started to settle the islands and formally declared a colonial administration in 1842, although Argentina continued to press her claim and from the 1960's on, with increasing vigour. Stanley was established in 1845. By this time, Britain's right to ownership rested mainly on her peaceful and continuous possession over a long period of time, and when serious negotiations began, they became dominated by the islander's desire to remain British.

Argentine Claims - After a period of Argentine lobbying, the United Nations passed Resolution 2065 in 1965 specifying the Falklands/Malvinas as a colonial problem, and calling on Britain and Argentina to find a peaceful solution. Talks continued on and off for the next seventeen years under both British Labour and Conservative Governments. Britain initially appeared flexible over the question of sovereignty, and by 1971 the Argentines were agreeing to concentrate on economic development and support, but thereafter, both sides' position hardened. The Argentines would accept nothing less than full sovereignty and in late 1980 the islanders rejected the one remaining solution of lease-back for a fixed period. On the road to war, Argentina set up a scientific base on Southern Thule in the South Sandwich Islands in 1976 and stayed put, and in 1982 her forces found themselves about to land on South Georgia and to invade and hold the Falklands themselves.

Part 4. SOUTH GEORGIA INVASION

Argentine Forces
Fleet transport Bahia Buen Suceso (3,100 ton, built 1951)
Task Force 60 (Capt C. Trombeta), icebreaker Bahia Paraiso (flagship - 9,600 tons, one Army Puma and one Alouette, 1978), frigate Guerrico (950 tons, Exocet, 1x100mm gun, 1978), approx 100 marines

British Forces
Ice patrol vessel Endurance, (3,600 tons, two Wasps, Capt N J Barker (CBE) RN), 22 Royal Marines

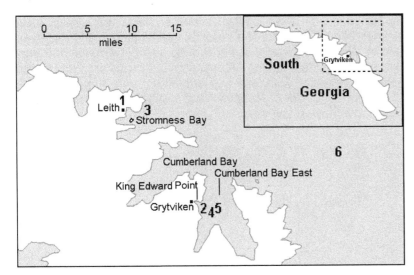

Summary of Pre-Invasion Events

1. 19th March - Bahia Buen Suceso at Leith
2. 24th - Endurance reached Grytviken
3. 25th - Bahia Paraiso off Leith
4. 31st - Royal Marines left at King Edward Point as Endurance headed for Stanley
5. 3rd April - Guerrico arrived with Bahia Paraiso in Battle for Grytviken
6. 3rd - Endurance returned later that day

Summary of Battle for Grytviken

1. Army Puma landed first Argentine Marines
2. On second flight from Bahia Paraiso, the Puma was hit and crashed across the Cove with the Marines on board
3. Guerrico sailed in to be hit by anti-armour weapons, and back out in the Bay opened fire.
4. More Argentine Marines landed from the Alouette and headed through Grytviken for the British positions

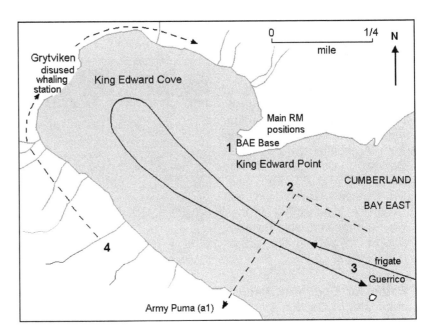

Argentine Claim - Argentina had long claimed South Georgia not so much in its own right, but as a dependency of the Falklands. The opportunity to exercise this claim was provided by Argentine businessman Constantino Davidoff, who contracted with the Scottish company of Christian Salvesen to clear away scrap whaling material littering parts of the island. Having agreed arrangements with the British Embassy in Buenos Aires, Davidoff chartered the fleet transport "Bahia Buen Suceso" to carry him and his workmen to South Georgia, and although there is no conclusive evidence the Argentine Government had deliberately planned what followed, the ship's illegal entry led to invasion. She arrived at Leith on Friday 19th March and started operations without observing the usual formalities of reporting first to the island's Magistrate, the base commander of the British Antarctic Survey (BAS) located at King Edward Point near Grytviken.

Incident - When a BAS team reached Leith that Friday 19th March, they found "Bahia Buen Suceso" in the harbour and workmen ashore with the Argentine flag flying. The incident was reported to Governor Hunt in Stanley, 900 miles away, who gave orders to the Magistrate that the Argentines must obtain proper authorisation. This they refused to do. Meanwhile ice patrol ship "Endurance" sailed in to Stanley on passage back to Britain and at the end of what was supposed to be her last season in the Antarctic.

Negotiations - Two days later, early on Sunday 21st March and at the start of nearly two week's diplomatic efforts to resolve the incursion, "Endurance", on orders from Fleet HQ at Northwood near London sailed for South Georgia. In addition to her own thirteen Royal Marines she took on board nine more from the small Falkland's garrison of Naval Party 8901. That same day - the 21st, BAS men set up an observation post overlooking Leith and saw the Argentine transport sail away leaving behind some of the civilian workers. "Endurance" reached Grytviken on Wednesday 24th at the start of a week of coastal patrols and replaced the BAS men above Leith with Marines flown in by Wasp. As negotiations continued between London and Buenos Aires, "Endurance" took no steps to remove the scrap men, but the Argentines had already ordered icebreaker "Bahia Paraiso" to sail to protect them, and by Thursday 25th, she had arrived at Leith. Approximately one hundred Marines went ashore under the command of Lt Cdr of Marines Alfredo Astiz and the icebreaker used her Alouette helicopter to shadow "Endurance" for the next few days.

Defence and Invasion - Almost a week later on Wednesday 31st March and as the Falkland's invasion threatened, "Endurance" landed her heavily-armed Royal Marine detachment at King Edward Point to prepare defences, and then unnoticed by "Bahia Paraiso", slipped out of Cumberland Bay that evening and headed for Stanley.

Two days later on news of Stanley's capture, "Endurance" reversed course, by which time frigate "Guerrico" had sailed from Argentina to join "Bahia Paraiso" as the hastily assembled TF 60. The other two frigates - "Drummond" and "Granville" - previously on their way to support "Bahia Paraiso" played no part in the events that followed.

Terrain typical of South Georgia. Tug "Salvageman" at Grytviken later in the war
(Courtesy - United Towing Ltd)

Battle for Grytviken, Saturday 3rd April - That morning "Guerrico" and the "Bahia Paraiso" under the command of Captain Trombeta and by now with many of the marines re-embarked from Leith, arrived off Grytviken. The Magistrate was called on to surrender by radio, but he passed authority for the island to Lt Mills, and at mid-day, with the Alouette going ahead to reconnoitre, "Guerrico" laying out in the Bay and the Puma about to land the first twenty troops near King Edward Point, battle commenced. As the troop-carrying Puma made her second trip in from "Bahia Paraiso" she was hit by small arms fire and badly damaged just off the Point with two Marines killed. Barely managing to stay airborne, she made it to the other side of King Edward Cove before crashing [first Argentine aircraft loss - a1]. The Alouette was also hit, but only lightly damaged and continued to bring in more Marines across from the base. Now "Guerrico" sailed in to support the landings and opened fire on the British positions, but it was her turn to be hit by hundreds of rounds of small arms fire as well as 66mm LAW and 84mm Carl Gustav anti-tank weapons before heading back out into the Bay.

Surrender - From there, she used her 100mm gun against Lt Mill's men as the Argentine Marines moved around the Cove, through the whaling station at Grytviken and closed in. Trapped, with one man wounded and having convincingly defended British sovereignty, he decided to surrender. All 22 Royal Marines as well as the 13 civilians at Grytviken were taken prisoner. "Endurance" arrived too late the same day to take part in the action, but from extreme range flew in a Wasp. Landing across Cumberland Bay from Grytviken, the crew could only observe the Argentines in possession of the scientific base.

She stayed on station for two more days, before sailing north early on Monday 5th April to replenish and meet the first ships of the British Task Force. The Royal Marines returned in triumph to Britain on the 20th April by way of Montevideo, and just six days later, the Argentine forces at Grytviken and Leith were themselves in British hands.

British Gallantry Awards
RM Detachment HMS Endurance - Defence of Grytviken
Lt K P Mills (DSC) RM
Sgt P J Leach (DSM) RM

Part 5. FALKLAND ISLANDS INVASION - Operation "ROSARIO"

2nd April 1982

Summary of Argentine Naval Forces

Task Force 40 - destroyers Santisima Trinidad, Hercules, frigates Drummond, Granville, submarine Santa Fe, transports LST Cabo San Antonio, icebreaker Almirante Irizar, Isla de los Estados.

Summary of Main Invasion Events

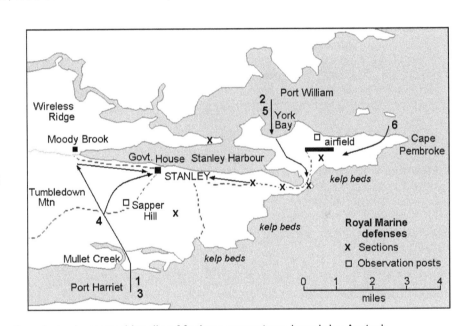

1. Late on 1st - small Buzo Tactico force from destroyer Santisima Trinidad to secure Mullet Creek
2. early on 2nd - small Buzo Tactico force from SS Santa Fe to check main landing beach at York Bay, northeast of Stanley
3. early on 2nd, 4.30am – more Buzo Tactico by helicopter from Almirante Irizar landed at Mullet Creek
4. Most of Mullet Creek landing force to Moody Brook, rest to Government House for attacks just after 6.00am
5. 6.30am - Cabo San Antonio started landing Marines over steep beach by Amtrak
6. 6.45am - more troops landed at airfield by helicopter from Almirante Irizar

Invasion Go-ahead - The build-up to invasion started when Britain protested about the landing on South Georgia. With talks on the future of the Falklands stalled, Argentina reacted strongly and by the 26th March, two frigates were on their way south, and more ships had put to sea ostensibly for exercises with the Uruguayan Navy. But it seemed that only now was the final decision taken to invade and they headed for Stanley although bad weather delayed their arrival. By Wednesday 31st March, British intelligence had to assume landings were imminent, Governor Hunt was warned, and next evening he announced over the radio that invasion was expected early on Friday 2nd April.

Defences - Before the broadcast took place, the defence of Stanley was already being put in hand by the small Falklands garrison of Naval Party 8901. Usually consisting of just 40 Royal Marines, the remaining members of the 1981/82 Detachment (others had left with "Endurance"), had only been relieved that day by Major M J Norman (MID) RM and his 1982/83 Detachment. Assuming the main landing would be near the airfield followed by an advance on Stanley, he deployed his 70 men accordingly, and positioned four delaying sections on the Stanley road ready to fall back on the main HQ at Government House. By the early hours of Friday, they were mostly in position and the small coaster "Forrest" was out in Port William on radar watch.

Landings around Stanley, Friday 2nd April - The plan was for the Buzo Tactico to attack both the Royal Marine barracks at Moody Brook and Government House to force a surrender, supported if necessary by men of the 2nd Marine Infantry Battalion landed from ships of Task Group 40.1. Once the airfield was in Argentine hands, the Army garrison would then fly in. The first landings were before midnight with a Buzo Tactico party going ashore from destroyer "Santisima Trinidad" to secure Mullet Creek, followed early on Friday morning by a smaller group from submarine "Santa Fe" to check out the main landing beach north of Stanley. Reports now started reaching the defenders about the presence of Argentine ships, and at 4.30am, more Buzo Tactico landed at Mullet Creek apparently from Sea King helicopters embarked on icebreaker "Almirante Irizar". Most of them headed for the by now empty barracks at Moody Brook while the rest passed quietly below Sapper Hill on their way to Government House. As they approached their objectives the destroyers and frigates of TF 40 took up support and escort positions and the LST headed in for the unguarded beach at York Bay.

Attacks - From 6.00am the main attacks and supporting landings got underway. The larger body of Buzo Tactico hit Moody Brook and then headed east for Government House which by then was under fire from the smaller group. Around 6.30am, the first of some 20 LVTP-7 Amtraks with 20 Marines each inside were landing from "Cabo San Antonio" and by 6.45am more troops were coming into the airfield by helicopter. As the off-balanced Royal Marine defenders fell back on Government House, one of the sections on the Stanley road stopped an Amtrak with anti-armour weapons.

British Surrender - With daybreak and Government House surrounded, under sniper fire and the Amtraks approaching, Governor Hunt attempted to negotiate. Faced with the overwhelming forces at Adm Busser's disposal, he ordered the Marines to lay down their arms, which they did at 9.30am without having suffered any casualties. The Argentines only admitted to one dead and others wounded. That evening, Governor and Mrs Hunt and most of the Royal Marines and the few men from "Endurance" were flown out. Major Norman and his men were back in Stanley 76 days later with J Coy, 42 Cdo RM.

Argentine Reinforcements - Before the surrender, the Army garrison, mainly from the 25th Infantry Regt was flying in. Another early arrival by Hercules was an AN/TPS-43F surveillance radar which became the centre of Argentina's command, control and communications structure at Stanley right through until the end of the war. Now Lieutenant General Osvaldo Garcia took over as Commander, Malvinas Operational Theatre, but as Britain's military response became clearer, the command was relocated to Argentina to cover the South Atlantic as a whole. Then on Wednesday 7th April, Major General Mario Menendez was appointed commander-in-chief as well as military governor, the same day Britain announced a 200 nautical mile maritime exclusion zone (MEZ) around the Falklands to take effect from the 12th April. By Monday 5th April following the landings, the invading warships were returning to port, although some of the naval transports were used in the build-up, and after the MEZ came into force the blockade was run by fleet transport "Bahia Buen Suceso" and merchantmen "Formosa" (12,800 grt) and "Rio Carcarana" (8,500grt). Most of the aircraft destined to be lost on the islands flew over although some of the helicopters were air-lifted, and Coast Guard patrol craft "Islas Malvinas" and "Rio Iguaza" reached Stanley for local duties.

Less than eight weeks after the invasion - ships of the Amphibious Group under attack on the 21st May 1982, including, centre, transport "Norland" and HMS Intrepid (Courtesy - MOD, Navy)

Occupation - The occupying forces were soon imposing their rules and regulations on the Islanders, many of whom got out of Stanley to the "Camp". Coasters "Forrest" (144grt) and "Monsunen" (230grt) were requisitioned together with a number of civil aircraft, some of which were lost in the subsequent bombardments. By the end of the month, as the British Task Force drew near, air raid precautions were introduced and a curfew and black-out was in force. A number of people were rounded up, some deported, and others confined, sometimes as at Goose Green in poor conditions.

Part 6. EARLY DIPLOMATIC EVENTS

to May 1982

Summary of Diplomatic Activity

UN HQ, New York
1st April - UK ambassador warns UN
2nd - Resolution 502 introduced
3rd - Security Council passed Resolution 502

EEC, Brussels
9th April - full support given to UK and sanctions announced against Argentina

UN HQ, New York
End of April - peace proposals launched by Secretary General

Peru
End of April - President Terry Belaunde initiated peace proposals

Gen Haig's Shuttle Diplomacy
(1) London - 8th April
(2) Buenos Aires - 9th/10th April
(3) London - 12th/13th
(4) Washington DC - 14th April
(5) Buenos Aires - 15th-19th

Main Falklands Area Operations
2nd April - Argentine invasion
1st May - British Task Force launched first attacks on Falklands
2nd May - Argentine cruiser General Belgrano sunk
4th May - British destroyer Sheffield hit by Exocet

British Diplomatic Response - In London, Mrs Thatcher directed Britain's diplomatic and economic response to events. Across the Atlantic, President Reagan tried to stay neutral and agreed to Secretary Haig starting his shuttle diplomacy.

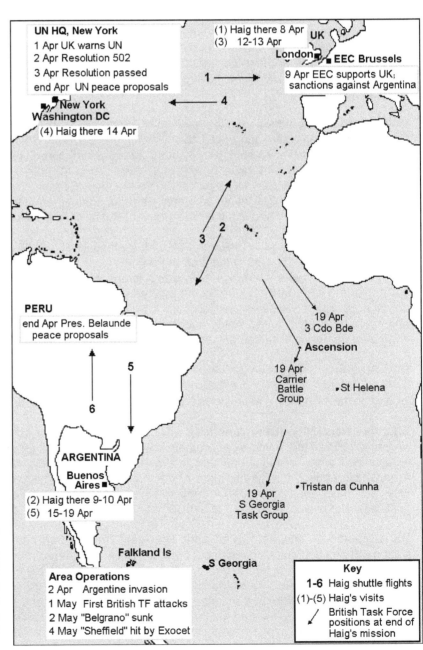

The United Nations was soon brought into the act by the British ambassador there, and very much to Britain's advantage. In contrast the junta in Buenos Aires was virtually unsuccessful in their attempts to gain support.

Leading Personalities - Amongst the main politicians and diplomats taking part were:

London - Prime Minister Margaret Thatcher and inner cabinet, including Francis Pym (successor to Lord Carrington), Foreign Affairs, John Nott, Defence, William Whitelaw, Home Secretary, and Cecil Parkinson, Conservative Party Chairman.

Washington D.C. - President Ronald Reagan, Secretary of State Alexander Haig, British ambassador Sir Nicholas Henderson, Argentine ambassador Snr Esteban Takacs.

Buenos Aires - General Galtieri, Brigadier General Lami Dozo and Admiral Anaya, and Foreign Minister, Snr Nicanor Costa Mendez.

United Nations, New York - Secretary General Snr Javier Perez de Cuellar, British ambassador Sir Anthony Parsons, Argentine ambassadors Senors Eduardo Roca and later Enrique Ros.

Support for Britain - Britain had reacted to developments in South Georgia through talks in London and Buenos Aires, but as invasion loomed, her international diplomacy moved into top gear. Within days, a highly successful campaign gained the support of the United Nations, the EEC and NATO, and the Commonwealth. In contrast Argentina even failed to win over the Organisation of American States (OAS). The first steps were taken on Wednesday 31st March when Sir Nicholas Henderson briefed Secretary Haig in Washington and President Reagan was called on by Mrs Thatcher to warn off President Galtieri, but in this he was unsuccessful. Over the next four weeks, America's attempts to be even-handed were not appreciated by Mrs Thatcher, although in US terms, having to choose between Latin American friend and main European ally was no easy matter.

United Nations Activities - On the evening of Thursday 1st April before invasion, Sir Anthony Parsons alerted the United Nations and addressed the 15 member Security Council. With confirmation next day that the invaders were ashore, Resolution 502 was formally introduced. Drafted by Britain, it called for an end to hostilities, immediate withdrawal of Argentine forces, and for both sides to seek a diplomatic solution. Voting was delayed until Saturday to allow Snr Costa Mendez to reach New York, but to no avail. That evening the vote took place in Britain's favour with only Panama against, and Russia abstaining along with Poland, China and Spain. Sir Anthony had laid the main plank of Britain's diplomatic position over the coming weeks.

Haig Shuttle Diplomacy - Concerned about the prospect of war, Secretary Haig and his team flew to London late on Wednesday 7th April at the start of their two week, 30,000 mile shuttle mission. The basis of this and all later peace plans were threefold - both side's forces to withdraw from the Falklands, an interim administration set up, and a long term settlement negotiated. In all that followed, Argentina would not move far from its demand for total sovereignty, and Britain, with Resolution 502 behind her, insisted on Argentine withdrawal and implicitly a return to the status quo. Mr Haig visited both London and Buenos Aires twice in his attempt to bring about a peaceful settlement, but by the 19th April had to accept there was little chance of success.

EEC Support - Before then, on Good Friday 9th April, and after lobbying by diplomats in Brussels and directly by Mrs Thatcher, the EEC gave full support to Britain and announced economic sanctions against Argentina at least until the 17th May. These included a total ban on imports and arms sales.

Effective Neutrality in the Americas - Thus only a week after invasion, Britain had wide support, the lead elements of the Task Force were on their way and General Galtieri realised he had totally misjudged Britain's resolve and world opinion, and that included the Americas. On Monday 26th April, and some days after Argentina's request, foreign ministers of the Organisation of American States met in Washington DC and in a vote two days later, accepted Argentine sovereignty over the Falklands and called on Britain to cease hostilities. But in what amounted to a diplomatic defeat for the junta, endorsed Resolution 502.

US Support - By the last day of April, President Reagan had come to accept there was little chance of a settlement and declared American support for Britain. He offered military aid and announced sanctions against Argentina. Mr Pym now returned to Washington as an ally, but still committed to the search for peace, and as he did, proposals were independently launched in the UN and by Peru. Both proposals were similar, but as events in the South Atlantic escalated from the first day of May and Britain's military options became less with the onset of winter, neither had much chance of success. The torpedoing of the cruiser "General Belgrano" lost Britain much of her support, especially in the EEC and as by now the Task Force was bombarding the Falklands, the last chances for peace had realistically gone.

British Military Response - But this was a long month in the making and followed Britain's rapid military response. On Monday 29th March orders were given for a fleet auxiliary to head south to support HMS Endurance and for three nuclear submarines to be prepared to follow. Two days later, British intelligence confirmed the likelihood of invasion and next day, on Thursday 1st April, the decision was taken to send a Task Force and the first submarine left.

Argentine & British Units Taking Part
(Parts 7-16)

Part 7. ARGENTINA ARMED FORCES and INVASION UNITS

Summary of Main Argentine Naval Invasion Forces

Falkland Islands

Task Force 20 - Distant Cover and Support
(Vice Admiral Juan Lombardo i/c)
Carrier 25 de Mayo (flagship)
Destroyers Comodoro Py, Hipolito Bouchard, Piedra Buena, Segui (all ex-US)
Tanker Punta Medanos

Task Force 40 - Amphibious
(Rear Admiral Jorge Gualter Allara)
Destroyers Santisima Trinidad (flagship), Hercules (both British Type 42s)
Frigates Drummond, Granville
Submarine Santa Fe

Task Group 40.1 - Landing Forces
(Rear Admiral of Marines Carlos Busser)
LST Cabo San Antonio
Icebreaker Almirante Irizar
Transport Isla de los Estados

South Georgia
Icebreaker Bahia Paraiso became Task Force 60 with arrival of Guerrico

First War for 100 Years

As Argentina went to war for the first time since the Paraguayan War of 1865-70, the Navy and Marines would spearhead the invasion on Friday 2nd April 1982, the Army would garrison and finally lose the Falklands, and the Air Force, which could possibly have won the coming Anglo-Argentine war, got ready to establish a presence there.

NAVAL FORCES

Navy or **Armada Republica Argentina** - With a strength of 30,000 officers and men, including 12,000 conscripts, the Navy was a mix of World War Two and modern ships. Main units in commission were:

> four patrol submarines (SANTA FE lost),
> one light fleet carrier and
> the old cruiser GENERAL BELGRANO (sunk),

six destroyers and three frigates, all Exocet-armed,
amphibious warfare craft,
eight fleet tankers and transports, and
two icebreakers or polar vessels,
.... a large proportion of which were at sea on the eve of invasion.

Under the overall command of Vice Admiral Juan Lombardo, most sailed by Friday 26th March from the main base of Puerto Belgrano.

Distant support and cover was provided by Task Force 20,
... while the landings took place from the ships of amphibious Task Force 40.

Before being recalled to join TF 40, frigates "Drummond" and "Granville" had earlier left for South Georgia, while fleet transport "Bahia Buen Suceso" had already returned to Argentina from there.

Marine Corps or **Infantaria de Marina** - The Navy also included a 6,000 strong Marine Corps or Infanteria de Marina organised into two Fleet Marine forces, each with two infantry battalions and supporting arms. It was from these that the assault commandos, or Buzos Tactico, and the landing force of some 800 men of the 2nd Marine Infantry Battalion were drawn. Another battalion was later deployed near Stanley.

Argentine Navy Super Etendard. The four operational aircraft mounted a series of attacks on the British Task force with Exocet missiles, sinking destroyer "Sheffield" and aircraft/helicopter support ship "Atlantic Conveyor"

Naval Aviation Command or **Comando Aviacion Naval Argentina (CANA)**

Included:

four operational Super Etendard strike fighters and their air-launched version of Exocet,

eight Skyhawk A-4Q attack bombers, ten Aermacchi MB.339s and fifteen Mentor T-34Cs in the light attack role,

Tracker anti-submarine aircraft and Lynx, Alouette and Sea King helicopters.

Carrier "25 de Mayo" first sailed with Skyhawks and Trackers embarked, but these were later landed, and together with the Super-Etendards, moved to southern airfields. Flying from there, three of the Skyhawks were lost in combat, and of the six MB.339s and four Mentors flown to the Falklands and operated from Stanley or Pebble Island, only one MB.339 survived.

Argentine Coastguard or **Prefectura Naval Argentina (PNA)** - Separate from the Navy, the PNA operated its own aircraft and over 40 patrol vessels. The one Puma helicopter, two Skyvan light aircraft and two patrol craft transferred to the Falklands were also lost.

LAND FORCES

Army or **Ejercito** - Although a professional army in South American terms, a weakness in comparison with the British land forces was the predominance of one year conscripts in the ranks. Total strength was 60,000 including 20,000 regular officers and NCOs. Organised in to five corps, the main operational unit was the brigade of which there were around two armoured, one mechanised, four infantry, three mountain, one jungle and one airmobile, each consisting of three battalions plus one artillery and one engineer battalion. In addition there were five anti-aircraft and one aviation battalions. The Army (with the Marines) employed on the Falklands, Panhard armoured cars, 105 and 155mm artillery, 20mm, 30mm and 35mm AA guns, and Roland, Tigercat and Blowpipe SAMs.

Occupation Forces - With the islands secured by the Marines, a relatively small Army garrison was air-lifted in to Stanley, but once the British Task Force was on its way, army strength built-up to over 10,000 troops. Of these, a reinforced brigade of 8,000 men from five regiments together with artillery, AA, armoured car and engineer units stayed in the Stanley area. Nearly 1,000 infantry with AA and some artillery went to Goose Green, and over on West Falkland, Port Howard and Fox Bay each received 800 men of an infantry regiment plus engineer support. Many were killed or wounded and the rest captured with all their surviving equipment.

Army Aviation Command or **Comando de Aviacion del Ejercito** - Equipped with aircraft and a large variety of helicopters, many of which were deployed to the Falklands and all lost - two Chinook CH-47Cs, five Puma SA.330Ls, three Agusta A-109As and nine Iroquois UH-1Hs.

AIR FORCE

Argentine Air Force or **Fuerza Aerea Argentina (FAA)** - According to best estimates, the FAA started the war with:

> 45 Skyhawk A-4B and C attack bombers,
> 37 Dagger and 17 Mirage fighter and attack aircraft,
> ten Canberra light bombers,
> more than 35 Argentine-designed and built Pucara close support aircraft,
> nine Hercules C-130 transports and tankers,
> Learjets, Boeing 707s and a number of other aircraft and helicopters.
> ...... not all were operational.

As soon as the assault forces landed, the Hercules started a job they continued to the very end; flying into Stanley the men and materiel vital to the Argentine defence of the Falklands. Eventually transferred to the islands were 24 Pucaras at Stanley, Goose Green or Pebble Island, and two Bell 212 and two Chinook helicopters. All but the Chinooks were lost. As the British Task Force headed south, the FAA transferred many of its aircraft to southern mainland bases and by the time the war was over had lost 32 Daggers, Mirage and Skyhawks, two Canberras, a Hercules, a Learjet and one more Pucara. Added to the Navy, Coast Guard and Army casualties, Argentina lost a total of 100 aircraft and helicopters.

Part 8. BRITISH TASK FORCE BUILD-UP

British Aims and Outcome - Once the decision was taken to launch "Operation Corporate" and dispute the Argentine invasion by force if necessary, Britain's military power was rapidly mobilised. Commanders were appointed and from bases throughout the country, the highly technological ships and aircraft were readied and despatched to transport and support a limited number of professional Marines, Paras and Guardsmen. Fighting as infantrymen, they re-took the Falklands the hard way, and at the end of an 8,000 mile long logistical nightmare and lengthy chain of command. Directly responsible to the British Cabinet for all military aspects was the Defence Staff at Whitehall not far from Downing Street with its Chief, Admiral of the Fleet Sir Terence Lewin and the other service heads. Working out of Northwood, Middlesex, just outside London were the Task Force Commanders led by Admiral Sir John Fieldhouse, Commander-in-Chief Fleet, who in turn controlled events in the South Atlantic through the commanders on the spot. Taking part in this vast undertaking were nearly 30,000 men and a few women, and a large proportion of Britain's Navy and Marines, fleet auxiliaries and merchantmen, aircraft and helicopter squadrons, plus five Army battalions and supporting arms.

Summary of Main British Commanders (Honours awarded in brackets)

Defence Staff, Whitehall, London - Admiral of the Fleet Sir (later Baron) Terence Lewin, Chief of the Defence Staff; Admiral Sir Henry Leach, Royal Navy; General Sir Edwin Bramall, Army; Air Chief Marshal Sir Michael Beetham, Royal Air Force.

Task Force Commanders, Northwood - Admiral Sir John Fieldhouse (GBE), Task Force Commander; Major General J J Moore (KCB) MC and bar RM, Land Forces Deputy, and later Lieut General Sir Richard Trant; Air Marshal Sir John Curtiss (KBE), Air Commander; Vice Admiral P G M Herbert, Flag Officer Submarines.

South Atlantic Commanders - Rear Admiral J F Woodward (KCB), Carrier Battle Group; Commodore M C Clapp (CB), Amphibious Task Group; Brigadier J H Thompson (CB) RM, Landing Force Task Group and 3 Commando Brigade RM. Followed by Major General Moore RM, Land Forces Falklands Islands and Brigadier M J A Wilson MC, 5th Infantry Brigade

Main Participating Military Bases in Britain

NORTHWOOD (Task Force HQ)

ROYAL NAVY
Culdrose (HMS Seahawk)
Devonport (HMS Drake)
Faslane (HMS Neptune - SSNs)
Gosport (HMS Dolphin)
Portland (HMS Osprey)
Portsmouth (HMS Nelson)
Rosyth (HMS Cochrane)
Yeovilton (HMS Heron)

ROYAL MARINES
Arbroath (45 Cdo RM)
Plymouth (3 Cdo Bde RM, incl.
  40 & 42 Cdo)
RM Poole

BRITISH ARMY
Aldershot (2 & 3 Para)
Church Crookham (1/7 Gurkhas)
Hereford (SAS)
London (2 Scots & 1 Welsh Guards)
Marchwood (RCT)
Middle Wallop (AAC)
Netheravon (AAC)
Sennybridge (5th Inf Bde training)

ROYAL AIR FORCE
Brize Norton (VC.10s)
Coningsby (Phantoms)
Kinloss (Nimrod MR2s)
Lyneham (Hercules)
Marham (Victors)
Odiham (Chinooks)
St Athan (maintenance)
St Mawgan (Nimrod MR1s)
Waddington (Vulcans)
Wittering (Harrier GR3s)
Wyton (Nimrod R1s)

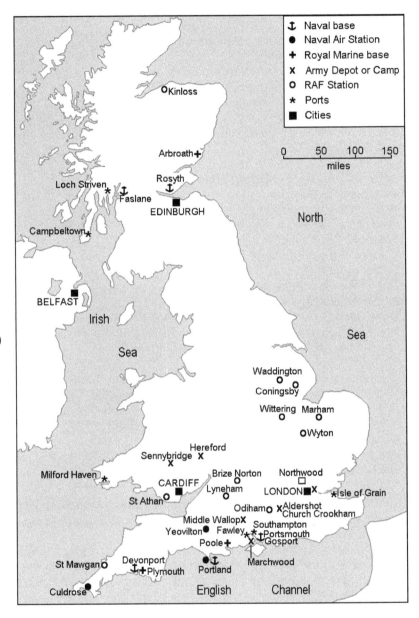

From the invasion of the Falklands on the 2nd April until the final Argentine surrender on the 15th June – just eleven weeks - each of the British ships, aircraft squadrons and main military units, as they entered the South Atlantic for the FIRST time in the campaign are introduced below. Ships lost are in CAPITALS:

Submarines reaching the Falkland's Area, early April to May
Nuclear submarines Spartan, Splendid, Conqueror, Courageous(?), Valiant and conventionally powered
  Onyx, with some SBS.

RAF Squadrons reaching or deploying to Ascension, early April to May
VC.10 transports of 10 Sqdn, Hercules transports of 24, 30, 47 and 70 Sqdns,
Nimrod maritime reconnaissance aircraft of 42(TB), 51(?), 120, 201 and 206 Sqdns,

Victor tankers of 55 and 57 Sqdns,
Vulcan bombers of 44, 50 and 101 Sqdns,
Harrier GR.3 attack aircraft of 1(F) Sqdn,
Chinook helicopter of 18 and a Sea King of 202 Sqdns,
Phantom fighters of 29(F) Sqdn,
Units of the RAF Regiment.

South Georgia recaptured (Operation Paraquat) on 25th April
Naval forces - destroyer Antrim, frigates Brilliant, Plymouth, ice patrol ship Endurance, RFAs Tidespring and (earlier) Brambleleaf and Fort Austin.
Land forces - M Coy 42 Cdo RM, SBS RM and D Sqdn 22nd SAS.

Carrier Battle Group starting attacks on Falklands, 1st May
Naval forces - carriers Hermes, Invincible, destroyers Glamorgan, COVENTRY, Glasgow, SHEFFIELD, frigates Broadsword, Alacrity, Arrow, Yarmouth and RFAs Olmeda and Resource.
Joined later in May by destroyer Exeter, frigate Ambuscade and RFA Regent.

Nuclear-powered hunter-killer submarine HMS Conqueror, one of the first Royal Navy warships to reach South Georgia and then the Falklands area. She torpedoed and sank the Argentine cruiser "General Belgrano" on the 2nd May 1982 (Courtesy MOD, Navy)

Carrier aircraft - Sea Harriers of Nos.800 and 801, anti-submarine and assault Sea King helicopters of Nos.820, 826 and 846 NAS; and later, Sea Harriers of No.809 and RAF Harrier GR.3s of 1(F) Squadrons.
Land forces - SBS RM, D and G Sqdns 22nd SAS.

Amphibious Group reaching the TEZ, followed by Landings in San Carlos Water on 21st May
Naval forces - including assault ships Fearless, Intrepid, frigates ARDENT, Argonaut and later ANTELOPE, RFAs Stromness, Tidepool, LSLs SIR GALAHAD, Sir Geraint, Sir Lancelot, Sir Percivale, Sir Tristram and (later) Sir Bedivere, transports Canberra, Elk, Europic Ferry, Norland, aircraft and helicopter support ship ATLANTIC CONVEYOR.
Land forces - 3 Commando Brigade RM including 40, 42 and 45 Cdo RM and 2 and 3 Para, and 3 CBAS Gazelle and Scout helicopters.

Other Ships and Helicopter Squadrons supporting the Task Force up to the End of May
At Ascension - RMAS mooring vessel Goosander and tanker Alvega; also detached despatch vessel Dumbarton Castle.
Tanker Holding Areas in the South Atlantic - RFA tankers Appleleaf, Pearleaf and Plumleaf plus tankers Anco Charger, Eburna, eight British Petroleum "British" tankers, and water tanker Fort Toronto.
Operating in Falklands area - hospital ship Uganda and ambulance ships Hecla, Herald and Hydra in Red Cross Box (RCB), repair ship Stena Seaspread and tugs Irishman, Salvageman, Yorkshireman in TRALA.
Reaching South Georgia - requisitioned minesweepers Cordella, Farnella, Junella, Northella and Pict, RFA tanker Blue Rover, RMAS tug Typhoon, detached despatch vessels Iris and Leeds Castle, ammo ship Lycaon and stores ship Saxonia.
Other Helicopters - Sea Kings of No.824 and also 846, Wessex of Nos.737, 845 and 848, Lynx of No.815 and Wasps of No.829 NAS on warships, RFAs and merchantmen, together with one RAF Chinook of 18 Sqdn.

Bristol Group arriving in TEZ, late May
Destroyers Bristol, Cardiff, frigates Active, Avenger, Andromeda, Minerva, Penelope, RFAs Bayleaf and Olna.

5th Infantry Brigade reaching South Atlantic late May to join Advance on Stanley, early June
Land forces - 5th Infantry Brigade including 2 Scots and 1 Welsh Guards, 1/7 Gurkha Rifles, and Gazelle and Scout helicopters of 656 Sqdn AAC.
Transports - Queen Elizabeth 2, Baltic Ferry and Nordic Ferry.

Ships and Helicopter Squadrons arriving to support Task Force up to Surrender
RFAs Engadine and Fort Grange, merchantmen Atlantic Causeway, Balder London, Contender Bezant, Geestport, St. Edmund, Tor Caledonia and Wimpey Seahorse,
Sea Kings of No.825 and Wessex of No.847 NAS.

Eventual British Casualties and Losses in Major Equipment

Four warships and a landing craft,
one fleet auxiliary and one merchantman,
23 Navy, seven RAF, three Marine and one Army helicopters and aircraft.
One thousand of the men taking part were killed or wounded.

Part 9. ROYAL NAVY WARSHIPS

Naval Tasks - Before the end of hostilities many of the major warships of the Royal Navy reached the Falkland's area, there to operate in the storms and heavy seas and fogs of the far South Atlantic as winter approached. Their tasks were numerous and included denying the surrounding seas to the Argentine Navy, providing the only air cover available, landing special forces and carrying out shore bombardment before and after the San Carlos landings, escorting the troop and supply ships and protecting them from attack by aircraft, submarine and surface ship, and acting as command, control and communications centres.

Operational Warships - Soon in operation were the only four big surface ships left to the Navy:

"Invincible"-class carrier, 1986 (Courtesy MOD, Navy)

old carrier Hermes (28,700 tons full load), the new but smaller Invincible (19.800 tons) and assault ships Fearless and Intrepid (12,100 tons).

Also half the force of nuclear fleet submarines

Conqueror, Courageous (?), Spartan, Splendid, Valiant, plus diesel-engined Onyx.

Even more significantly, most of the modern destroyers and frigates also took part. As they carried a confusing diversity of weapons and suffered heavily (nine out of 23 were sunk or seriously damaged, and others less so by enemy action) their main characteristics are summarised. The weapon systems were:

surface-to-surface missiles (SSM), surface-to-air missiles (SAM), anti-submarine warfare (ASW) including ships torpedo weapon system (STWS), main gun(s) and helicopter(s).

DESTROYERS

Type 82	Bristol	7,100 tons full load	Sea Dart SAM, Ikara ASW, 1x4.5in, could carry Wasp
County class	Antrim (UXB damage) Glamorgan (Exocet damage)	6,200 tons	Exocet SSM, Seaslug/Sea Cat SAM, 2x4.5in, 1xWessex Helicopter
Type 42	Cardiff COVENTRY (sunk by bombs) Exeter Glasgow (UXB damage) SHEFFIELD (sunk by Exocet)	4,100 tons	Sea Dart SAM, STWS ASW, 1x4.5in, 1xLynx helicopter

FRIGATES

Type 22	Brilliant Broadsword	4,000 tons	Exocet SSM, Sea Wolf SAM, STWS ASW, 2xLynx helicopters
Type 21	Active* Alacrity Ambuscade ANTELOPE (sunk by bombs) ARDENT (sunk by bombs) Arrow Avenger	3,200 tons	Exocet SSM, Sea Cat SAM, STWS ASW, 1x4.5in, 1xWasp* or Lynx helicopter
Leander class	Andromeda* Argonaut (UXB damage) Minerva Penelope	3,200 tons	Exocet SSM, Sea Wolf* or Sea Cat SAM, STWS ASW, 1xLynx helicopter
Rothesay class	Plymouth (bomb damage) Yarmouth	2,800 tons	Sea Cat SAM, Limbo ASW, 2x4.5in, 1xWasp helicopter

Other Types - Apart from Endurance, other warships taking part up to the surrender were survey ships Hecla, Herald and Hydra (2,700 tons, Wasp helicopter) as ambulance ships, and fishery protection vessels Dumbarton Castle and Leeds Castle (1,450 tons) in the role of despatch vessels.

Part 10. FLEET AIR ARM SQUADRONS

Sea Harriers - Lacking fleet carriers and with the Falklands less than 500 miles from Argentine, the Navy had to provide the only possible air cover with its few Sea Harrier FRS.1 jump-jets armed with 30mm Aden cannon, the lethal AIM-9L Sidewinder AAM for combat air patrol, and cluster bombs for ground attack. Including those transferred from No.899 HQ Training Squadron, 12 were scraped together for "Hermes"' No.800 and 8 for "Invincible's" No.801 NAS. Thus 20 aircraft, some piloted by the RAF, had to defend the Fleet against 100 plus Argentine attackers. Only in mid-May were they reinforced by eight more Sea Harriers of No.809 NAS (plus six RAF GR.3s). Just six Navy Harriers were lost by accident or ground fire, and not one in air-to-air fighting.

Helicopters - The rest of the Navy's airpower came from its numerous helicopters, although three more squadrons had to be reformed to support the land forces in their later drive on Stanley. Flying mainly from the warships and RFAs, they carried out transport and vertical replenishment (vertrep) duties, special forces landings and naval gunfire support, and anti-submarine and anti-ship missions, the latter by Sea Skua-equipped Lynx. But not airborne early warning which was sadly lacking. Some transferred from ship to ship, including the merchantmen, and many later went ashore on the Falklands. In all, 17 helicopters were lost - five Sea Kings by accident, two Wessex on South Georgia, six Wessex and a Lynx went down with "Atlantic Conveyor", one Lynx each with "Ardent" and "Coventry" and last of all a Wessex destroyed on Exocet-hit "Glamorgan". Helicopter types, Naval Air Squadron and Main Roles were:

Sea Kings
No.820 - 11 HAS.5s on Invincible for ASW
No.824 - 5 HAS.2As on RFAs, 2 based at
  Gibraltar
No.825 - Reformed Squadron of 10
  HAS.2As reached Falklands late May in
  support role
No.826 - 9 HAS.5s on Hermes for ASW
No.846 - 15 HC.4 Assault, including 9
  initially on Hermes, 3 on Fearless and
  1 on Intrepid

Sea Harriers of, from top, Nos 899, 801, 800 NAS
(Courtesy - RNAS Yeovilton)

Wessex
No.737 - 2 HAS.3s on County class destroyers
No.845 & No.848 (reformed NAS) - 30 HU.5s before end of war on RFAs, Intrepid, carried on Atlantic
  Conveyor (6) and at Ascension (1)
No.847 - Reformed Squadron of 24 HU.5s reached Falklands early June in support role

Lynx - No.815 HAS.2s on destroyers and frigates

Wasp - No.829 HAS.1s on Rothesay frigates and small ships

Part 11. ROYAL FLEET AUXILIARY SHIPS

Vital Fleet Support - Away from its few shore bases, the Navy simply could not operate without the Royal Fleet Auxiliary, which like its parent service sent a large proportion of its strength to the South Atlantic before the end of the war - no less than 22 of the 27 ships in commission. Civilian-manned and flying the Blue Ensign, the RFAs usually supplied warships underway by Replenishment at Sea (RAS) techniques:

> heavy furnace fuel oil for older ships, diesel and aviation fuels and fresh water were supplied
>   through hoses,
> dry goods by jackstay and
> most ships were equipped to handle helicopters for vertrep, and if needed to provide the RFAs
>   own ASW screen.

The types of ships, displacement tons, and helicopters embarked were:

Fleet replenishment ships - supplied ammunition, food and dry stores:		
Regent, Resource	22,800 tons	Wessex
Fort Austin, Fort Grange	17,200 tons	Wessex/Sea Kings
Stromness - stores support ship	14,000 tons	helicopter deck

Fleet tankers - carried all three types of fuel plus fresh water, could replenish three ships at a time, including one astern:

Olmeda, Olna (plus Olwen – post-war only)	36,000 tons	Sea Kings/Wessex
Tidepool, Tidespring	27,400 tons	Wessex
Blue Rover - one of five small fleet tankers, also carried dry cargo	11,500 tons	helicopter deck

Support tankers - normally transported ship and aviation fuel between terminals and depots, but could replenish the fleet tankers and directly refuel other ships. The two classes were considerably supplemented by civilian tankers:

Appleleaf, Bayleaf, Brambleleaf	26,000 tons	(no flightdeck)
Pearleaf and Plumleaf - older ships	26,000 tons	(no flightdeck)

Landing ship logistics (LSLs) - RO-RO vessels equipped with bow and stern doors and ramps for loading and unloading troops and tanks:

Sir Bedivere, SIR GALAHAD (lost by air attack), Sir Geraint, Sir Lancelot (UXB damage), Sir Percivale, Sir Tristram (UXB damage).	5,500 tons	helicopter deck

Helicopter support ship - equipped for naval training in the handling and maintenance of helicopters:

Engadine	8,000 tons	helicopter deck

RFA Olmeda replenishing HMS Invincible post-war (Courtesy - MOD, Navy)

Separate from the RFA was the **Royal Maritime Auxiliary Service** with 400 civilian-manned ships providing marine services in and around naval bases. Two ships sailed south - ocean tug "Typhoon" (1,030grt) and mooring, salvage and boom vessel "Goosander" (900grt).

Part 12. MERCHANT NAVY SHIPS

Vital Need for Merchant Ships

Up to the surrender in mid-June, 40 merchantmen totalling over 500,000grt reached the South Atlantic. Without them, the war would not have been won as the Royal Fleet Auxiliary lacked the ships to transport the land forces and then support them and the warships 8,000 miles from home.

Chartered (Ch) when available......

requisitioned (Req) when under contract........

... the Ships Taken Up From Trade (Stuft) from Britain's dwindling merchant fleet were rapidly converted to their military role in naval and civilian dockyards, but mainly Devonport and Portsmouth.

Crew of tug "Yorkshireman" at South Georgia (Courtesy - United Towing Ltd)

All received minimum naval communications and some Satnav (SN) and Satcom (SC) equipment.....

.....most were fitted for RAS, many with one or two helipads (H or 2H) and some with extra accommodation and light AA weapons.

Soon loaded, most sailed with Naval Parties embarked for ciphering, RAS, vertrep and other duties. Taking only those ships which arrived on station before the end of the war, their main military roles, starting with the troop and equipment transports were:

Transports reaching TEZ mid-May with 3 Cdo Bde and more aircraft		
Canberra	44,800grt	Req/2H
Elk	5,500grt	Req
Europic Ferry	4,200grt	Req/SN/SC
Norland	13,000grt	Req/2H/SN/SC
ATLANTIC CONVEYOR - aircraft and helicopter support ship (sunk by Exocet)	15,000grt	Req/flight deck/SC
Transports arriving end of May with 5th Inf Bde and military stores		
Queen Elizabeth 2	67,100grt	Req/2H

Baltic Ferry	6,500grt	Req/2H/SN/SC
Nordic Ferry	6,500grt	Req/2H/SN/SC
Lycaon - ammunition ship	11,800grt	Ch/SC
Atlantic Causeway - helicopter support ship	15,000grt	Req/flight deck/hangar/SC

Transports arriving in June

St. Edmund - troopship	9,000grt	Req/2H/SN/SC
Tor Caledonia - transport	5,100grt	Req
Contender Bezant - aircraft and helicopter carrier	11,400grt	Ch/flight deck/hangar

Oil Tankers, mostly used to replenish RFAs in the tanker holding areas set out **in the order:**

British Esk, British Tay, British Test, British Tamar, British Trent	all 15,600grt	All chartered
Anco Charger	15,600grt	Chartered
British Dart, British Wye, British Avon	all 15,600grt	All chartered
Alvega	33,300grt	Chartered
Eburna	19,800grt	Chartered
Balder London	20,000grt	Chartered

Other vessels and approximate **order of departure** were:

Irishman, Yorkshireman - ocean tugs	both 700grt	Req
Salvageman - ocean tug	1,600grt	Req
Wimpey Seahorse - mooring vessel	1,600grt	Req/SC
Stena Seaspread - repair ship	6,100grt	Req/SN/SC
Fort Toronto - water tanker	20,000grt	Ch
Uganda - hospital ship	16,900grt	Req/H/SC
Cordella, Farnella, Junella, Northella, Pict - minesweepers	1,200-1,600grt	Req
Iris - despatch vessel	3,900grt	Req/H/SC
Saxonia - refrigerated stores ship	12,000grt	Ch/H/SN/SC
Geestport - refrigerated stores ship	7,700grt	Req/H

With 40 merchantmen already in the South Atlantic or on their way by Week Nine, more were needed. **Before the surrender** a further eight set out, including during the week, tanker "Scottish Eagle" from Milford Haven and offshore ship "British Enterprise III" from Rosyth. The complete list was:

    Tankers Scottish Eagle (33,000grt, Ch/SC) and G A Walker (18,700grt, Ch)
    Despatch vessel British Enterprise III (1,600grt, Req)
    Repair ship Stena Inspector (6,100grt, Ch/SN/SC)
    Helicopter carrier and repair ship Astronomer (27,900grt, Req/flight deck and hangar)
    Ammunition ship Laertes (11,800grt, Req)
    Refrigerated stores ship Avelona Star (9,800grt, Ch/H)
    Minesweeper support ship St Helena (3,100grt, Req/H/SN/SC)

Part 13. 3 COMMANDO BRIGADE ROYAL MARINES

3 Commando Brigade's job was to establish a bridgehead before the Army's 5th Infantry Brigade (5th Inf Bde) arrived to help complete the recapture of the Falklands. Its teeth were three Royal Marine Commandos each with three rifle companies of 120 men each, one HQ and one support company, all backed up by a number of other Marine and commando-trained Army units.

The Army also provided strong reinforcements including the 3rd Battalion The Parachute Regt, and later the 2nd Battalion, both from 5th Inf Bde. Main infantry weapons were the 7.62mm SLR rifle and 7.62mm general purpose machine gun, 66mm light (LAW) and 84mm Carl Gustav medium (MAW) anti-armour weapons, and in support companies, 81mm mortars and Milan anti-tank wire guided missiles.

Marines of K Coy, 42 Cdo RM move off Mount Kent
(Courtesy - Royal Marines Museum)

3 Commando Brigade Royal Marines

Infantry - 40, 42 and 45 Commando RM (M Coy 42 Cdo to South Georgia, replaced later by newly-formed J Coy 42 Cdo)

Artillery - 29 Commando Regiment, Royal Artillery with Nos 7, 8 and 79 Batteries each of 6x105mm artillery and 148 Commando Forward Observation Battery, Royal Artillery for naval gunfire observation

Combat engineers - 59 Independent Commando Squadron, Royal Engineers

Logistics - Commando Logistics Regiment RM

Helicopters - 3 Commando Brigade Air Squadron RM with nine Gazelle AH.1s and six Scout AH.1s (two RM Gazelles and one Scout were lost)

HQ & Communications - Brigade Headquarter and Signal Squadron including 1st Raiding Squadron equipped with rigid raiders and Gemini assault craft and an Air Defence Troop with 12xBlowpipe SAMs

In medium range reconnaissance role - Mountain and Arctic Warfare (Training) Cadre

Raiding and reconnaissance - 3 Sections, Special Boat Squadron (No.2 Section to South Georgia)

Other units - included:

Tactical Air Control Parties RM for directing air strikes
Y Signals Troop RM
Commando Forces Band RM for medical duties
Two Royal Navy Surgical Support Teams

Army Reinforcements, including:

Infantry - 2nd and 3rd Battalions, The Parachute Regiment each with one HQ, three rifle, one patrol and one support company

Light armour - B Squadron, The Blues and Royals with four Scorpion and four Scimitar light tanks and one Samson recovery vehicle

Air defence - T Battery, 12 Air Defence Regiment with 12xRapier SAMs

Helicopters - 656 Army Air Corps Squadron with a flight of three Scout AH.1s

Raiding and reconnaissance - D and G Squadrons, 22nd Special Air Service Regiment (D Sqdn initially to South Georgia)

Attached to 2 Para - 29 Battery, 4 Field Regiment, Royal Artillery with 6x105mm guns

Troop each from:
43 Air Defence Battery
32 Guided Weapons Regiment, Royal Artillery with Blowpipe SAMs
9 Para Squadron, Royal Engineers
16 Field Ambulance, Royal Army Medical Corps
Explosive ordnance disposal - from 49 EOD Squadron, Royal Engineers (and EOD Team RAF)

Other units included:
Forward Observation Officer parties from 4 Field Regiment Royal Artillery
Tactical Air Control parties

Detachments from:
Postal and Courier Regiment, Royal Engineers
Rear Link Detachments, Royal Signals
81 Ordnance Company, Royal Army Ordnance Corps
Mexeflote detachment 17 Port Regiment, Royal Corps of Transport

---

Part 14. 5th INFANTRY BRIGADE

Build-Up - Once 3 Commando Brigade was ashore, the Army's **5th Infantry Brigade** would arrive to bring total land forces strength to approximately 10,000 men. Both brigades would then come under the divisional headquarters of Major General Jeremy Moore RM as Commander, Land Forces Falkland Islands. Even then, to retake the islands, he would be far short of the superiority of numbers needed to easily defeat the well dug-in defenders.

Brigade infantry was provided by the

> 1st Battalion, 7th Duke of Edinburgh's Own Gurkha Rifles,
>> together with two Guards battalions - 1st Welsh and 2nd Scots transferred to 5th Infantry to replace 2 and 3 Parachute Regiments.

Before sailing, they trained for two weeks near Sennybridge in Wales in terrain similar to the Falklands.

Support came from a variety of arms and units, some of which were already represented in 3 Cdo Bde:

Artillery - Headquarter and 97 Battery, 4 Field Regiment, Royal Artillery with 6x105mm guns

Air defence - one troop of 43 Air Defence Battery, 32 Guided Weapons Regiment, Royal Artillery with Blowpipe SAMs

Combat engineers - 36 Engineer Regiment, Royal Engineers and 9 Parachute Squadron, Royal Engineers

Helicopters - 656 Army Air Corps Squadron with 3 Scout AH.1s and 6 Gazelle AH.1s (one Gazelle was lost)

HQ and Communications - Brigade Headquarters and Signal Squadron with Rear Link Detachments, Royal Signals

Other units included, complete or in part:
  16 Field Ambulance, Royal Army Medical Corps
  81 and 91 Ordnance Company and 421 Explosive Ordnance Disposal Coy, Royal Army Ordnance Corps
  8 Field Cash Office, Royal Army Pay Corps
  407 Road Transport Troop, Royal Corps of Transport with Snowcats
  10 Field Workshop, Royal Electrical and Mechanical Engineers
  160 Provost Company, Royal Military Police

Most of the more than 3,000 men of the Brigade sailed on "Queen Elizabeth 2" and were joined from Ascension by General Moore as Commander (designate) who assumed full command of land forces in early June. Supporting equipment, some troops and the helicopters were carried by transports "Baltic Ferry" and "Nordic Ferry".

Men of 1st Welsh Guards in Sea King helicopter drill on "Queen Elizabeth II"

Lieutenant Colonel J F Rickett OBE, co, 1st Welsh Guards

(both courtesy Brigadier Rickett)

Part 15. ROYAL AIR FORCE - Role & Operations

RAF Importance - With the Navy flying just about all the operations around South Georgia and then the Falklands, although with a number of RAF Sea Harrier pilots, the RAF's role can be overlooked. And yet it's ability to rapidly transport men, supplies and aircraft, first to Ascension and then later further south was so important to success.

Between the UK and Ascension - Hercules and **VC.10 transports** flew over 500 sorties to Ascension by the end of the war to bring in more than 5,000 people and 6,000 tons of freight. The Hercules, some the lengthened C.3s, but mostly C.1s, were from the pool of over fifty aircraft of 24, 30, 47 and 70 Sqdns of the Lyneham Transport Wing. The first two squadrons concentrated on the UK/Ascension airbridge and the other two on missions south, and by the end of the war, six aircraft had been fitted for in-flight refuelling to extend their range.

As well as flying to Ascension, the thirteen VC.10 passenger aircraft of 10 Sqdn from Brize Norton later returned with ship's survivors, and from Montevideo, brought back prisoners and deportees from the Falklands and South Georgia and wounded men from battle. They also continued to fly the Atlantic to the United States. Extra transport capacity was provided by chartered Boeing 707s and five ex-RAF Belfast freighters.

RAF VC-10 transport
(Courtesy - MOD, RAF)

Ascension-based Aircraft and Units - On their way south in early May, three **Harrier GR.3s** of 1 (Fighter) Sqdn were retained at Wideawake for air defence, but later relieved by three supersonic **Phantom FGR.2s** of 29(F) Sqdn from RAF Coningsby. By then, and with the shortage of helicopters on the island, a **Sea King HAR.3** of 202 Air-Sea Rescue Sqdn had joined a **Chinook** of 18 Sqdn on vertrep duties. Apart from units responsible for air movements, communications and supply, the RAF also took on ground defence with the arrival of HQ Unit, 3 Wing and Field Flight, 15 Sqdn of the RAF Regt.

Missions Flown from Ascension - First to deploy were two **Nimrod MR.1 maritime patrol aircraft** of 42(TB) Sqdn from St Mawgan to patrol Ascension waters and act as links with the nuclear subs. Later in April, they were replaced by some of the thirteen plus and more modern **MR.2s** of 120, 201 and 206 Sqdns from Kinloss. In over a hundred sorties from Wideawake, they flew ahead of the Task Force, reached as far as Argentine waters, and provided SAR and radio links and coordinated air refuelling for Victor and Vulcan missions and Harrier staging flights. By the surrender, some MR.2s were fitted for air-refuelling and some with

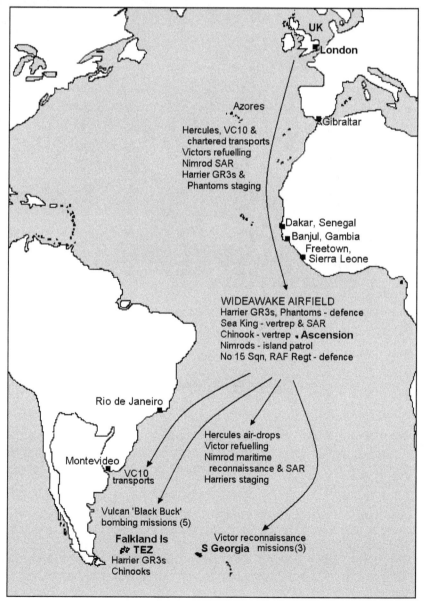

Sidewinder AAMs for self defence, but no aircraft equipped with the Harpoon anti-shipping missile were ready in time. In addition, R.1 reconnaissance aircraft of Wyton's 51 Sqdn may have taken part.

At least south from Ascension, few missions would have been possible without the Victor K.2 tankers of 55 and 57 Sqdns from Marham, some twenty of which reached Ascension. Apart from refuelling each other as needed, they first flew three maritime radar reconnaissance missions leading up to the recapture of South Georgia. Then in nearly 600 sorties the Victors supported other aircraft in often complicated logistics patterns. These included (with outline numbers of tanker sorties) fighters staging to Ascension and some Harrier GR.3s on from there, Hercules long range drops (6), extended Nimrod patrols (12), Vulcan raids on Stanley (15). They also provided cover as "Atlantic Conveyor" went south with her Harriers and helicopters.

Although the Waddington-based **Vulcan B.2 bombers** of 44, 50 and 101 Sqdns were due to retire from service, a number were fitted with extra ECM and readied for action. Four aircraft in total reached Ascension, the first two at the end of April to start a planned series of seven, single aircraft "Black Buck" missions against Stanley through to mid June. Conventional bombs were used on three occasions and Shrike anti-radar missiles on two, with one mission of each type being called off.

The **Hercules** of 47 and 70 Sqdns were trained in tactical support and based at Ascension to air drop men and urgent supplies to the Task Force further south. As 47 Sqdn included a Special Forces Flight, it may have been used for undisclosed covert operations.

RAF Gallantry Awards
Hercules missions from Ascension by 47 Sqdn RAF
Flt Lt H C Burgoyne (AFC) RAF
Sqdn Ldr A M Roberts (AFC) RAF

Based in the Falklands - To reinforce the Navy's Sea Harriers, Harrier GR.3s of 1(F) Sqdn, RAF Wittering were prepared for carrier service. Although fitted with Sidewinder and ECM and with the pilots receiving limited ski-jump training at Yeovilton, they were mainly used in their normal ground attack role. Nine out of ten aircraft setting out in early May reached Ascension, and apart from the three that temporarily stayed on, the other six sailed with "Atlantic Conveyor" and later flew off to "Hermes". Six more arrived at the end of May to add to the three already at Ascension. Of this nine, four flew direct to "Hermes", four sailed with merchantman "Contender Bezant" too late to join the fighting, and one returned to the UK with fuel leaks. Thus a total of ten GR.3s flew with the Navy in the South Atlantic (the original six plus the later four), with three shot down by ground fire and one damaged beyond repair in landing.

With the boggy terrain and almost total lack of roads, heavy lift helicopters were a must. Hence the importance of the first five **Chinook HC.1s** of 18 Sqdn, RAF Odiham carried by "Atlantic Conveyor". One stayed on Ascension, but three of the remaining four were lost in the Exocet attack. The one survivor worked wonders, and not until the surrender did three more plus the Ascension Chinook arrive on "Contender Bezant".

Part 16. ARGENTINE DEFENCES ON FALKLANDS

By the time Britain was ready to land, Argentine forces were well established on the islands. In spite of the numerous Sea Harrier attacks and naval bombardments and the Pebble Island raid, they were superior in numbers of men, artillery, attack aircraft and had a good helicopter lift. However on the ground, they were about to depend on well prepared defensive positions rather than aggressive counter-attack. Following is a summary of the main ground forces and their supporting aircraft. On the eve of the landings most of the latter were based at Stanley although some of the FAA Pucaras and helicopters were at Goose Green. Pebble Island was by then out of action. A total of 20 attack aircraft and 23 helicopters from the four services remained available after losses to 20th May, the day before the landings at San Carlos Bay.

FALKLAND ISLANDS - commanded by Major General Menendez

GROUND FORCES included:
3rd Mechanised Infantry Brigade (Major General Omar Parada with 4th, 5th, 8th and 12th Regiments),
10th Motorised Infantry Brigade (Major General Oscar Joffre with 3rd, 6th and 7th Regiments),
Independent 25th Regiment and 5th Marine Infantry Battalion.

Forces allocated as follows:

Stanley & Approaches - Commander, General Joffre, 10th Brigade reinforced to c8000 men from:

3rd, 4th, 6th, 7th and 25th Regiments, each of c1000 men, all Motorised Infantry except for 4th Infantry,
5th Marine Battalion, c800 men,
3rd Artillery Battalion with 30x105mm and 3x155mm guns,
Armoured Car Squadron with 12 Panhards,
181st Military Police and Intelligence Company,
601st Anti-Aircraft Battalion.

Although not based on the Falklands, Argentine Air Force Skyhawk A-4 attack bombers inflicted heavy damage on the Royal Navy

Goose Green and **West Falkland** under command of General Parada, 3rd Bde but based in Stanley:

Goose Green - c1000 men from 12th Infantry Regiment, elements 601st AA Battalion, elements of the Argentine Air Force (later – half-battery of 3x105mm guns)

Port Howard - c800 men from 5th Infantry Regiment and elements 9th Engineer Company

Fox Bay - c900 men from 8th Motorised Infantry Regiment and elements 9th Engineer Company.

AIRCRAFT STRENGTH (losses to 20th May in brackets):

Navy - 5 MB.339s (1 MB.339 and 4 Mentors lost)
Coast Guard - 1 Puma (2 Skyvan)
Army - 2 Chinook, 4 Puma, 3 Agusta, 9 Iroquois (1 Puma)
Air Force - 15 Pucara, 2 Bell, 2 Chinook (9 Pucara)

Early British Task Force Movements
(Parts 17-19)

Part 17. ADVANCED GROUP SAILS SOUTH

WEEK ONE, 29th March-4th April 1982

Summary of British Ships & Aircraft Departing or on Passage (subsequent awards in brackets)

Royal Navy
All with **Advanced Group**:
Antrim, Capt B G Young (DSO) RN
Arrow, Cdr P J Bootherstone (DSC) RN
Brilliant, Capt J F Coward (DSO) RN
Coventry, Capt D Hart-Dyke MVO RN
Glamorgan, Capt M E Barrow
 (DSO) RN
Glasgow, Capt A P Hoddinott OBE RN
Plymouth, Capt D Pentreath (DSO) RN
Sheffield, Capt J F T G Salt RN

Nuclear Submarines:
Conqueror, Cdr C L Wreford-Brown
 (DSO) RN - from UK
Spartan, Cdr J B Taylor (MID) RN - in
 Central Atlantic
Splendid, Cdr R C Lane-Nott (MID) RN
 - from UK

Royal Fleet Auxiliary
Appleleaf, Capt G P A McDougall RFA
 - from Gibraltar
Fort Austin, Cdre S C Dunlop CBE
 (DSO) RFA - in Central Atlantic
Sir Tristram, Capt G R Green (DSC)
 RFA - from Belize
Tidespring, Capt S Redmond (OBE)
 RFA - Advanced Group
Typhoon, Capt J N Morris RMAS and
 NP 1820 - from UK

Royal Air Force
VC.10s of 10 Sqdn RAF, Wing Cdr O
 G Bunn MBE RAF
Hercules of Lyneham Wing RAF

Helicopters
Disembarked at Gibraltar - No.824
 NAS, B Flt, 2 Sea King HAS.2As

Falklands area
British Ice Patrol Vessel Endurance

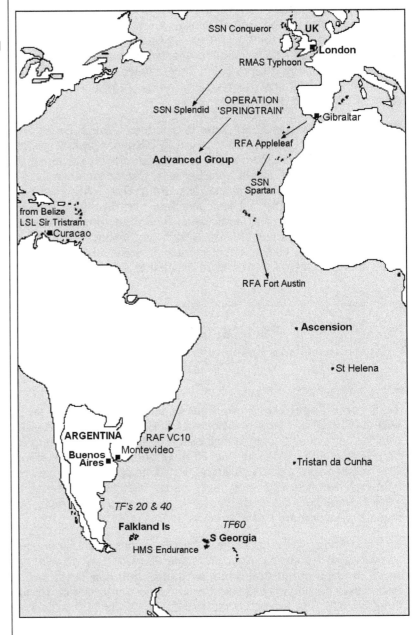

Task Force Departures - Quite fortuitously, warships of the First Flotilla commanded by Rear Admiral Woodward were in the Gibraltar area for "Operation Springtrain", and before the week was out, many were heading south. But even before the question of a Task Force arose, lone "Endurance" needed replenishment, so on Monday, RFA "Fort Austin" under the command of the Fleet Commodore sailed from Gibraltar. She left behind her two assigned Sea Kings of No.824 NAS which played an important part supplying other ships passing by. Once the go ahead was given, next to leave on Thursday 1st April and after loading live torpedoes at Gibraltar was nuclear submarine "Spartan" whose job was to help establish a credible maritime exclusion zone. Then on Friday an "Advanced Group" of "Springtrain" ships started to head for Ascension. Included with Admiral Woodward's flagship, destroyer "Antrim" was sister ship "Glamorgan", Type 42s "Coventry", "Glasgow" and "Sheffield", frigates "Arrow", "Brilliant", "Plymouth", and RFA fleet tanker "Tidespring". Previously on passage from Curacao to UK, RFA support tanker "Appleleaf" also sailed from Gibraltar to refuel Task Force ships on the way south. Two more nuclear submarines followed "Spartan" to the South Atlantic, but this time from Faslane in Scotland. First to go on Thursday was "Splendid" and within three weeks she was on patrol off the Argentine coast to shadow carrier "25 de Mayo".

Rear Admiral J F Woodward RN, Commander, Carrier Battle Group (Courtesy - MOD, Navy)

On Sunday, "Conqueror" left, later to sink the "General Belgrano". Also departing on Sunday was the first of many support ships - RMAS ocean tug "Typhoon" which sailed from Portland for Ascension before later heading on to South Georgia. Far to the west of the "Advanced Group" as it started south, RFA landing ship, logistic "Sir Tristram" sailed from Belize in Central America for Ascension as the first of the many ships that later merged as the Amphibious Task Group. The **RAF** also began building the vital air-bridge to Ascension and beyond, when the first Hercules flew from Lyneham to Gibraltar. However beating them to the South Atlantic was a VC.10 of 10 Sqdn which left on Saturday for Montevideo to pick up Rex Hunt and the men of NP 8901. They arrived back at Brize Norton on Monday. By the end of the week, the first Special Forces units were on their way south or about to leave. Some SBS may have sailed with "Conqueror" from Faslane, but most appear to have flown direct to Ascension.

Part 18. CARRIER BATTLE GROUP FOLLOWS
WEEK TWO, 5th-11th April 1982

Task Force Departures from Monday 5th April - Through an incredible amount of effort, a **Carrier Battle Group (CVBG)** and most of 3 Commando Brigade (3 Cdo Bde) were on their way to Ascension by week's end, with the carriers and some of their escort and supply ships being first to leave. "Hermes" and "Invincible" sailed from Portsmouth on Monday with RFA support tanker "Pearleaf" carrying heavy fuel oil for the older "Hermes". On the same day, frigates "Alacrity" and "Antelope" left Devonport along with RFA fleet tanker "Olmeda". Also RFA replenishment ship "Resource" loaded with naval stores left Rosyth to join the carriers. By the end of the week, "Antelope" had crossed over to the 3 Cdo Bde ships, but after sailing from Gibraltar on Thursday, frigates "Broadsword" and "Yarmouth" took her place.

By Good Friday 9th, most of the **3 Cdo Bde** units and their equipment had left on a variety of ships, although some flew to Ascension. Apart from one RM Cdo Coy on "Hermes" and part of one on "Resource", the rest sailed in ships of the **Amphibious Task Group**. On Tuesday 6th, assault ship "Fearless" headed out from Portsmouth as Brigade HQ with Commodore Clapp, and off Portland took on board Brigadier Thompson and three No.846 Sea Kings. Of the four LSLs sailing at this time, "Sir Percivale" and "Sir Lancelot" left from Marchwood, and "Sir Galahad" and "Sir Geraint" from Devonport. Next day, RFA stores support ship "Stromness" left Portsmouth after being converted to carry 45 Cdo RM.

Summary of British Ships & Aircraft Departing (subsequent awards in brackets)

Royal Navy
Alacrity, Cdr C J S Craig (DSC) RN
Antelope, Cdr N J Tobin (DSC) RN
Broadsword, Capt W R Canning ADC
  (DSO) RN
Fearless, Capt E S J Larken (DSO) RN
Hermes, Capt L E Middleton (DSO) RN
Invincible, Capt J J Black (DSO) MBE RN
Yarmouth, Cdr A Morton (DSC) RN

Royal Fleet Auxiliary
Brambleleaf, Capt M S J Farley RFA
Olmeda, Capt G P Overbury (OBE) RFA
Pearleaf, Capt J McCulloch RFA
Resource, Capt B A Seymour RFA
Sir Galahad, Capt P J G Roberts (DSO) RFA
Sir Geraint, Capt D E Lawrence (DSC) RFA
Sir Lancelot, Capt C A Purtcher-Wydenbruck
  (OBE) RFA
Sir Percivale, Capt A F Pitt (DSC) RFA
Stromness, Capt J B Dickinson (OBE) RFA

Merchant Ships
British Esk, Capt G Barber and Naval Party
  (NP) 1740
British Tay, Capt P T Morris
British Test, Capt I A Oliphant and NP 1790
Canberra, Capt D J Scott-Masson (CBE) and
  NP 1710, Capt C P O Burne (CBE) RN
Elk, Capt J P Morton (CBE) and NP 1720,
  Cdr A S Ritchie (OBE) RN
Irishman, Capt W Allen and NP 1770
Salvageman, Capt A J Stockwell and NP
  1760

Royal Air Force
Nimrod MR.1s of 42(TB) Sqdn RAF, Wing
  Cdr D L Baugh (OBE) RAF

3 Commando Brigade Air Squadron
9 Gazelles (3 each) on Sir Galahad, Sir Geraint and Sir Percivale
6 Scouts (3 each) on Fearless and Sir Lancelot

Naval Air Squadrons Embarked
No.800 - 12 Sea Harriers, Hermes
No.801 - 8 Sea Harriers, Invincible
No.820 - 11 Sea King HAS.5s, Invincible
No.826 - 9 Sea King HAS.5s, Hermes
No.846 - 9 Sea King HC.4s on Hermes and 3 on Fearless
No.824 A Flt - 2 Sea King HAS.2As, Olmeda
No.845 A Flt - 2 Wessex HU.5s, Resource
No.845 B Flt - 2 Wessex HU.5s, Fort Austin from Ascension
No.845 D Flt, 2 Wessex HU.5s, based at Ascension

UK Departures
Tankers British Tay, British Test, British Esk
Tugs Irishman, Salvageman

3 Commando Bde
Assault ship Fearless
Transports Canberra, Elk
LSLs Sir Galahad, Sir Geraint, Sir Lancelot, Sir Percivale
RFA Stromness
Frigate Antelope

Other RFAs at Sea
Appleleaf, Pearleaf

Carrier Battle Group
Carriers Hermes, Invincible
Frigate Alacrity
RFAs Olmeda, Resource
Frigates Broadsword, Yarmouth

RAF Aircraft
Nimrod MR1s, No 42(TB)
Hercules, VC10s

Advanced Group
DD Glamorgan, Coventry
Glasgow, Sheffield
Frigates Arrow, Brilliant

S Georgia Task Group
DD Antrim
Frigate Plymouth
RFA Tidespring
M Coy 42 Cdo/SBS/SAS

RFA Fort Austin/SAS

RFA Brambleleaf from Gulf Patrol

The first **merchantmen** also sailed. Taking just two days to convert from cruise ship to trooper, "Canberra" left Southampton on Friday 9th with nearly 3,000 men including most of 40 and 42 Cdo RM and 3 Para, and accompanied by RO-RO ship "Elk" loaded with ammunition and vehicles. Over the weekend, the first **tankers** headed for the South Atlantic, mainly to top-up the RFAs in the tanker holding areas - "British Esk" from Portland, "British Tay" after loading at Milford Haven and Campbeltown, and "British Test" from Portsmouth. Also from Portsmouth on Saturday, tugs "Irishman" and "Salvageman" loaded with towing and salvage gear left first for Ascension. Apart from the SBS, the other units destined to take part in re-capturing South Georgia flew to Ascension during the week - D Sqdn 22nd SAS apparently earlier on, followed by M Coy 42 Cdo from Brize Norton on Friday.

Ascension and South Atlantic - On Tuesday 6th the first RAF aircraft moved to Ascension's Wideawake airfield. Two Nimrod MR.1s of 42(TB) Sqdn arrived from St. Mawgan via the Azores, and next day started patrolling the seas around Ascension and supporting the nuclear subs on passage south. They were replaced in mid month by more modern MR.2s, but from the UK, later flew SAR for the Harriers as they staged to Ascension. Also on Tuesday, RFA "Fort Austin" reached the island and three days later continued on with D Sqdn SAS, two newly-embarked No.845 Wessex as well as three Sea Skua-equipped Lynx for ships of the **"Advanced Group"**. It was from these that the **South Georgia Task Group** was detached. After Admiral Woodward had transferred his flag to "Glamorgan", and under the command of Captain Young in "Antrim" they went ahead and reached Ascension on Saturday, but neither they, nor the rest of the "Advanced Group" which got in next day spent much time there. Earlier in the week, RFA support tanker "Brambleleaf", after leaving her Persian Gulf Patrol headed via the Cape of Good Hope to refuel the South Georgia ships.

Assault ship HMS Fearless (Courtesy - MOD, Navy)

Disposition of British Ships, Aircraft & Land Forces in Summary

UK Departures - tankers British Tay, British Test, British Esk, tugs Irishman, Salvageman

3 Commando Brigade Transport – assault ship Fearless, transports Canberra, Elk, LSLs Sir Galahad, Sir Geraint, Sir Lancelot, Sir Percivale, RFA Stromness, frigate Antelope

RFAs at Sea - Appleleaf, Pearleaf

Carrier Battle Group – carriers Hermes, Invincible, frigate Alacrity, RFA Olmeda, Resource, joined by frigates Broadsword, Yarmouth

Other Ships nearing or in South Atlantic - LSL Sir Tristram, SSNs Conqueror, Splendid, Spartan, RFA Fort Austin, Brambleleaf

Ships and Aircraft in Ascension Area
RAF Aircraft - Nimrod MR.1s of 42(TB), Hercules, VC.10s
Advanced Group - destroyers Glamorgan, Coventry, Glasgow, Sheffield, frigates Arrow, Brilliant
South Georgia Task Group - destroyer Antrim, frigate Plymouth, RFA Tidespring, M Coy 42 Cdo, SBS, D Sqn SAS

Departing Falkland's Area - ice patrol vessel Endurance

Part 19. ASCENSION ISLAND - Stepping Stone to Victory

Geography - Located at position 07.56' South, 14.22' West, 4,200 miles (3,700 nautical) from Britain and 3,800 (3,300 nautical) from the Falklands, Ascension was vital to the success of the Task Force. Close to the equator, but not unbearably hot, the 38 square mile island is a product of the mid-Atlantic ridge and completely volcanic in origin. In effect a mountain peak rising out of the sea, it is covered by sharp rock and extinct cones of dust and clinker. The highest point of Green Mountain is covered by the only tropical vegetation and trees in a largely barren landscape devoid of water and shelter. Surrounded by the almost continual swell of the South Atlantic, there are no natural harbours and only a single jetty at Clarence Bay and a small landing cove at English Bay. Amongst the abundant wildlife around the island is the sooty tern or "wideawake".

History - Discovered in 1501, presumably on Ascension Day, the island remained uninhabited until the early 19th century, when with Napoleon exiled to nearby St Helena, a small Royal Navy garrison was established. Until 1922, the Admiralty was in control but then Ascension became a dependency of St. Helena with the Administrator appointed by Britain. Wideawake airfield was built in World War 2 as a staging post between Brazil and Africa and had since been developed by the Americans and the single runway extended to over 10,000 feet to take heavy transport aircraft. With only a few movements each week, it mainly served the US satellite and missile tracking facilities and British submarine cable and satellite relay stations. American-controlled and operated by Pan American Airways, British aircraft normally had to give 24 hours notice of use, but during the war this requirement was waived. The population consisted solely of contracted employees and their families from St. Helena, Britain and the United States and at the last census totalled 1,051. The capital is Georgetown. By 1982 the associated islands of St. Helena, Ascension and Tristan da Cunha were one of the few Colonies remaining to Britain. With the use of Simonstown in South Africa ruled out for obvious political reasons, Ascension Island with its airfield was the only possible forward base, but one nearly 4,000 miles from the scene of action.

Summary of British Forces Support Unit Ascension Island

ROYAL AIR FORCE DEFENCES

Surrounding area - Nimrod maritime reconnaissance aircraft from early April.

Local air defence - three Harrier GR.3s of 1(F) Sqdn from early May until relieved later in the month by three Phantom FGR.2s of 29(F) Sqdn. RAF-manned mobile early warning radar on Green Mountain.

Ground defence - HQ Unit, No.3 Wing and No.15 Field Sqdn, RAF Regiment.

Other RAF Units - one 202 Sqdn Sea King and one 18 Sqdn Chinook helicopters for vertrep duties from early May. Also air movements, mobile servicing, tactical communications and meteorological units.

ARMY included:

Royal Corps of Signals - established rear link Communications Centres for the Task Force.

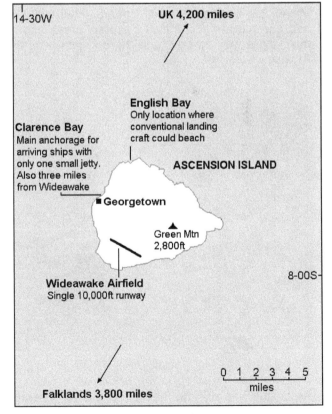

Royal Engineers - constructed 3½ mile fuel pipeline system to the airfield along with 180,000 gallon bulk fuel storage, and a desalination plant.

Royal Army Ordnance Corps - operated the pipeline system capable of delivering up to 300,000 gallons each day.

Royal Corps of Transport - 47 Air Despatch Squadron prepared stores for air dropping.

ROYAL NAVY

Naval Party 1222 - arrived in early April to receive men, stores, equipment, and helicopters flown out from Britain and to arrange for transhipment south.

Fleet Air Arm - maintenance personnel prepared the arriving helicopters

No.845 NAS - one Wessex HU.5 of D Flt, provided vertrep and crossdeck delivery services together with the two **RAF** helicopters which arrived later.

Role – In spite of its short-comings as a base, Ascension was invaluable. The **Task Force** could not be completely self-contained and a lot of men and supplies had to be ferried out to the South Atlantic by a constant stream of RAF Hercules and VC.10s, chartered freighters and mainly undisclosed American aircraft bringing in such stores as the latest Sidewinder AAMs. These were either delivered to the ships as they called in or passed by, or in urgent cases, air-dropped to them on the way to the Falklands or South Georgia. Few ships spent much time there although most of the **Amphibious Task Group** with 3 Cdo Bde did stay to prepare for the coming landings. In the case of the troops, only limited preparation was possible as there was no room for large scale manoeuvres other than marching, although they were able to train on the rapidly constructed firing ranges and practice disembarking from the troopships by helicopter and landing craft. More importantly, the opportunity was taken for the hastily loaded ships to re-distribute some of their stores to other ships, to receive much needed supplies from the UK, and where possible to "combat load" for an amphibious landing. Much of the necessary "cross decking" was carried out by the helicopters with their vertical replenishment capabilities, but also taking part were the Navy landing craft, Royal Corps of Transport Mexeflotes, and locally hired lighters. In all this movement there were major logistical problems. Wideawake had one runway and limited dispersal areas and helicopters could only land there because of the volcanic dust, there was no port, and the one jetty was three miles away and not always useable because of the Atlantic waves.

Wideawake and the terrain, Vulcan bombers on the tarmac (Courtesy - MOD, RAF)

Ascension was also the main base for **RAF operations** in support of the Task Force. Usually refuelled in the air by a great number of Victor tanker sorties, "Black Buck" air attacks on Stanley, reconnaissance, airdrops, and SAR were carried out by the resident Vulcans, Nimrods and Hercules. Added to all the helicopter and transport movements, these made Wideawake one of the busiest airfields in the world with up to 400 movements of all types each day.

Responsible for this array of activities was the **British Forces Support Unit Ascension Island** commanded by Capt R. McQueen (awarded CBE) RN. Involving all three services, some 1000 men, occasionally rising to 1500 did everything needed to support the Task Force, work the airfield in cooperation with the resident Americans and defend the island against possible attack by Argentine forces. In general the RAF was responsible for airfield operations and both air and ground defence, the Army built and manned the necessary additional facilities, and the Navy [NP 1222, Cdr G A C Woods (OBE) RN] operated a forward logistical base for the Task Force ships.

So important to the morale of the men taking part as well as the operation of the Task Force was the efficient handling of the vast amounts of private and official mail passing through the island. Although involving all services, the **Royal Engineers Postal and Courier Service** [WO1 R G Randall (MBE) RE] handled up to 2 tons of airmail daily and 1000 bags of parcels each week.

Preliminary British Operations
(Parts 20-30)

Part 20. 3 COMMANDO BRIGADE APPROACHES ASCENSION

WEEK THREE, Task Force Movements & Operations
12th-18th April 1982

Summary of British Ships & Aircraft Departing (subsequent awards in brackets)

Royal Fleet Auxiliary
Blue Rover, Capt D A Reynolds RFA

Merchant Ships
British Tamar, Capt D O W Jones and NP 1730
British Trent, Capt P R Waller
Stena Seaspread, Capt N Williams and NP 1810, Capt P Badcock (CBE) RN
Yorkshireman, Capt P Rimmer and NP 1780

Royal Air Force
Victors of 55 & 57 Sqdns, shortly Wing Cdr A W Bowman MBE RAF
Nimrod MR.2s of 120, 201 & 206 Sqdns, Wing Cdr D Emmerson (AFC) RAF

Naval Air Squadron Embarked at Ascension
No.845 C Flt - 2 Wessex HU.5s, Tidespring

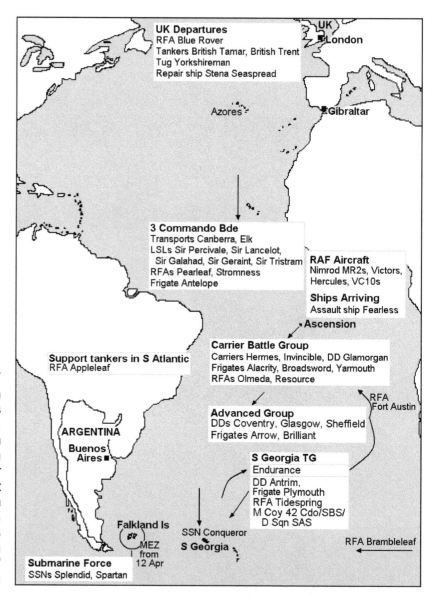

Task Force Departures from Monday 12th April - The few ships leaving all headed for Ascension. Tug "Yorkshireman" sailed from Portsmouth on Tuesday, followed on Friday by RFA small fleet tanker "Blue Rover" and off-shore support vessel "Stena Seaspread" with a heavy machine shop in her role as repair ship. More chartered tankers also sailed - "British Tamar" from Milford Haven and "British Trent" after loading at Fawley, Isle of Grain and Gosport.

Ascension - With M Coy 42 Cdo and two No.845 Wessex now on board "Tidespring", the **South Georgia ships** were on their way by Monday. Two days later the **"Advanced Group"** followed them south, with the exception of "Glamorgan", which returned north to transfer Admiral Woodward to "Hermes" as Commander, **Carrier Battle Group**. Reaching Ascension on Friday, the carriers continued working up their air wings as the CVBG helicopters and especially the No.846 Sea Kings took part in a massive vertrep. Next day, they were followed in by RFA "Resource", and ahead of the other amphibious ships by "Fearless" to allow Brigadier Thompson and Commodore Clapp to join Woodward on "Hermes" for a council of war chaired by Admiral Fieldhouse who had flown in from Northwood with the other commanders. The basic plan was (1) to blockade the Falklands with the nuclear submarines, (2) re-capture South Georgia, (3) establish air and sea control with the **Advanced** and **Carrier Battle Groups**, (4) carry out a landing from the **Amphibious Group** ships, and (5) retake the islands.

On their way south, Thompson, Clapp and their staffs, including Major S E Southby-Tailyour (awarded OBE) RM who as a previous commander of NP 8901 and yachtsman had surveyed much of the Falklands coast, had been planning how and where to land. With so little intelligence on Argentine forces and positions, a major task was to put ashore SBS and G Sqdn SAS teams to gather this information. On Sunday 18th, the **Carrier Battle Group** pressed on, leaving "Fearless" and other arriving ships of the **Amphibious Group** including LSL "Sir Tristram" to stay for up to three weeks preparing for the coming landings. To assist them, "Hermes" left behind four of her nine No.846 Sea Kings. Other arrivals over the next two days were nine Victor tankers of 55 and 57 Sqdns whose first job was to fly reconnaissance for the South Georgia Task Group.

South Atlantic and Falklands - Back on Monday 12th, "Endurance" met "Fort Austin" to embark D Sqdn SAS and replenish, and two days later joined up with the **South Georgia ships**. Next day, and only two days after arriving at Ascension, the first Nimrod MR.2 of the Kinloss Wing flew on to drop secret orders to "Antrim". Meanwhile "Fort Austin" headed back to Ascension transferring her Lynx to ships of the **"Advanced Group"**, whilst way off to the south west, nuclear submarine "Spartan" had been on patrol off Port Stanley since Monday.

Landing Ship Logistics RFA Sir Percivale heading south. Lashed alongside is a "Mexeflote". On the stern are three Royal Marine Gazelle helicopters and a group of Marines doing PT! (Courtesy - MOD, Navy)

Argentine warships now went to sea as **TF 79** to prepare for battle. Carrier "25 de Mayo" exercised her air group with land-based aircraft, further south three frigates sortied, and submarines "Salta" and "San Luis" probably started patrols to the north of the Falklands around this time, although "Salta" reportedly returned to port with mechanical problems. Over the next two weeks the Exocet-carrying, Super Etendards practiced attacks on their own type 42 destroyers.

Disposition of British Ships, Aircraft & Land Forces in Summary

UK Departures - RFA Blue Rover, tankers British Tamar, British Trent, tug Yorkshireman, repair ship Stena Seaspread

3 Commando Brigade Transport - transports Canberra, Elk, LSLs Sir Percivale, Sir Lancelot, Sir Galahad, Sir Geraint, Sir Tristram, RFA Pearleaf, Stromness, frigate Antelope

3 Commando Brigade to Ascension
By air - X and Y Coy, 45 Cdo RM, also M Coy 42 Cdo, SBS, SAS
With Carrier Battle Group (CVBG) - A Coy 40 Cdo on Hermes, part of Z Coy 45 Cdo on Resource

Rest of Brigade scattered around Amphibious Task Group ships: Brigade HQ on Fearless, B & C Coy 40 Cdo, K & L Coy 42 Cdo and 3 Para on Canberra, 45 Cdo RM (part) on RFA Stromness, Brigade helicopters on Fearless and four LSLs, light tanks on Elk (total strength approximately 5,500).
2 Para to follow on Norland, with equipment and AAC helicopters on Europic Ferry.

Ships and Aircraft in Ascension Area
RAF Aircraft - Nimrod MR.2s of 120, 201 and 206 Sqdns, Victors of 55 and 57 Sqdns, Hercules, VC.10s
Ship Arriving - assault ship Fearless

Support Tanker in South Atlantic - RFA Appleleaf

Carrier Battle Group - carriers Hermes, Invincible, destroyer Glamorgan, frigates Alacrity, Broadsword, Yarmouth, RFA Olmeda, Resource

Advanced Group - destroyers Coventry, Glasgow, Sheffield, frigates Arrow, Brilliant

South Georgia Task Group - destroyer Antrim, frigate Plymouth, RFA Tidespring, M Coy 42 Cdo, SBS, D Sqdn SAS, joined by ice patrol vessel Endurance

Returning to Ascension - RFA Fort Austin

In South Atlantic - RFA Brambleleaf

In Falklands & South Georgia Area - MEZ in force from Monday 12th April, SSNs Splendid, Spartan, Conqueror

---

Part 21. CARRIER BATTLE & ADVANCED GROUPS JOIN UP

WEEK FOUR, Task Force Movements & Operations
19th-25th April 1982

Task Force Departures from Monday 19th April - Only now were two more frigates ready to leave for Ascension. On Monday, type 21 "Ardent" and Leander class "Argonaut" sailed from Devonport along with two RFAs from Portland - support tanker "Plumleaf" and replenishment ship "Regent". That same day, the first of four white painted and Red Cross-marked hospital ships departed. Liner "Uganda" cut short a children's Mediterranean cruise and arriving at Gibraltar spent the weekend having full medical facilities installed before heading south. She was followed from Gib on Tuesday by survey ship "Hecla", and from Portsmouth on Saturday by "Herald" and "Hydra" all in the role of ambulance ships. One of their main tasks would be to ferry casualties between "Uganda" in the planned **Red Cross Box** and Montevideo.

HMS Hermes post-war (Courtesy - MOD, Navy)

Monday 19th also saw the departure from Southampton of "Fort Toronto" as the only fresh water tanker with the Task Force through to the end of the war. Then by the end of the week, three more tankers were on their way as fleet refuellers - "British Dart" after delayed loading at Loch Striven, "Anco Charger" from Fawley, and "British Wye" from Devonport. Finally on Sunday, another two RO-RO transports set out as part of the build-up of **3 Cdo Bde**. After conversion at Southampton, ferry "Europic Ferry" left Portland with much of 2 Para's equipment and three Scouts. And joining her from Devonport was container ship "Atlantic Conveyor" in an aircraft and helicopter support role, complete with flight deck, fuelling and maintenance facilities, and carrying six Navy Wessex and five RAF Chinook helicopters.

Ascension - Now the ships of the **Amphibious Group** started arriving to spend their time storing and re-stowing, replenishing by helicopter, landing craft and Mexeflote, and sending their troops ashore for limited exercises and weapons training. The slower **LSL Group** only stayed until the end of the following week, but the others remained a week longer. Meanwhile, and typical of the enterprise shown, "Elk" had the sides of her upper deck cut away for helicopter operations and added two 40mm Bofors. Two civilian tugs also arrived to join RMAS "Typhoon", with "Irishman" staying into early May, but "Salvageman" soon headed for Tristan da Cunha and on to South Georgia. During the week, RFA "Fort Austin" got back from her rendezvous with "Endurance", re-stored and returned south to join the CVBG.

Summary of British Ships & Aircraft Departing (subsequent awards in brackets)

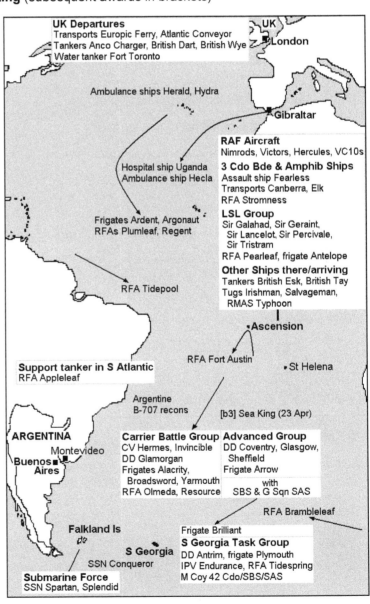

Royal Navy
Ardent, Cdr A W J West (DSC) RN
Argonaut, Capt C H Layman (DSO) MVO RN
Hecla, Capt G L Hope RN
Herald, Cdr R I C Halliday RN
Hydra, Cdr R J Campbell RN

Royal Fleet Auxiliary
Plumleaf, Capt R W M Wallace RFA
Regent, Capt J Logan RFA
Tidepool, Capt J W Gaffrey RFA - from Curacao

Merchant Ships
Atlantic Conveyor, Capt I H North (post DSC) and NP 1840, Capt M H G Layard (CBE) RN
Anco Charger, Capt B Hatton
British Dart, Capt J A M Taylor and NP 1800
British Wye, Capt D M Rundle (OBE)
Europic Ferry, Capt W J C Clarke (OBE) and NP 1860, Lt Cdr C E K Roe RN
Fort Toronto, Capt R I Kinnier and NP 1750
Uganda, Capt J G Clark and NP 1830, Cdr A B Gough RN and Surgeon Capt A J Rintoul RN

Helicopters Embarked
No.848 A Flt - 2 Wessex HU.5s on RFA Regent
6 Wessex HU.5s of No.848 D Flt and 5 Chinooks of 18 Sqdn RAF on Atlantic Conveyor,
3 Scouts of 656 Sqdn AAC on Europic Ferry

South Atlantic - On Wednesday 21st the **South Georgia Group** arrived off the forbidding island. Next day, on the 22nd, two helicopters were lost on South Georgia's Fortuna Glacier [first British aircraft losses - b1,b2 - see Part 22]. Still on the 21st and far to the north, one of "Hermes'" Sea Harriers intercepted an Argentine Boeing 707 of Grupo 1 approaching the **Carrier Battle Group**. This happened each time one of them came near over the next three days, when in response to warnings through diplomatic channels, they stayed away. On Friday 23rd in the evening, the first Task Force aircraft was lost at sea in the South Atlantic when one of "Hermes" five remaining No.846 Sea King HC.4s flying on vertrep crashed in poor weather with the loss of her crewman [third British aircraft loss - b3]. By Sunday 25th, and less than seven days from combat, the carriers rendezvoused with the **Advanced Group** ships. Before then in the South Georgia area, the two helicopters had been lost, detached frigate "Brilliant" had joined other ships there in the helicopter attacks on submarine "Santa Fe", and that same Sunday, the Argentine garrison on South Georgia was surrendering.

Disposition of British Ships, Aircraft & Land Forces in Summary

Other UK Departures - transports Europic Ferry, Atlantic Conveyor, tankers Anco Charger, British Dart, British Wye, water tanker Fort Toronto

On Passage, North Atlantic - ambulance ships Herald, Hydra, hospital ship Uganda & ambulance ship Hecla, frigates Ardent, Argonaut, RFA Plumleaf, Regent, also RFA Tidepool

Ships and Aircraft in Ascension Area
RAF Aircraft - Nimrods, Victors, Hercules, VC.10s
3 Commando Brigade & Amphibious Group Ships - assault ship Fearless, transports Canberra, Elk, RFA Stromness
LSL Group - LSLs Sir Galahad, Sir Geraint, Sir Lancelot, Sir Percivale, Sir Tristram, RFA Pearleaf, frigate Antelope
Other Ships at Ascension or Reaching the Area on the Way South - tankers British Esk, British Tay, tugs Irishman, Salvageman, RMAS Typhoon

Reaching and Departing Ascension - RFA Fort Austin

Support Tanker in South Atlantic - RFA Appleleaf

Carrier Battle Group - carriers Hermes, Invincible, destroyer Glamorgan, frigates Alacrity, Broadsword, Yarmouth, RFA Olmeda, Resource joined by:
Advanced Group - destroyers Coventry, Glasgow, Sheffield, frigate Arrow, plus SBS & G Sqdn SAS

In South Atlantic - RFA Brambleleaf

In or Approaching Falklands Area - SSN Splendid, Spartan, Conqueror

South Georgia Task Group - destroyer Antrim, frigate Plymouth, ice patrol vessel Endurance, RFA Tidespring, M Coy 42 Cdo, SBS, D Sqdn SAS, joined by frigate Brilliant.

Part 22. SOUTH GEORGIA RETAKEN - Operation "Paraquet"

Summary of Main Events

British Forces Taking Part

Destroyer Antrim, 2x4.5in, 1xWessex HAS.3	Land forces 250 from:	Commanders Capt B G Young (awarded DSO) RN of Antrim, Task Group
Frigate Plymouth, 2x4.5in, 1xWasp	M Coy 42 Cdo RM No.2 Section SBS RM	Maj J M G Sheridan RM, Landing Forces
Ice patrol ship Endurance, 2xWasp	D Sqdn SAS 148 Bty 29 Cdo Regt team	Maj C N G Delves (DSO), D Sqdn SAS
RFA Tidespring, 2xWessex HU.5s joined by frigate Brilliant, 2xLynx		Capt C J Nunn RM, M Coy 42 Cdo

1. 21st - **Mountain Troop SAS** landed on Fortuna Glacier for move to Leith, but stopped by blizzards.
2. 22nd - **Mountain Troop** picked up by Antrim Wessex after both Tidespring Wessex crashed [b1, b2].
3. Gemini assault craft from Antrim then put **Boat Troop SAS** ashore at Grass Island to observe Leith.
4. From 22nd - **SBS** landed at Hound Bay and tried to move across Cumberland Bay East by Gemini to a position south of Grytviken. Stopped by ice and laid up. Later picked up and reportedly landed at Moraine Fiord.
5. 23rd - Submarine threat; Task Force ships except Endurance moved out to sea.
6. 24th - Argentine Boeing 707 overflew Endurance and Task Force ships (except Tidespring with M Coy, 42 Cdo) ordered back in to hunt for submarine.
7. 25th - Task Force helicopters damaged submarine Santa Fe (abandoned at King Edward Point jetty) and then put landing force ashore.
8. 25th - As Antrim and Plymouth bombarded from out in Cumberland Bay, **SAS/SBS/RM** landing force went ashore at Hestesletten and advanced through Grytviken towards King Edward Point. Argentines surrendered.
9. 26th - Argentine force at Leith surrendered to Plymouth and Endurance

Before the **Task Group** arrived off South Georgia on the morning of Wednesday 21st, submarine "Conqueror" had already been on patrol for two days and on Tuesday, an RAF Victor from Ascension made the first radar reconnaissance flight off the coast. Two more of these 7,000 mile, 14 hour missions followed over Thursday and Saturday nights, but neither they nor "Conqueror" spotted any Argentine ships. The first task was for observation posts to be set up by the SAS near Leith and the SBS south of Grytviken. Although there were doubts about the SAS plans, Mountain Troop was put down safely on Fortuna Glacier at mid-day that Wednesday 21st by the three Wessex available. Forced to camp overnight in blizzard conditions, attempts were made to pick up the men next morning, but as the helicopters flew up the glacier in atrocious weather, they had to return to refuel. Next time in, the men were lifted off, but in the blinding snow, both "Tidespring's" Wessex crashed [first British aircraft losses - b1, b2]. Then "Antrim's" own Wessex, skillfully piloted by Lt Cdr Stanley first unloaded his passengers and eventually managed to rescue the stranded men in one over-loaded lift later that afternoon. To make up the losses, "Brilliant" was detached from the Task Force with her two Lynx.

Late that Thursday night (22nd) from "Antrim" out in Stromness Bay, SAS Boat Troop headed in for Grass Island, but again with near fatal results. Five Gemini assault craft set out in the dark, but two broke down and were reported missing next morning. "Antrim's" Wessex was once again to the rescue and soon found one of the crews, but the other was not located until after the surrender when their rescue beacon was activated. But at least by Friday morning the SAS men were in position near Leith.

All this time the SBS were no more fortunate in their first attempts to approach Grytviken. Accounts somewhat differ, but apparently they landed at Hound Bay from "Endurance" early on Thursday morning, and made their way across Sorling Valley before trying to cross Cumberland Bay East by Gemini. Stopped by glacier ice, they laid up, were later picked up and reportedly landed at Moraine Fiord by Wasp on Saturday 24th.

Before then RFA tanker "Brambleleaf" arrived and started to refuel "Tidespring", but in a sub alert on Friday 23rd, broke away damaging some of her gear. (The transfer was completed on Saturday and the tanker headed for England.) Then the Task Group was warned that the "Santa Fe" (Lt Cdr Bicain) was on her way into Grytviken with men and supplies. Apart from "Endurance" which stayed close to the coast amongst the ice, the ships headed away taking with them the main landing force of M Coy 42 Cdo on "Tidespring". A Boeing 707 of Grupo 1 now overflew "Endurance" on Saturday, and "Antrim", "Plymouth" and the newly arrived "Brilliant" were ordered to close South Georgia to deal with the submarine threat leaving "Tidespring" some

200 miles away in comparative safety. Armed with a variety of weapons, the ship's helicopters prepared to hunt down the submarine which got into Grytviken that evening.

On Sunday morning (25th) as "Santa Fe" headed out on the surface, she was spotted off Cumberland Bay by Lt Cdr Stanley's Wessex. Near-missed by two Mk.11 depth charges and with some damage, the submarine limped back towards Grytviken. As she did, one of "Brilliant's" Lynx attacked with a Mk.46 torpedo, the two "Endurance" Wasps (Flight Commander, Lt Cdr Ellerbeck) fired AS.12 missiles hitting her fin, "Plymouth's" Wasp fired another AS.12 and both of "Brilliant's" Wasps strafed with machine guns. The warships meanwhile headed for the action at high speed. Although the attacks only slightly damaged the "Santa Fe" and wounded one crewman, by noon she was abandoned alongside the jetty at King Edward Point. (Later, on being moved to Grytviken, one of "Santa Fe's" crew was shot and killed in the mistaken belief he was trying to scuttle the boat.)

Lieutenant Commander I Stanley RN, Flight Commander, No 737 NAS, HMS Antrim (Courtesy - RNAS Yeovilton)

With the submarine's return and the potential defenders now numbering some 140, the decision was made to land whatever force could be mustered under covering naval gunfire and without waiting for the bulk of M Coy to arrive on "Tidespring". Under the command of Major Sheriden RM, a company of 75 men was assembled from the SAS, SBS and other Royal Marines with Major Delves and Capt Nunn RM as troop commanders. In the early afternoon (25th still) from out in Cumberland Bay and under the control of a naval gunfire observer landed by "Endurance's" Wasp, "Antrim" and "Plymouth" laid down a 4.5 inch barrage all around the Argentine positions at King Edward Point. Landed by "Antrim's" Wessex and "Brilliant's" two Lynx at Hestesletten, the first wave of the ad hoc force advanced through the whaling station at Grytviken and across an unsuspected minefield towards the BAS base. As they approached, white flags were hoisted and around 5pm local time, the Argentines surrendered without a shot being fired. When contacted by radio, the small detachment of marines at Leith under the command of Lt Cdr Astiz refused to surrender.

Next morning (Monday 26th), "Endurance" and "Plymouth" sailed along to Leith and the Marines gave in. "Plymouth" and "Brilliant" left on Wednesday 28th to join the CVBG, but "Tidespring" now with nearly 150 Argentine POW's and the 40 civilian workers from Leith embarked, and escorted by "Antrim" did not head north for Ascension until Sunday 2nd. A disappointed M Coy 42 Cdo stayed on to garrison South Georgia, and "Endurance" remained as guardship.

British Gallantry Awards included:
Retaking of South Georgia
HMS Antrim Lt Cdr I Stanley (DSO) RN
HMS Endurance Lt Cdr J A Ellerbeck (DSC) RN

Part 23. AMPHIBIOUS GROUP EXERCISES AT ASCENSION

WEEK FIVE, British Task Force Movements
26th April-2nd May 1982

Task Force Departures from Monday 26th April - Diesel patrol submarine "Onyx" sailed from Gosport on Monday at the same time as the last of the **Amphibious Group** headed for Ascension. Assault ship "Intrepid", not long after being readied for disposal, left from Portland, RO-RO ferry "Norland" from Portsmouth with the men of 2 Para, followed by the sixth LSL "Sir Bedivere" from Marchwood after returning from Vancouver, Canada. The early part of the week also saw the departure from Devonport of RFA support tanker "Bayleaf" on her maiden voyage and tanker "British Avon" from Portsmouth. Quite separately, RFA fleet tanker "Tidepool" arrived at Ascension from Curacao with a full British crew after being borrowed back from Chile to where she was being delivered.

During the week a variety of small ships headed for Ascension. Converted for minesweeping duties at Rosyth, the five trawlers "Cordella", "Farnella", "Junella", "Northella" and "Pict" left Portland on Tuesday 27th with Navy crews after working-up as the **11th Mine Countermeasures Squadron**. Next to go were three despatch ships, two of them Navy fishery protection vessels from Portland after being modified at Portsmouth - "Leeds Castle" on Thursday and "Dumbarton Castle" on Saturday, and from Devonport on Thursday, cable ship "Iris". By the end of the week RMAS mooring, salvage and boom vessel "Goosander" was on her way from Rosyth to lay out and maintain the moorings at Ascension.

Summary of British Ships & Aircraft Departing
(subsequent awards in brackets)

Royal Navy
Dumbarton Castle, Lt Cdr N D Wood RN
Intrepid, Capt P G V Dingemans
  (DSO) RN
Leeds Castle, Lt Cdr C F B Hamilton RN
Onyx, Lt Cdr A Johnson RN

11th MCMS
Cordella, Lt Cdr M C G Holloway RN
Farnella, Lt R J Bishop RN
Junella, Lt Cdr M Rowledge RN
Northella, Lt Cdr J P S Greenop RN
Pict, Lt Cdr D G Garwood (MID) RN

Royal Fleet Auxiliary
Bayleaf, Capt A E T Hunter RFA
Sir Bedivere, Capt P J McCarthy
  (OBE) RFA
Goosander, Capt A MacGregor RMAS
  and NP 1930

Merchant Ships
British Avon, Capt J W M Guy
Iris, Capt A Fulton (OBE) and NP 1870,
  Lt Cdr J Bithell RN
Norland, Capt D A Ellerby (CBE) and NP
  1850, Cdr C J Esplin-Jones (OBE) RN

RAF Aircraft
Vulcans of 44, 50 & 101 Sqdns RAF,
  Sqdn Ldr A C Montgomery RAF

Fleet Air Arm Aircraft
8 Sea Harriers of No.809 NAS
2 Wessex HU.5s of No.845 E Flt & 1 Sea
  King HC.4 of No.846 NAS on Intrepid

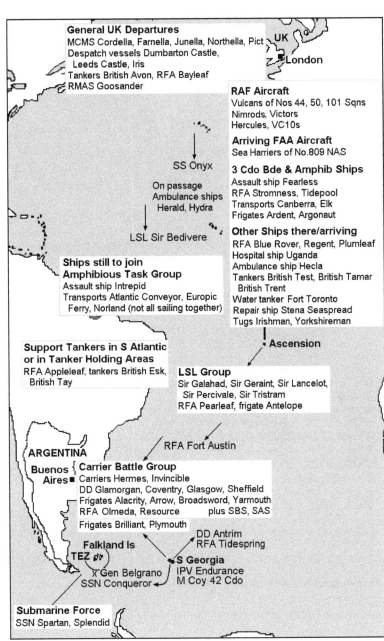

Ascension - As **3 Cdo Bde** prepared to move south and "Canberra" practised offloading her troops by LCU and helicopter, various ships reached the island, and usually in a matter of days or less, continued south. By the weekend, this included the slower **LSL Group** of the **Amphibious Task Group** which was on its way escorted by frigate "Antelope". By then Major General Moore had flown down to meet Thompson and Clapp to review the landing options now reduced to three East Falkland's sites. With two of these around Stanley and thus close to the main Argentine defences, San Carlos Water became the preferred option. Important air movements also took place. On Thursday 29th the first two Vulcan B.2 bombers arrived from Waddington to prepare for "Black Buck 1", the opening raid on Stanley on Saturday. And over Saturday and Sunday, eight Sea Harriers of No.809 NAS reached Wideawake after making the nine hour flight from Yeovilton refuelled by Victor tankers. There they awaited the arrival of RAF GR.3s and their transport south, the doomed "Atlantic Conveyor".

South Atlantic - As the **Carrier Battle Group** approached the eastern edge of the TEZ, frigates "Brilliant" and "Plymouth" joined up on Thursday from South Georgia carrying No.2 SBS and D Sqdn SAS. Next day the TEZ came into force, and on Saturday 1st May, the Royal Navy sailed in to start the softening-up attacks designed to establish air and sea superiority. Earlier in the week, Argentine trawler "Narwhal" was warned to keep clear of the Task Force and on Sunday, off to the south west, cruiser "General Belgrano" was torpedoed and sunk by the "Conqueror". That same Sunday, "Tidespring" and "Antrim" departed South Georgia for Ascension carrying the Argentine POW's.

Aircraft/helicopter support ship "Atlantic Conveyor" practicing Sea Harrier landings before sailing south

Disposition of British Ships, Aircraft & Land Forces in Summary

UK Departures - MCMS Cordella, Farnella, Junella, Northella, Pict, despatch vessels Dumbarton Castle, Leeds Castle, Iris, tankers British Avon and RFA Bayleaf, RMAS Goosander, LSL Sir Bedivere, SS Onyx

Ships on Passage to Join Amphibious Task Group (not all sailing together) - assault ship Intrepid, transports Atlantic Conveyor, Europic Ferry, Norland. Also on passage – ambulance ships Herlad, Hydra

Ships and Aircraft in Ascension Area
RAF Aircraft - Vulcans of Nos.44, 50 and 101 Sqdns, Nimrods, Victors, Hercules, VC.10s
Arriving FAA Aircraft - Sea Harriers of No.809 NAS
3 Commando Brigade & Amphibious Group Ships - assault ship Fearless, RFA Stromness, Tidepool, transports Canberra, Elk, frigates Ardent, Argonaut
Other Ships at Ascension or Reaching the Area on the Way South - RFA Blue Rover, Regent, Plumleaf, hospital ship Uganda, ambulance ship Hecla, tankers British Test, British Tamar, British Trent, water tanker Fort Toronto, repair ship Stena Seaspread, tugs Irishman, Yorkshireman

LSL Group - Sir Galahad, Sir Geraint, Sir Lancelot, Sir Percivale, Sir Tristram, RFA Pearleaf, frigate Antelope

Support Tankers in South Atlantic or in Tanker Holding Areas - RFA Appleleaf, British Esk, British Tay

In South Atlantic - RFA Fort Austin

Carrier Battle Group - carriers Hermes, Invincible, destroyers Coventry, Glamorgan, Glasgow, Sheffield, frigates Alacrity, Arrow, Broadsword, Yarmouth, RFA Olmeda, Resource joined by frigates Brilliant, Plymouth with SBS and SAS

Submarine Force - TEZ in force from Friday 30th April - SSN Spartan, Splendid, Conqueror (sank ARA General Belgrano)

Departing South Georgia - destroyers Antrim, RFA Tidespring

South Georgia - IPV Endurance, M Coy 42 Cdo

Part 24. ARA GENERAL BELGRANO SUNK

WEEK FIVE, Falkland Area Operations
26th April-2nd May 1982

Summary of Main Events

Arriving Carrier Squadrons:
HMS Hermes
No.800 - 12 Sea Harriers [Lt Cdr A D Auld (awarded DSC) RN]
No.826 - 9 Sea King HAS.5s [Lt Cdr D J S Squier (AFC) RN]
HMS Invincible
No.801 - 8 Sea Harriers [Cdr N D Ward (DSC) AFC RN]
No.820 - 11 Sea King HAS.5s [Lt Cdr R J S Wykes-Sneyd (AFC) RN

RN Warships on Station:
SSN's - Spartan, Splendid in Falkland's area/off Argentine coast
CVBG - Carriers Hermes, Invincible, destroyers Coventry, Glasgow, Sheffield, frigates Broadsword, Plymouth, RFA Olmeda, Resource, with SBS and SAS

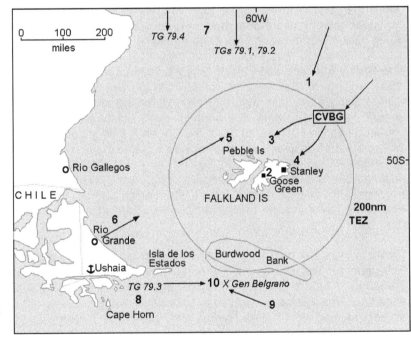

1. 'Black Buck 1' - Vulcan raid on Stanley (1st)
2. Argentine aircraft losses at Goose Green - [a2,a3,a4] Pucara (1st)
3. Frigates Brilliant, Yarmouth with ASW Sea Kings hunt for San Luis (1st)
4. Destroyer Glamorgan, frigates Alacrity, Arrow carry out shore bombardment. All slightly damaged by air attack (1st)
5. Argentine aircraft losses off North Falklands (1st) - [a5,a6] Mirage, [a7] Dagger, [a8] Canberra
6. Super Etendards abort Exocet mission (2nd)
7. Argentine Task Force 79 to North of Falklands: **TGs 79.1 & 2** – Carrier 25 de Mayo and escorts. Prepared to launch Skyhawk attack Sunday morning. Aircraft loss - [a9] Lynx (2nd); **TG 79.4** - 3 frigates
8. Argentine Task Force 79 South of Falklands: **TG 79.3** - Cruiser Belgrano, destroyers Hipolito Bouchard, Piedra Bueno
9. SSN Conqueror from South Georgia
10. Sinking of GENERAL BELGRANO (2nd), aircraft loss - [a10] Alouette

As Admiral Woodward's **Carrier Battle Group** entered the TEZ on Saturday 1st May, a lone Vulcan bomber piloted by Flt Lt Withers approached the Falklands for "Black Buck 1". Leaving Ascension late on Friday with a second Vulcan and eleven Victor tankers, some of which refuelled each other, the first air-raid on Stanley was about to be made. Intended to deny the airfield to fast jets, 21x1,000lb bombs were dropped from 10,000 feet early that morning. Only one hit the runway, but the attack signalled the RAF's ability to strike in the South Atlantic and against mainland targets. The Vulcan returned safely from its nearly 16 hour, 8,000 mile round trip, and one of the Victor captains - Sqdn Ldr Tuxford, was decorated for his part in the operation. ("Black Buck 2" on Tuesday morning was made from 16,000 feet but failed to hit the runway).

As the first "Black Buck" raid took place on the 1st, the carriers with just twenty Sea Harriers between them prepared to go into action. Keeping to the east of the Falklands to reduce the chance of air attack and screened by their anti-submarine Sea Kings, "Invincible" flew off Sea Harriers for combat air patrols as "Hermes" aircraft followed up the Vulcan raid with ground strikes. Soon after 8.00am, nine of them hit Stanley airfield, destroying installations and stores and damaging a civilian Islander aircraft with CBUs. The other three went in at Goose Green, wrecking one Pucara [a2] and badly damaging two more [a3, a4].

Flt Lt W F M Withers RAF, Vulcan pilot, on return from the 1st May 1982 "Black Buck 1" bombing raid on Stanley
(Courtesy - MOD, RAF)

All this time, Type 22 "Brilliant" and Rothesay class "Yarmouth" with three ASW Sea Kings from "Hermes" searched all day for the suspected Argentine submarine "San Luis", but failed to find her. Also detached were "Glamorgan", and Type 21s "Alacrity" and "Arrow" for the first of many bombardments of the Stanley area. "Alacrity's" Lynx took off that afternoon to provide naval gunfire spotting, but stumbled on Argentine patrol craft "Islas Malvinas" sheltering near Kidney Island just to the north of Stanley. Going into attack with GPMG, she damaged the vessel, but was hit by the return fire, and "Arrow's" Lynx later took over the spotting duties. Just before 5.00pm, as the warships continued their bombardment, they were attacked without warning by three Grupo 6 Daggers, and all received minor damage from cannon fire or near misses.

The **Grupo 6 attack** was part of Argentina's response that Saturday the 1st to what was believed to be a full scale landing. Sorties were launched from the mainland by Skyhawks, Canberras and Daggers, with some Mirage flying cover, and also by Falklands-based aircraft. Around the time of this strike, four Argentine FAA aircraft were lost towards the north of the Falklands to Sea Harriers and their Sidewinders. "Glamorgan" vectored two No.801 aircraft on to two Grupo 8 Mirage, one of which exploded over Pebble Island in the first air-to-air kill of the war, and the other, damaged by a missile and approaching Stanley was shot down by Argentine AA [a5, a6]. Next, two Sea Harriers of No.800 NAS claimed the Squadron's first victim in combat by downing one of two Grupo 6 Daggers flying escort [a7]. Then further to the north, two more No.801 Harriers accounted for one of three Grupo 2 Canberras looking for British ships [a8]. Next day, two CANA Super Etendards flew from the mainland for an Exocet attack on the Task Force, but turned back with refuelling problems.

Earlier in the week before the British arrival, ships of the Argentine Navy sailed from the north and south of the Falklands as Task Force 79. By early Sunday morning (the 2nd), carrier "25 de Mayo" to the north was preparing to launch a Skyhawk attack which was aborted because of light winds, and that same day both escorting Type 42s were involved in separate incidents. "Hercules" readied but failed to fire a Sea Dart against an approaching No.801 Sea Harrier, and "Santisima Trinidad" lost her Lynx in a flying accident [a9]. By then, submarine "San Luis" may have carried out the first of a number of unsuccessful attacks before she returned to port around the end of the month. To the south, Sunday also saw one of the most controversial incidents of the war - the loss of cruiser "General Belgrano" and over 300 men.

Not used during "Operation Rosario", the "General Belgrano" put to sea from Ushuaia on Monday 26th April escorted by two Exocet-armed destroyers, and three days later was ordered to patrol south of the shallow Burdwood Bank. On Friday, nuclear submarine "Conqueror" made first contact at long range, and on Saturday closed in to shadow. Although just outside the TEZ, "GENERAL BELGRANO", as the southern arm of TF.79 was a potential threat to the carriers and her destruction was ordered. Attacked and hit at 4.00pm on Sunday 2nd May by two conventional Mark 8 torpedoes she was soon abandoned, and went down with heavy loss of life and her helicopter [a10]. A third torpedo hit the escorting "Hipolito Bouchard" without exploding but possibly caused some damage, and "Conqueror" was therefore presumably counter-attacked by "Piedra Bueno", which later returned with other Argentine ships to search for the cruiser's survivors. Shortly after the sinking, the main units of the Argentine Navy returned to port or stayed in coastal waters for the rest of the war. Although British special forces may already have landed from the nuclear subs, the SBS and G Sqdn SAS now went ashore on the Falklands to check out landing sites and to target aircraft, troops and stores for naval bombardment and Harrier strikes. Some of the teams stayed in position, close to the Argentines and in bad weather for many days at a time.

Areas of operation on East Falkland were believed to include Bluff Cove, Stanley, Berkeley Sound, Cow Bay, Port Salvador, San Carlos Water, Goose Green and Lafonia, and over on West Falkland, Pebble Island, Port Howard and Fox Bay. The first patrols started flying in Saturday night in "Hermes'" four remaining No.846 Sea King HC.4s, which equipped with PNG for night flying, played such an important role over the next six weeks.

British Gallantry Awards included:

Vulcan attack - 'Black Buck 1'
Flt Lt W F M Withers (DFC) RAF
Sqdn Ldr R Tuxford (AFC) RAF

Special forces missions during the war, including:

SBS & SAS patrols
Capt A J G Wight (MC) Welsh Guards
Cpl T Brookes (MM) Royal Signals
Sgt T Collings (MM) RM
Sgt J G Mather (MM)

No.846 NAS - special forces insertions
Lt N J North (DSC) RN
Lt Cdr S C Thornewill (DSC) RN, CO
Cpl Aircrewman M D Love (post DSM) RM
CPO Aircrewman M J Tupper (DSM)

Part 25. TASK FORCE IN ACTION

WEEK SIX, British Task Force Movements
3rd-9th May 1982

Task Force Departures from Monday 3rd May - Monday saw the last nuclear submarines on their way to the South Atlantic when "Valiant" left Faslane for patrol off the Argentine coast. ("Courageous" also possibly left around now). Two more warships also sailed from other parts of the world for Ascension and on to the Total Exclusion Zone (TEZ) after carrying out guardship duties - frigate "Ambuscade" from Gibraltar on Monday and destroyer "Exeter" from the West Indies on Friday to replace the lost "Sheffield". Two merchantmen left with much needed supplies for the Task Force, but this time via South Georgia. On Tuesday 4th cargo ship "Lycaon" sailed from Southampton loaded with ammunition, and on Saturday refrigerated stores ship "Saxonia" from Plymouth mainly with food. Additional tankers also headed for the South Atlantic during the week. "Alvega" from Portsmouth for Ascension to serve out the war as a base storage tanker supplying heavy fuel oil, diesel and aviation fuel, and "Eburna" sailing from the West Indies having earlier been converted for fleet refuelling at Plymouth. Then on Sunday, part of **5th Inf Bde** headed out from Southampton on RO-RO ferries "Baltic Ferry" and "Nordic Ferry".

Ascension - Late on Monday 3rd, two Vulcans with their Victor tankers took off to get one of the bombers to Stanley early next morning for "Black Buck 2". Meanwhile the build-up of aircraft continued. Starting on Monday, nine Harrier GR.3s from RAF Wittering (a tenth returned) reached Wideawake over the next three days after making the nine hour flight from St Mawgan. Of these, three stayed on to provide the first local air defence for Ascension and the other six prepared to embark on "Atlantic Conveyor" later in the week. During this week the two No.845 Wessex based on the island were joined in their vertrep duties by one of "Atlantic Conveyor's" Chinooks and by a flown-in Sea King HAR.3 which also provided search-and-rescue.

Now the bulk of **3 Cdo Bde** followed in the wake of the slower LSLs. On Thursday 6th, "Canberra" left with 40 and 42 Cdo RM and 3 Para, and with both her and "Elk" carrying their own Sea King HC.4s. Accompanying them were RFA "Tidepool" and two escorting frigates. As they departed, the rest of the **Amphibious Group** ships were arriving to join "Fearless" and RFA "Stromness" (now with most of 45 Cdo RM on board), but only to stay for a short time. Assault ship "Intrepid" and transport "Atlantic Conveyor" reached the island on

Wednesday, and the merchantman took on board the awaiting eight Sea Harriers and six GR.3s to add to her already large complement of helicopters. Finally, transports "Europic Ferry" and "Norland" got in with 2 Para after calling in at Freetown on the way. Within a matter of hours on Friday, they and the last of the amphibious ships were heading south.

Summary of British Ships & Aircraft Departing

Royal Navy
Ambuscade, Cdr P J Mosse RN
Courageous, Cdr R T N Best RN
Exeter, Capt H M Balfour MVO RN
Valiant, Cdr T M Le Marchand (awarded MID) RN

Merchant Ships
Alvega, Capt A Lazenby
Baltic Ferry, Capt E Harrison and NP 1960, Lt Cdr G B Webb RN
Eburna, Capt J C Beaumont
Lycaon, Capt H R Lawton and NP 1900, Lt Cdr D J Stiles RN
Nordic Ferry, Capt R Jenkins and NP 1950, Lt Cdr M St J D A Thorburn RN
Saxonia, Capt H Evans and NP 1910

RAF Aircraft
9 Harrier GR.3s of 1(F) Sqdn

Aircraft Embarked:
Army Aircraft
3 Scouts of 656 Sqdn AAC on Baltic Ferry
6 Gazelles of 656 Sqdn AAC on Nordic Ferry

At Ascension
No.845 D Flt - 2 Wessex HU.5s on Ascension to Intrepid
No.845 E Flt - 2 Wessex HU.5s from Intrepid to Tidepool
No.846 - 9 Sea King HC.4s on Canberra (1), Elk (3), Fearless (3), Intrepid (2)
8 Sea Harriers of No.809 NAS, 6 Wessex HU.5s of No.848 D Flt, 6 Harrier GR.3s of 1(F) Sqdn RAF, and 4 Chinooks of 18 Sqdn RAF on Atlantic Conveyor

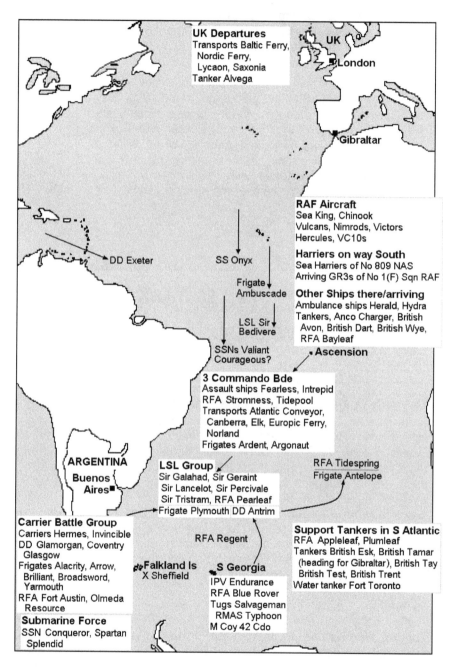

South Atlantic – Later in the week, escorting warships "Antelope" and "Antrim" met and exchanged roles. "Antelope" carried on north with "Tidespring" and her POWs bound for Ascension, while "Antrim" took over the task of escorting the LSL Group south, in which she was joined by "Plymouth" from the CVBG. Further south, but back on Tuesday 4th, the Carrier Battle Group suffered its first, shocking casualty, when destroyer "Sheffield" was hit by an air-launched Exocet, the missile which exercised such an influence over Task Force operations throughout the war. Meanwhile "Endurance", on her own at South Georgia, saw the start of the build-up there when two tugs arrived. RMAS "Typhoon" stayed through May, while "Salvageman" soon sailed to assist "Sheffield" but without success, and moved on to what was later known as the Tug, Repair and

Logistic Area (TRALA) to the east of the Falklands. On Sunday, RFA "Blue Rover" followed them in to Cumberland Bay to take up her duties as station tanker.

RAF Hercules at Wideawake Airfield with two Nimrods in the left background. Note the volcanic terrain of Ascension Island.

Disposition of British Ships, Aircraft & Land Forces in Summary

RAF Vulcan bomber (both courtesy - MOD, RAF)

UK Departures – transports Baltic Ferry, Nordic Ferry, Lycaon, Saxonia, tanker Alvega

Ships on Passage, Central/South Atlantic – destroyer Exeter, SS Onyx, SSN Valiant, frigate Ambuscade, SSN Courageous, LSL Sir Bedivere

Ships and Aircraft in Ascension Area
RAF Aircraft – Sea King of 202 and Chinook of 18 Sqdn RAF, Vulcans, Nimrods, Victors, Hercules, VC.10s
Harriers on Way South – Sea Harriers of No.809 NAS, arriving Harrier GR.3s of 1(F) Sqdn RAF
Other Ships at Ascension or Reaching the Area on the Way South – ambulance ships Herald, Hydra, tankers RFA Bayleaf, Anco Charger, British Avon, British Dart, British Wye

Support Tankers in South Atlantic or in Tanker Holding Areas – RFA Appleleaf, Plumleaf, chartered British Esk, British Tamar (left for Gibraltar), British Tay, British Test, British Trent, water tanker Fort Toronto

3 Commando Brigade and Amphibious Group Ships – assault ships Fearless, Intrepid, RFA Stromness, Tidepool, transports Atlantic Conveyor, Canberra, Elk, Europic Ferry, Norland, frigates Ardent, Argonaut

LSL Group – Sir Galahad, Sir Geraint, Sir Lancelot, Sir Percivale, Sir Tristram, RFA Pearleaf, frigate Plymouth, destroyer Antrim

In South Atlantic – RFA Tidespring, frigate Antelope, also RFA Regent

Carrier Battle Group – carriers Hermes, Invincible, destroyers Coventry, Glamorgan, Glasgow, (SHEFFIELD lost), frigates Alacrity, Arrow, Brilliant, Broadsword, Yarmouth, RFA Fort Austin, Olmeda, Resource, plus SBS and SAS

Submarine Force – SSN Conqueror, Spartan, Splendid

South Georgia – IPV Endurance, RFA Blue Rover, tugs Salvageman, RMAS Typhoon, M Coy 42 Cdo RM

Part 26. HMS SHEFFIELD SUNK

WEEK SIX, Falkland Area Operations
3rd-9th May 1982

Summary of Main Events

CVBG – Carriers Hermes, Invincible, destroyers Coventry, Glamorgan, Glasgow, frigates Alacrity, Arrow, Brilliant, Broadsword, Yarmouth, RFA Fort Austin, Olmeda, Resource, with SBS and SAS.

1. Argentine patrol ship Alferez Sobral damaged 70 miles north of East Falkland island (3rd)
2. Argentine aircraft lost near Stanley – [a11] Aermacchi MB-339A (3rd), [a12] PNA Skyvan (3rd/4th)
3. 'Black Buck 2' – second Vulcan raid on Stanley (4th)
4. Two Super Etendards launch Exocet (4th) at:
5. SHEFFIELD hit at 52¾S, 57¼ (4th), sank at 53S, 57W on 10th
6. British aircraft lost at Goose Green – [b4] Sea Harrier (4th)
7. British aircraft lost at 53S, 57W – [b5, b6] Sea Harriers (6th)
TEZ – extended to within 12 miles of Argentine coast from Friday 7th
8. Argentine intelligence trawler Narwhal damaged 60 miles SE of Stanley (9th) and later sank
9. Argentine aircraft lost off South Jason Island – [a13, a14] Skyhawks (9th)
10. Argentine aircraft lost at mouth of Choiseul Sound – [a15] Army Puma (9th)

Midnight on Sunday 2nd as patrol vessel "Alferez Sobral" searched for the crew of the downed Canberra [a8] to the north of the Falklands, she was detected by a No.826 Sea King. Fired on, the helicopter called for help and from a range of eight miles, "Coventry's" Lynx fired two of the new Sea Skua missiles, followed shortly by two more from "Glasgow's" Lynx. Badly damaged and with eight crew dead, the "Sobral" was escorted into Puerto Deseado two days later, but the Canberra's crew was never found. Later in the day one of two MB-339As of CANA 1 Esc returning to Stanley from a patrol to the south east, crashed in bad weather near the airfield killing the pilot [a11], and that night, a PNA Skyvan [a12] at the airfield was badly damaged in another bombardment by "Glamorgan", "Alacrity" and "Arrow". Then early on Tuesday morning, the same Vulcan as before attacked the runway in "Black Buck 2".

With the Argentine Navy's return to port, the **British Task Force established control of the surrounding seas**, but it would be weeks before air supremacy was achieved. As a foretaste of events, the first ships and aircraft were lost in combat on Tuesday 4th. Most of the TF.79 ships were returning to port by Tuesday and "25 de Mayo" disembarked her aircraft. Although submarine "San Luis" stayed out a few more days, the rest of the Navy kept well clear of the British nuclear subs. However to the south of the Falklands a number of ships joined in the search for "Belgrano's" survivors with most of them returning on Wednesday. Then to confirm control of the seas, Britain extended the TEZ on Friday and warned Argentina that any warships or military aircraft found more than 12 miles from their coast were liable to attack.

By late Tuesday morning (4th) the **CVBG** was 70 miles to the south east of Stanley. Aware of the Exocet threat, frigates "Brilliant" and "Broadsword" with their point defence Sea Wolf stayed in close to the carriers. Near them was a screen of three RFAs, further out a second one of "Glamorgan" and three more frigates, and then twenty miles ahead, the three Type 42s including "Sheffield" with their high altitude Sea Darts. Finally towards the Falklands, Sea Harriers of No.801 flew CAP and at this time investigated a number of possible air contacts. Before then a CANA Neptune had picked up the ships by radar and two Super Etendards of 2 Esc took off from Rio Grande each armed with an Exocet AM.39. Refuelled by a Grupo 1 Hercules, they flew in at low altitude, popped-up for a radar check and released the missile from 20 to 30 miles. One of the Exocet may just have missed "Yarmouth", but the other slammed with hardly any warning into "Sheffield" soon after 11.00am. Hitting amidships, the warhead did not explode, but the impact and unused fuel started uncontrollable fires.

Captain L E Middleton RN, commanding officer, HMS Hermes (Courtesy – RNAS Yeovilton)

With "Sheffield" badly damaged and with little power, frigate "Arrow" soon came alongside to assist and "Yarmouth" stood by. Captain Salt's crew fought gallantly to save their ship, but with 20 men dead, the order to abandon ship was given that afternoon. With the wounded already on board "Hermes", "Arrow" took off most of the 260 survivors. "Sheffield" drifted for four days until "Yarmouth" was ordered to pull her clear of the TEZ. Taken in tow by Sunday, "SHEFFIELD" finally sank next day not too many miles from where she was hit. The survivors later returned to Ascension on tanker "British Esk".

Shortly after "Sheffield" was hit, three No.800 Sea Harriers from "Hermes" attacked Goose Green airstrip with CBUs and retard bombs. Little damage was done, but one aircraft was hit by Skyguard-directed 35mm Oerlikon fire and crashed killing the pilot [b4]. With the threat from Exocet, the carriers now moved further away from Stanley, and there was little activity over the next few days, but that did not prevent further losses. On Thursday morning (6th), two No.801 Sea Harriers on CAP were sent to check a radar contact and just disappeared without trace after presumably colliding in the poor visibility [b5, b6]. With the carriers down to 17 Harriers, their next action took place Sunday morning (9th) when two No.800 aircraft left "Hermes" to bomb Stanley. Stopped by cloud cover, they detected intelligence trawler "Narwhal" while on their way back and were given permission to attack by control ship "Coventry". Strafing failed to stop her and the high-altitude fuzed bombs were dropped, one of which hit without exploding. With the trawler at a standstill, Nos.820 and 846 Sea Kings flew an SBS party some 150 miles to capture her, but before arriving, two more No.800 Sea Harriers attacked and further damaged "NARWAL" with cannon fire. The SBS boarding went ahead, but next day she sank in tow with one crewman dead.

Returning to Saturday evening, and with the Task Force back on the offensive, frigate "Alacrity" bombarded the Stanley area as "Brilliant" and her Lynx entered the north end of Falkland Sound to intercept any supply ships. Meanwhile "Coventry" and "Broadsword" had moved closer to Stanley with the unenviable job of tempting out Argentine aircraft. Late Sunday morning, "Coventry" fired three Sea Darts at distant aircraft, including a Hercules on a supply run to Stanley, and apparently missed. However around this time, two Grupo 4 Skyhawks were lost [a13, a14]. They may have been hit by the Sea Darts or alternatively crashed in low visibility on their way to attack the two ships. Whatever the case, one of them was later found on South Jason Island. Then in the afternoon, as an Army Puma headed out over Choiseul Sound to search for "Narwal", another Sea Dart fired at extreme range brought her down with the loss of all on board [a15].

> **British Gallantry Awards included:**
> HMS Sheffield – rescue work
> Lt Cdr J S Woodhead (post DSC) RN
> PO MEM(M) D R Briggs (post DSM)
> PO Medical Asst G A Meager (QGM)

Part 27. 5th INFANTRY BRIGADE SAILS ON QE2

WEEK SEVEN, British Task Force Movements
10th-16th May 1982

Summary of British Ships & Aircraft Departing

Royal Navy
Active, Cdr P C B Canter RN
Andromeda, Capt J Weatherall RN
Avenger, Capt H M White RN
Bristol, Capt A Grose RN
Cardiff, Capt M G T Harris RN
Minerva, Cdr S H G Johnston RN
Penelope, Cdr P V Rickard RN

Royal Fleet Auxiliary
Engadine, Capt D F Freeman RFA
Fort Grange, Capt D G M Averill CBE RFA
Olna, Capt J A Bailey RFA

Merchant Ships
Atlantic Causeway, Capt M H C Twomey and NP 1990, Cdr R P Seymour RN
Balder London, Capt K J Wallace
Queen Elizabeth 2, Capt P Jackson and NP 1980, Capt N C H James RN
Wimpey Seahorse, Capt M J Slack (awarded OBE) and NP 2000

Naval Air Squadrons Embarked
No.824 C Flt – 3 Sea King HAS.2As, Fort Grange
No.847 A Flt – 4 Wessex HU.5s, Engadine
No.848 B Flt – 2 Wessex HU.5s, Olna
No.845 C Flt – 2 replacement Wessex HU.5s at Ascension, Tidespring
8 Sea King HAS.2As of No.825 and 20 Wessex HU.5s of No.847 on Atlantic Causeway
2 Sea King HAS.2As of No.825 on Queen Elizabeth 2

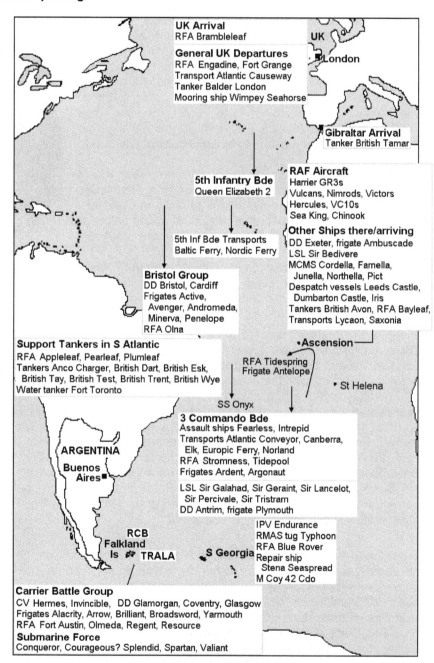

UK Arrival
RFA Brambleleaf

General UK Departures
RFA Engadine, Fort Grange
Transport Atlantic Causeway
Tanker Balder London
Mooring ship Wimpey Seahorse

Gibraltar Arrival
Tanker British Tamar

5th Infantry Bde
Queen Elizabeth 2

RAF Aircraft
Harrier GR3s
Vulcans, Nimrods, Victors
Hercules, VC10s
Sea King, Chinook

5th Inf Bde Transports
Baltic Ferry, Nordic Ferry

Other Ships there/arriving
DD Exeter, frigate Ambuscade
LSL Sir Bedivere
MCMS Cordella, Farnella, Junella, Northella, Pict
Despatch vessels Leeds Castle, Dumbarton Castle, Iris
Tankers British Avon, RFA Bayleaf,
Transports Lycaon, Saxonia

Bristol Group
DD Bristol, Cardiff
Frigates Active, Avenger, Andromeda, Minerva, Penelope
RFA Olna

Support Tankers in S Atlantic
RFA Appleleaf, Pearleaf, Plumleaf
Tankers Anco Charger, British Dart, British Esk, British Tay, British Test, British Trent, British Wye
Water tanker Fort Toronto

Ascension — RFA Tidespring, Frigate Antelope

SS Onyx

3 Commando Bde
Assault ships Fearless, Intrepid
Transports Atlantic Conveyor, Canberra, Elk, Europic Ferry, Norland
RFA Stromness, Tidepool
Frigates Ardent, Argonaut

LSL Sir Galahad, Sir Geraint, Sir Lancelot, Sir Percivale, Sir Tristram
DD Antrim, frigate Plymouth

IPV Endurance
RMAS tug Typhoon
RFA Blue Rover
Repair ship Stena Seaspread
M Coy 42 Cdo

RCB Falkland Is — TRALA — S Georgia

Carrier Battle Group
CV Hermes, Invincible, DD Glamorgan, Coventry, Glasgow
Frigates Alacrity, Arrow, Brilliant, Broadsword, Yarmouth
RFA Fort Austin, Olmeda, Regent, Resource

Submarine Force
Conqueror, Courageous? Splendid, Spartan, Valiant

Task Force Departures from Monday 10th May – The week saw the departure of the first (and the last) major sea and land reinforcements, starting on Monday with the "Bristol" group of ships which hurried down in two weeks. Type 82 destroyer "Bristol" and RFA fleet tanker "Olna" left from Portsmouth and type 21 frigates "Active" and "Avenger", and Leander-class "Andromeda", "Minerva" and "Penelope" from Devonport. On Wednesday, type 42 "Cardiff" departed Gibraltar following a Persian Gulf patrol and by Friday had joined the group. RFA helicopter support ship "Engadine" also sailed from Devonport at the same time as the "Bristol" ships but made her own way via Gibraltar carrying four Wessex. The remaining 20 Wessex from reformed No.847 NAS and eight No.825 Sea Kings followed on Friday in RO-RO container ship "Atlantic Causeway" after her conversion to helicopter ship complete with flightdeck and hangar.

On Wednesday 12th, an even more important departure was the bulk of 5th Infantry Brigade on "Queen Elizabeth 2" from Southampton direct for South Georgia. Then on Friday, RFA fleet replenishment ship "Fort Grange" headed out from Devonport, followed on Sunday by offshore support vessel "Wimpey Seahorse" following earlier work on her at Rosyth. More tanker movements also took place with "Balder London" sailing from Portsmouth, RFA "Brambleleaf" getting in to Portland later in the week for repairs to the damage received off South Georgia, and "British Tamar" reaching Gibraltar on Friday to reload.

Ascension - As "Leeds Castle" headed on south, "Dumbarton Castle" arrived to begin her duties as a despatch vessel. Arriving on Wednesday 12th from the other direction with the South Georgia POWs was RFA "Tidespring" and escorting frigate "Antelope". After "Tidespring" picked up two replacement Wessex, she and "Antelope" headed back south over the weekend, hardly a week before the frigate's end. On Saturday in a record-breaking flight of 19 hours and 8,300 miles, an RAF Nimrod crewed by 201 Sqdn reconnoitred the Argentine coast for any warships that might threaten the approaching Task Force, but on Sunday the Vulcan "Black Buck 3" raid on Stanley was cancelled.

South Atlantic - RFA fleet replenishment ship "Regent" joined the carriers and around the end of the week, submarine "Valiant" (and "Courageous"?) arrived to start patrolling off the Argentine coast. To the north of Stanley, the Red Cross Box came into operation with the arrival of hospital ship "Uganda" on Tuesday 11th followed three days later by ambulance ship "Hecla", the first of the three to arrive. Off to the east of the Falklands, tug "Salvageman" arrived in the TRALA where she was shortly joined by repair ship "Stena Seaspread" which just now reached South Georgia. And that Sunday the bulk of 3 Cdo Bde caught up with the LSL Group only five days from the landings at San Carlos.

Transport "Elk" and one of the two assault ships, hull pennant number painted out. (Courtesy - MOD, Navy)

Disposition of British Ships, Aircraft & Land Forces in Summary

UK Departures - RFA Engadine, Fort Grange, transport Atlantic Causeway, tanker Balder London, mooring ship Wimpey Seahorse

UK Arrival - RFA Brambleleaf

Gibraltar Arrival - tanker British Tamar

Ships on Passage, Central Atlantic:
5 Infantry Brigade - Queen Elizabeth 2, transports Baltic Ferry, Nordic Ferry
Bristol Group - destroyers Bristol, Cardiff, frigates Active, Avenger, Andromeda, Minerva, Penelope, RFA Olna

Ships and Aircraft in Ascension Area
RAF Aircraft - Harrier GR.3s, Vulcans, Nimrods, Victors, Hercules, VC.10s, Sea King, Chinook
Other Ships at Ascension or Reaching the Area on the Way South - destroyer Exeter, frigate Ambuscade, LSL Sir Bedivere, MCMS Cordella, Farnella, Junella, Northella, Pict, despatch vessels Leeds Castle, Dumbarton Castle, Iris, tankers British Avon, RFA Bayleaf, transports Lycaon, Saxonia.
Frigate Antelope, RFA tidespring (returning to South Atlantic)

Support Tankers in South Atlantic or in Tanker Holding Areas - RFA Appleleaf, Pearleaf, Plumleaf, chartered Anco Charger, British Dart, British Esk, British Tay, British Test, British Trent, British Wye, water tanker Fort Toronto

Vessels on Passage, South Atlantic - SS Onyx, ambulance ships Herald, Hydra

3 Commando Brigade and Amphibious Group Ships - assault ships Fearless, Intrepid, RFA Stromness, Tidepool, transports Atlantic Conveyor, Canberra, Elk, Europic Ferry, Norland, frigates Ardent, Argonaut,
joined up with LSL Group - Sir Galahad, Sir Geraint, Sir Lancelot, Sir Percivale, Sir Tristram, destroyer Antrim, frigate Plymouth

Red Cross Box, RCB - hospital ship Uganda, ambulance ship Hecla

Tug, Repair & Logistic Area, TRALA - tug Salvageman

Carrier Battle Group - carriers Hermes, Invincible, destroyers Coventry, Glamorgan, Glasgow, frigates Alacrity, Arrow, Brilliant, Broadsword, Yarmouth, RFA Fort Austin, Olmeda, Regent, Resource, plus SBS and SAS

Submarine Force - SSN Conqueror, Courageous, Spartan, Splendid, Valiant

South Georgia - IPV Endurance, RMAS Typhoon, RFA Blue Rover, repair ship Stena Seaspread, M Coy 42 Cdo RM

Part 28. PEBBLE ISLAND RAID by SAS

WEEK SEVEN, Falkland Area Operations
10th-16th May 1982

In the **build-up to the landings at San Carlos**, Admiral Woodward's destroyers and frigates continued to wear down the invaders and D Sqdn SAS made an important contribution with its Pebble Island raid. On Monday 10th, as submarine "San Luis" made her last reported and equally unsuccessful attack on ships of the Task Force and "Sheffield" finally sank, "Glasgow" (Sea Dart) and "Brilliant" (Sea Wolf) took over as type 42/22 combination from "Coventry" and "Broadsword" and continued their radar picket and bombardment duties off Stanley. That night as "Arrow" moved to the north end of Falkland Sound, sister ship "Alacrity" prepared to sail right through from the south for the first time to flush out any supply ships. As she passed up the Sound, "Alacrity" detected a small ship off Swan Island apparently heading for Port Howard, and using her single 4.5 inch, illuminated with star shell. Refusing to stop, the target was engaged in the **only surface action** of the war and after a number of hits, exploded and sank with heavy casualties. Reportedly there were only two survivors from what turned out to be the naval transport "ISLA DE LOS ESTADOS" carrying fuel and military supplies. "Alacrity" carried on through to meet "Arrow", and on Tuesday morning, both ships headed back to the carriers. Later that day, "Yarmouth" also returned from her attempts to tow "Sheffield" out of the TEZ.

On Wednesday afternoon (12th) with "Glasgow" and "Brilliant" still off Stanley, eight A-4B Skyhawks of Grupo 5 were sent in to attack the bombarding ships. The first flight came in low, and as "Brilliant" fired her Sea Wolf automatically for the first time in anger, two aircraft exploded in the air, a third crashed in to the sea trying to escape and the fourth dropped its bomb without hitting, and got away [a16, a17, a18]. The second flight of four came in some minutes later, but for technical reasons Sea Wolf could not fire, and this time "Glasgow" was hit by a bomb which went in one side and out the other without exploding or causing any casualties. Although the damage was not severe, she had to withdraw to the CVBG for repairs that took a number of days and eventually became the first British warship to return home. Meanwhile as these Skyhawks returned home, they passed too close to Goose Green and "Glasgow's" attacker was shot down by Argentine AA [a19].

Summary of Main Events

CVBG - Carrier Hermes, Invincible, destroyers Coventry, Glamorgan, Glasgow, frigates Alacrity, Arrow, Brilliant, Broadsword, Yarmouth, RFA Fort Austin, Olmeda, Resource, with SBS and SAS

1. SHEFFIELD sank (10th)
2. Alacrity entered Falkland Sound from the south (10th)
3. Alacrity sank Isla de los Estados off Swan Is (10th/11th)
4. Alacrity met Arrow and headed back to CVBG (10th/11th)
5. Glasgow damaged off Stanley/ Argentine aircraft lost - [a16,a17,a18] Skyhawks (12th)
6. Argentine aircraft lost at Goose Green - [a19] Skyhawk (12th)
7. PEBBLE ISLAND OPERATION (11th-15th)
   (1) SAS Boat Troop patrol ashore to reconnoitre (11th/12th)
   (2) Hermes, Broadsword and Glamorgan approached and D Sqdn SAS landed by No.846 Sea Kings (14th)

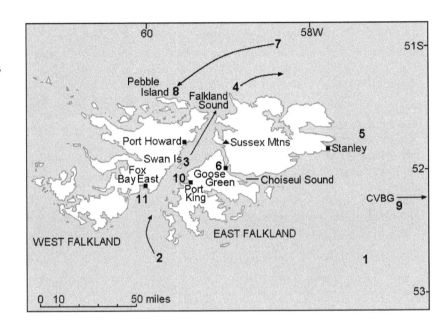

8. Pebble Island installations and aircraft destroyed and force returned to CVBG; Argentine aircraft lost - [a20-25] Pucaras, [a26-29] Mentors, [a30] Skyvan (14th/15th)
9. British aircraft lost east of Falklands - [b7] Sea King (12th)
10. Argentine cargo ship Rio Carcarana attacked and beached in Port King (16th)
11. Argentine transport Bahia Buen Suceso damaged at Fox Bay East (16th)

Just a week before the landings, a raid was mounted by **D Sqdn SAS** on the airstrip and facilities at **Pebble Island**, especially to destroy the ground attack Pucaras based there. First of all men of the Squadron's Boat Troop were put ashore over Tuesday night to reconnoitre the area and three days later on Friday 14th, "Hermes" and escort "Broadsword" together with "Glamorgan" in the fire support role left the CVBG, and passing to the north, approached Pebble Island by night. As "Glamorgan" closed in to gunfire range, "Hermes" flew off the 48 SAS attackers and NGFO team in her No.846 Sea Kings to be guided in at midnight by the awaiting patrol. After a forced march to the airstrip, the attack went ahead led by Captain Hamilton, and all the aircraft there put out of action or destroyed by prepared charges. A fuel depot, ammo dump and radar installation were also destroyed. All this time "Glamorgan" provided gunfire support, and as the raiders withdrew, a brief Argentine counter-attack was halted when the officer in charge was shot. With two men slightly wounded the SAS were safely picked up again by the helicopters. The raid was a complete success and the Argentines not only lost six Pucaras of Grupo 3 [a20-25], four T-34C Mentors [a26-29] of CANA 4 Esc and one Coast Guard Skyvan [a30], but also the use of the airstrip at a crucial time. Now into Saturday morning, the warships returned to the CVBG, but "Glamorgan" soon moved on to other duties.

Although bad weather had restricted fixed wing flying earlier in the week, by Wednesday 12th it had improved sufficiently for high level bombing attacks to be made on Stanley, the same day a No.826 ASW Sea King from "Hermes" ditched near the CVBG with engine failure [b7]. The crew was saved. The next main action took place over the weekend as Sea Harriers continued to bomb Stanley. On Saturday night "Brilliant's" Lynx failed in an attack on the transport "Bahia Buen Suceso" in Fox Bay East, but "Hermes" aircraft more than made up for this next day. In the middle of Sunday 16th, two No.800 Sea Harriers bombed and strafed the blockade running cargo ship "Rio Carcarana" (8,500grt) at anchor off Port King and although there were no casualties, she caught fire, was beached and abandoned, and finally destroyed by "Antelope's" Lynx a week later. Another two aircraft caught the "Bahia Buen Suceso" still at Fox Bay East alongside the jetty and raked her with cannon fire. Bombs were not used because of the ship's proximity to the settlement, but the damage was enough to deny her use to the Argentines, and she stayed there until after the war.

Following the Pebble Island raid, HMS Glamorgan took on the job of convincing the Argentines that any landings would take place on East Falkland, south of the capital. For a number of nights, she bombarded Stanley and moved down the coast as far as Choiseul Sound carrying out a variety of deception activities. Other SBS and SAS operations were taking place all this time, and over Sunday night "Alacrity" sailed through Falkland Sound again and landed an SBS/NGFO team by Gemini near Sussex Mountains which overlooked the landing beaches around San Carlos Water.

Sea Harriers of No 800 NAS aboard HMS Hermes in "typical foul weather" in the Atlantic during winter. Probably taken post-war, but typical of South Atlantic conditions during the Falkland's War
(Courtesy - MOD, Navy)

Part 29. AMPHIBIOUS TASK GROUP JOINS TASK FORCE

WEEK EIGHT, British Task Force Movements
17th-23rd MAY 1982

Task Force Departures from Monday 17th May

From mid week, the last four merchantmen to reach the South Atlantic before the end of hostilities sailed from the UK. These included three RO-ROs - from Devonport, ferry "St. Edmund" in the transport role, and container ship "Contender Bezant" as an aircraft and helicopter carrier with RAF and Navy helicopters as well as her own Wasps for supply duties and self-defence, and from Southampton, cargo ship "Tor Caledonia" with vehicles and Rapier missiles. The fourth to leave was refrigerated stores ship "Geestport" from Portsmouth loaded mainly with food. The first two ships to return also headed south - "British Tamar" from Gibraltar earlier in the week and RFA support tanker "Brambleleaf" from Portland at the end.

Ascension - The main reinforcements reached the island although they just passed by or barely stopped for last minute stores. Over Tuesday 18th and Wednesday 19th it was the **"Bristol" Group**, including "Active", and next day the **5th Inf Bde** transports "Baltic Ferry" and "Nordic Ferry". That same day, "Queen Elizabeth 2" carrying the complete Brigade approached Ascension taking on board Major General Moore and his staff by helicopter after they had flown down from the UK, and by Saturday they were continuing south. Helicopter support ship "Atlantic Causeway" met "QE2" at this time, and around now RMAS mooring ship "Goosander" arrived to lay out and maintain moorings. The RAF also made another record-breaking flight. On Thursday, on the eve of D-day, the same Nimrod MR.2 as before but now crewed by 206 Sqdn, flew almost the length of Argentina looking for any sign that the Argentine Navy threatened the amphibious ships.

Summary of British Ships & Aircraft Departing

Merchant Ships
Contender Bezant, Capt A MacKinnon
  and NP 2050, Lt Cdr D H Yates RN
Geestport, Capt G F Foster and
  NP 1920, Second Off R Bourne RFA
St. Edmund, Capt M J Stockman and
  NP 2060, Lt Cdr A M Scott RN
Tor Caledonia, Capt A Scott and
  NP 2020, Lt Cdr J G Devine RN

Helicopters Embarked
1 Sea King HC.4 of No.846 NAS,
2 Wasps of No.829 NAS, and
3 Chinooks of 18 Sqdn RAF on
Contender Bezant

South Atlantic - Only now on Tuesday 18th, as the **Amphibious Task Group** was joining the carriers to the north east of the Falklands, were the San Carlos plans presented to the full British Cabinet. Admiral Woodward was then given the go ahead by the War Cabinet and final preparations put in hand for the landing which took place early on Friday morning. By the end of the week, **3 Cdo Bde** was safely ashore and digging in, two type 21 frigates lost and other ships damaged, and the Argentine air forces were suffering heavily at the hands of the British defences. By then more ships had arrived from the north. The sixth and last LSL, "Sir Bedivere" reached the TEZ before moving on to San Carlos, and by Saturday morning (22nd) destroyer "Exeter" and frigate "Ambuscade" had joined the CVBG. The latter's sister ship "Antelope" also got in from escorting "Tidespring" to Ascension, but soon moved on to San Carlos to share the fate of "Ardent". Another arrival was despatch vessel "Leeds Castle" although her duties shortly took her to South Georgia.

Other groups of ships also played their part although not involved directly in the fighting. In the Red Cross Box area "Uganda" and "Hecla" were joined in their work by ambulance ship "Hydra", and the TRALA opened for repair business when "Stena Seaspread" arrived from South Georgia. By mid-June this impressive vessel had carried out damage and other repairs in mid-ocean to nearly 40 ships including 11 warships and four captured. Then in South Georgia, and for later delivery to "Stena Seaspread", "Endurance" working parties took on the job of recovering scrap steel from the disused whaling stations for ship repairs, and on Sunday, cargo ship "Saxonia" got in ready to transfer food and other supplies to the RFAs over the next three weeks.

Disposition of British Ships, Aircraft & Land Forces in Summary

UK Departures - RFA Brambleleaf, transports Contender Bezant, Geestport, St. Edmund, Tor Caledonia

Gibraltar Departure - tanker British Tamar

RFAs on Passage - Engadine, Fort Grange

Map annotations

UK Departures
RFA Brambleleaf
Transports Contender Bezant,
Geestport, St Edmund,
Tor Caledonia

Gibraltar Departure
Tanker British Tamar

RAF Aircraft
Harrier GR3s
Nimrods, Victors, Vulcans
Hercules, VC10s
Chinook, Sea King

Other Ships there/arriving
Bristol Group
DD Bristol, Cardiff
Frigates Active, Avenger,
  Andromeda, Minerva, Penelope
RFA Olna

5th Infantry Bde
Transports Baltic Ferry,
  Nordic Ferry,
  Queen Elizabeth 2

Ascension
Other Ships
Despatch vessel Dumbarton
  Castle (general duties)
RMAS Mooring ship Goosander
Transport Atlantic Causeway
Tankers British Avon
  Alvega (base storage)

RFA on Passage
Engadine, Fort Grange

Support Tankers in S Atlantic
RFA Appleleaf, Bayleaf, Pearleaf, Plumleaf
Tankers Anco Charger, British Dart, British Tay,
  British Test, British Trent, British Wye,
  British Esk (sailing for Ascension)
Water tanker Fort Toronto

Arrivals
DD Exeter
Frigates Ambuscade,
  Antelope
LSL Sir Bedivere

Main Task Force Ships in TEZ
See Parts 30, 33, 34, 35

RCB
TRALA
Falkland Is

S Georgia
IPV Endurance
RFA Blue Rover
RMAS Typhoon
Transport Saxonia
M Coy 42 Cdo

Submarine Force
SSN Conqueror, Courageous (?)
Splendid, Spartan, Valiant

Ships and Aircraft in Ascension Area
RAF Aircraft - Harrier GR.3s, Vulcans, Nimrods, Victors, Hercules, VC.10s, Sea King, Chinook
Other Ships at Ascension or Reaching the Area on the Way South
BRISTOL GROUP - destroyers Bristol, Cardiff, Frigates Active, Avenger, Andromeda, Minerva, Penelope, RFA Olna
5 INFANTRY BRIGADE - transports Baltic Ferry, Nordic Ferry, Queen Elizabeth 2
OTHER SHIPS - despatch vessel Dumbarton Castle (general duties), RMAS Mooring ship Goosander, transport Atlantic Causeway, tankers British Avon, Alvega (base storage)

Some of the many Wessex helicopters so vital to the Falkland's campaign (Courtesy - MOD, Navy)

Support Tankers in South Atlantic or in Tanker Holding Areas - RFA Appleleaf, Bayleaf, Pearleaf, Plumleaf, chartered Anco Charger, British Dart, British Tay, British Test, British Trent, British Wye, British Esk (sailing for Ascension), water tanker Fort Toronto

Arriving in South Atlantic - SS Onyx, RFA Tidespring, destroyer Exeter, frigates Ambuscade, Antelope, LSL Sir Bedivere

RCB, Red Cross Box - hospital ship Uganda, ambulance ship Hecla, Hydra

TRALA, Tug, Repair & Logistic Area - repair ship Stena Seaspread, tug Salvageman

SEE FOLLOWING PARTS FOR MAIN TASK FORCE SHIPS DURING THIS PERIOD:
Part 30: 17th-20th May - Operations leading up to San Carlos Landings
Part 33: 21st May – Landings at San Carlos
Part 34: 21st May - Air Battles
Part 35: 22nd-23rd May - Falkland Area Operations

Submarine Force - SSN Conqueror, Courageous, Splendid, Spartan, Valiant

South Georgia - IPV Endurance, RMAS Typhoon, RFA Blue Rover, transport Saxonia, M Coy 42 Cdo RM

Part 30. SEA KING-to-CHILE INCIDENT

WEEK EIGHT (part), Operations leading up to San Carlos Landings 17th-20th MAY 1982

Summary of Main Events

Arriving Carrier Squadrons:
HMS Hermes
No.809 - 4 Sea Harriers for No.800 NAS
1(F) Sqdn RAF - 6 Harrier GR.3s [Wing Cdr P T Squire (awarded DFC) AFC RAF]
HMS Invincible
No.809 - 4 Sea Harriers for No.801 NAS

1. SEA KING TO CHILE INCIDENT (17th-18th) - Invincible and Brilliant approached Argentine coast and special forces landed near air bases by No.846 Sea King (17th). By morning, ships back with CVBG. That evening, Sea King [b9] destroyed near Punta Arenas and crew later picked up by Chile (18th)
2. British aircraft lost east of Falklands - [b8] Sea King (17th)
3. British aircraft lost north east of Falklands - [b10] Sea King (19th)
4. APPROACH TO SAN CARLOS BY 3 COMMANDO BRIGADE (20th) – Assault ships Fearless, Intrepid, transports Canberra, Europic Ferry, Norland, RFAs Fort Austin, Stromness, LSLs Sir Galahad, Sir Geraint, Sir Lancelot, Sir Percivale, Sir Tristram, frigates Argonaut, Brilliant, Broadsword, Plymouth, Yarmouth plus destroyer Antrim and frigate Ardent on support missions
5. CARRIER BATTLE GROUP (20th) - Carriers Hermes, Invincible, destroyers Coventry, Glamorgan, Glasgow, frigates Alacrity, Arrow, RFA Olmeda, Regent, Resource, Tidepool, transports Atlantic Conveyor, Elk

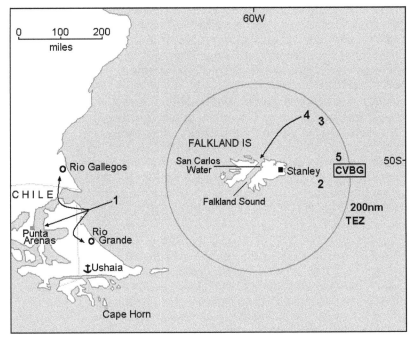

Plus submarine force, hospital ships in RCB, repair ship and tug in TRALA, and some tankers in TEZ.

One of the strangest incidents of the war now took place involving **Chile**. The only certainty at the time was that during the week the Chilean authorities found a burnt out Sea King HC.4 of No.846 NAS near the southern town of Punta Arenas, the crew of three gave themselves up and was returned to the UK to later receive gallantry awards for a number of hazardous missions. Presumably, and as announced by the Ministry of Defence, these

British Gallantry Awards included:
No.846 Sea King to Chile
Lt A R C Bennett (DSC) RN
Lt R Hutchings (DSC) RM
Ldg Aircrewman P B Imrie (DSM)

included losing their way, ending up 500 miles from the Task Force and destroying their helicopter!! One possibility was that after a high speed dash to the west over Monday night (17th) by "Invincible" and escort "Brilliant", the Sea King landed special forces near air bases in Southern Argentina either to report on aircraft as they left to attack the Task Force or even in an attempt to destroy the Super Etendards (*subsequently confirmed in the 1990's*).

Whatever happened, the carrier obviously could not risk waiting for the helicopter to return and by Tuesday morning (18th) was back with the CVBG. The Sea King therefore made its way to neutral territory to be destroyed by the crew sometime over Tuesday night [b9]. Any men landed might then have been picked up later by submarine. As it happened, the diesel-engined and more manoeuvrable "Onyx" arrived in the Falkland's area by the end of the month and was reported to have lifted off special forces from near Rio Grande, and in doing so to have damaged herself on an uncharted rock. She also went on to land SBS teams around the Falklands to supplement the helicopter drops.

Back on Monday 17th as the amphibious ships neared the carrier group, the second No.826 Sea King from "Hermes" was lost by accident. Late that night to the east of the Falklands while on ASW patrol, she hit the sea with altimeter trouble and had to be abandoned, but again fortunately with no casualties [b8]. Next day when within range, and through into Wednesday, "Atlantic Conveyor" flew off four of the embarked No.809 Sea Harriers to "Invincible" and the remaining four with the six RAF GR.3s to "Hermes". The 25 Sea Harriers would now concentrate on air defence and the RAF GR.3s on ground attack, but with a total of 31 now embarked, the carrier maintenance teams were sorely stretched and yet still provided a remarkably high level of availability.

When the many ships did meet some 200 miles to the north east of Stanley, equipment and stores, men and helicopters were redistributed ready for the landings. Eleven assault Sea Kings of No.846 NAS were moved around to four of the ships that entered San Carlos Water, and on Wednesday evening a twelfth was lost with particularly tragic consequences. Before then, orders were received from Northwood to spread "Canberra's" major units around the other ships to avoid heavy loss of life in the event of her being hit. Through Wednesday 19th and in surprisingly calm weather for the South Atlantic in autumn, the larger landing craft (LCUs) carried by the assault ships transferred 40 Cdo RM to "Fearless", and Z Coy 45 Cdo and 3 Para to "Intrepid". The whole of 42 Cdo stayed on "Canberra", the rest of 45 Cdo on RFA "Stromness" and 2 Para on "Norland".

Captain G R Green RFA, commanding officer RFA Sir Tristram, one of the LSLs sailing into San Carlos Water over the night of 20th May 1982 (Courtesy - RFA Service)

The opportunity was also taken to transfer the special forces and three surviving night-flying No.846 Sea Kings from "Hermes" after their three week's covert operations. In one of the last flights that Wednesday from the carrier to "Intrepid", one of the Sea Kings loaded with SAS crashed into the sea and 21 out of the 30 men on board died [b10]. At the time a sea bird strike was thought to have brought her down, but this cause is now open to doubt. The dead included 18 men of D and G Sqdn SAS, some of them so soon after their Pebble Island triumph, one member of the Royal Signals, the only RAF casualty of the war and the aircrewman, Corporal M D Love RM who was awarded a posthumous DSM for his special forces missions.

Carrying Brigadier Thompson's troops, but commanded by Commodore Clapp, the **Amphibious Task Group** now headed for Falkland Sound. Leaving "Atlantic Conveyor" and "Elk" with the CVBG, it consisted of command ship "Fearless", "Intrepid", the five LSLs, merchantmen "Canberra", "Europic Ferry" and "Norland", RFA "Stromness" as a troopship and from the carrier group, "Fort Austin" for helicopter support. Apart from the original escort of "Antrim", "Ardent", "Argonaut" and "Plymouth", Admiral Woodward allocated "Yarmouth" and weakened his own defences by also sending "Brilliant" and "Broadsword". Faced with sailing across the north of the Falklands through the daylight hours of Thursday 20th, the Type 22's Sea Wolf could have proved crucial in fighting off any determined aircraft attacks on the troopships. As it happened, the convoy was hidden all day by poor weather and reached the jumping off point for San Carlos Water without apparently being spotted. Later that Thursday, "Antrim" and "Ardent" went ahead on separate support missions and 3 Commando Brigade prepared to land early next morning, starting with the first assault wave of 40 Cdo and 2 Para who went ashore at San Carlos.

So much took place in and around **San Carlos Water** over the next few days, three parts describe the main events:

    Part 33: 21st May – Landings at San Carlos
    Part 34: 21st May - Air Battles around San Carlos
    Part 35: 22nd-23rd May - Falkland Area Operations

But before then, Argentine and British aircraft and shipping losses inflicted and losses sustained are summarised as an introduction to the land, sea and air battles that took place until the end of the war:

    Part 31: Argentine Aircraft and their Successes against British Ships
    Part 32: British Successes against Argentine Aircraft and Ships

Summary of Losses Inflicted and Sustained
(Parts 31-32)

Part 31. ARGENTINE AIRCRAFT and their SUCCESSES AGAINST BRITISH SHIPS

Aside from the land battles, most of the war was fought between Argentine aircraft and the British ships and carrier-borne Harriers. Argentine losses were heavy, but so were the Royal Navy's, and only the hit on "Glamorgan" by a land-based Exocet at the end of the war was not due to aircraft. Just before the San Carlos landings, this is a useful point to summarise the main Argentine aircraft involved and the losses they sustained, as well as inflicted.

Argentine Air Force Mirage

NAVAL AVIATION COMMAND (CANA)

1st Attack Sqdn (1 Esc)	6 Aermacchi MB-339As to Falklands, 2 lost and 3 captured	Minor damage to Argonaut by cannon (21st May)
2nd Fighter and Attack Sqdn (2 Esc)	Super Etendard flying from Rio Grande with no losses	Destroyer SHEFFIELD (4th May) and support ship ATLANTIC CONVEYOR (25th May) hit by Exocet; both sank
3rd Fighter and Attack Sqdn (3 Esc)	Skyhawk A-4Qs flying from Rio Grande, 3 lost	Frigate ARDENT sunk by bombs (21st May)
4th Attack Sqdn (4 Esc)	4 Mentor T-34Cs to Falklands, all lost	-

ARGENTINE AIR FORCE (FAA)

1st Air Transport Group (Grupo 1)	Hercules (1 lost), Boeing 707s. Also photo-reconnaissance Learjets (1 lost)	-
2nd Light Bomber Group (Grupo 2)	Canberras flying from Trelew and Rio Gallegos, 2 lost	-
3rd Attack Group (Grupo 3)	24 Pucaras to Falklands, 13 lost and 11 captured, plus one mainland-based aircraft lost	The only British aircraft casualty directly due to Argentine aircraft was Royal Marine Scout of 3 CBAS [b28] shot down by a Grupo 3 Pucara on the 28th May
4th Fighter Bomber Group (Grupo 4)	Skyhawk A-4Cs flying from San Julian and Rio Grande, 9 lost	Believed to have damaged LSLs Sir Bedivere, Sir Galahad and Sir Lancelot with UXBs (all 24th May)

5th Fighter Bomber Group (Grupo 5)	Skyhawk A-4Bs from Rio Gallegos, 10 lost	Destroyer Glasgow damaged by UXB (12th May) Frigate Argonaut damaged by UXB (21st May) Frigate ANTELOPE sunk by bomb (23rd May) Destroyer COVENTRY sunk by bombs and frigate Broadsword damaged by UXB (both 25th May) LSLs SIR GALAHAD (later scuttled) and Sir Tristram damaged; Fearless LCU F4 sunk by bombs (all 8th June)
6th Fighter Bomber Group (Grupo 6)	Daggers from Rio Grande and San Julian, 11 lost	Destroyer Glamorgan, frigates Alacrity and Arrow, minor damage by cannon fire and near misses (all 1st May) Destroyer Antrim damaged by UXB, frigate Ardent damaged by bomb, frigates Brilliant and Broadsword minor damage by cannon fire (all 21st May) Frigate Plymouth damaged by UXB and Cannon fire (8th June)
7th Group, Helicopter Sqdn	including Bell 212s and Chinook. Two Bells to Falklands, both lost	-
8th Fighter Group (Grupo 8)	Mirage IIIEs from Comodoro Rivadavia and Rio Callegos, 2 lost	-

Adding the aircraft of the Argentine Coastguard (PNA) and Army Combat Aviation Battalion 601 transferred to the Falklands, all of which were destroyed or captured, plus two Navy helicopters lost at sea brought total losses from all causes to a round one hundred.

Part 32. BRITISH SUCCESSES AGAINST ARGENTINE SHIPS and AIRCRAFT

As the war approached a speedy end this is a convenient place to summarise the British successes against Argentine sea and air forces. None of the "scores" are official, some no doubt are open to argument, and of course only give a limited indication of the contribution made by each of the main front-line units.

Sea Harrier FRS Mk 1 wing details including air-to-air Sidewinder missiles (Courtesy - MOD, Navy)

ARGENTINE SHIPS

Sunk or Damaged by British Ships	
HMS Conqueror	Cruiser GENERAL BELGRANO sunk
HMS Alacrity	Fleet transport ISLA DE LOS ESTADOS sunk
HMS Brilliant and HMS Yarmouth	Coaster Monsunen driven aground

..... by Aircraft Squadrons

HMS Hermes, No.800 Sea Harriers	Trawler NARWHAL sunk Fleet transport Bahia Buen Suceso damaged Transport Rio Carcarana damaged Patrol ship Rio Iguaza beached
HMS Antelope, No.815 Lynx	Transport RIO CARCARANA destroyed
HMS Antrim No.737 Wessex, HMS Brilliant No.815 Lynx, HMS Endurance and Plymouth No.829 Wasps	Submarine Santa Fe disabled, later captured
HMS Coventry and Glasgow, No.815 Lynx	Patrol vessel Alferez Sobral damaged

ARGENTINE AIRCRAFT AND HELICOPTERS

Destroyed by British Carrier-Based Aircraft
(Squadron pilot receiving gallantry award also listed)

HMS Hermes, No.800 Sea Harriers

Lt Cdr A D Auld (DSC) RN	2 Daggers [a50, a51]
Lt Cdr G W J Batt (post DSC) RN	-
Lt Cdr M S Blissett (MID) RN	Skyhawk [a36]
Lt Cdr R V Frederiksen (MID) RN	Dagger [a38]
Lt M Hale RN	Dagger [a49]
Flt Lt J Leeming RAF	Skyhawk [a43]
Flt Lt D H S Morgan (DSC) RAF	2 Skyhawks [a67, a68]
Lt C R W Morrell (MID) RN	1½ Skyhawks [a42, a44]
Flt Lt R Penfold RAF	Dagger [a7]
Lt D A Smith (MID) RN	Dagger [a52], Skyhawk [a69]
Lt Cdr N W Thomas (DSC) RN	Skyhawk [a37]
plus	3 Pucaras [a2,a3,a4], 1½ Pumas [a45, a47], Agusta 109A [a46]

HMS Invincible, No.801 Sea Harriers

Flt Lt P C Barton RAF	Mirage [a5]
Lt W A Curtiss (post MID) RN	Canberra [a8]
Lt S R Thomas (DSC) RN	Mirage [a6], 2 Daggers [a39,a40]
Cdr N D Ward (DSC) AFC RN	Pucara [a35], Dagger [a41], Hercules [a65]
plus	½ Puma [a47]

.... by Royal Navy Warships & Royal Marine Defences

HMS Ardent	½ Skyhawk [a44]
HMS Brilliant	3 Skyhawks [a16, a17, a18]
HMS Broadsword	probably Dagger [a34]
HMS Coventry	Puma [a15], 2 Skyhawks [a54,a56]
HMS Exeter	2 Skyhawks [a63,a64], Learjet [a66], Canberra [a70]
HMS Fearless or Intrepid	Skyhawk [a57]
Naval bombardment	Skyvan [a12]
Royal Marines	Puma [a1], Aermacchi [a59]

.... by BRITISH ARMY and RAF
(Two pilots receiving gallantry awards also listed)

San Carlos Water defences, ship and shore-based including Rapiers	3 Skyhawks [a48, a53, a55]
T Bty, 12 Air Defence Regt RA	Dagger [a61]
2 Para	Pucara [a60]
D Sqdn SAS	7 Pucaras [a20-a25, a33], 4 Mentors [a26-a29], Skyvan [a30]
1(F) Sqdn RAF Harrier GR.3s]	Chinook [a31], Puma [a32
Sqdn Ldr J J Pook (DFC) RAF	-
Wing Cdr P T Squire (DFC) AFC RAF	-

San Carlos Landings and Consolidation
(Parts 33-40)

Part 33. LANDINGS AT SAN CARLOS WATER
WEEK EIGHT, 21st May 1982

Summary of Main Events (subsequent awards in brackets)

Arriving Support Helicopters:
11 Sea King HC.4s of No.846 NAS on Fearless (4), Intrepid (4), Canberra (2) and Norland (1)
5 embarked Wessex HU.5s of No.845 NAS, including RFA Resource A Flt [Lt Cdr H J Lomas (DSC) RN]

3 Commando Brigade Commanders
Main units:
Brigadier J H A Thompson (CB) OBE ADC RM
Deputy Commander, Colonel T Seccombe RM
Bde Major (Chief of Staff), Maj J Chester (OBE) RM
Deputy Chief of Staff, Maj G V J O'N Wells-Cole RM
40 Cdo RM, Lt Col M P J Hunt (OBE) RM
42 Cdo RM, Lt Col N F Vaux (DSO) RM
45 Cdo RM, Lt Col A F Whitehead (DSO) RM
29 Cdo Regt RA, Lt Col M J Holroyd-Smith (OBE) RA
59 Ind Cdo Sqdn RE, Maj R MacDonald (MID) RE
Cdo Logistics Regt, Lt Col I J Hellberg (OBE) RCT
Bde HQ & Signals Sqdn, Maj R C Dixon RM
Mountain & Arctic Warfare Cadre, Capt R Boswell RM
SBS, Maj J J Thomson (OBE) RM
Cdo Bde Air Sqdn, Maj C P Cameron (MC) RM with 9 Gazelles and 9 Scouts (3 from No.656 AAC)
Main attached Army Units:
2 Para, Lt Col H Jones (post VC) OBE
3 Para, Lt Col H W R Pike (DSO) MBE
22 SAS Regt, Lt Col H M Rose OBE (MID)

1. FANNING HEAD RAID - SBS land by helicopter from Antrim; Argentine positions engaged by machine guns under Antrim's covering fire
2. DARWIN RAID - D Sqdn SAS landed by helicopter to hold down Argentine forces around Darwin and Goose Green. Support fire from Ardent out in Grantham Sound
3. AMPHIBIOUS SHIPS
   1st Assault Wave: 40 Cdo from Fearless by Fearless LCU, 2 Para from Norland by Intrepid LCU, both to San Carlos
   2nd Assault Wave: 45 Cdo from Stromness to Ajax Bay, 3 Para from Intrepid to Port San Carlos,
   In Reserve: 42 Cdo in Canberra, later to Port San Carlos
   Supply Transports - Europic Ferry, Fort Austin, Sirs Galahad, Geraint, Lancelot, Percivale, Tristram
4. SAN CARLOS (Blue Beach) - 40 Cdo RM and 3 Cdo Bde HQ, Arty Bty. Also 2 Para which moved towards Sussex Mountains
5. AJAX BAY (Red Beach) - 45 Cdo RM. Also Brigade Maintenance Area, Cdo Logistic Regt, Arty Bty
6. PORT SAN CARLOS (Green Beach) - 3 Para. Also 42 Cdo RM, Arty Bty
7. British aircraft lost just east of Port San Carlos - [b11,b12] Gazelles

At End of Day
8. BACK TO CVBG - destroyer Antrim, transports Canberra, Europic Ferry, Norland

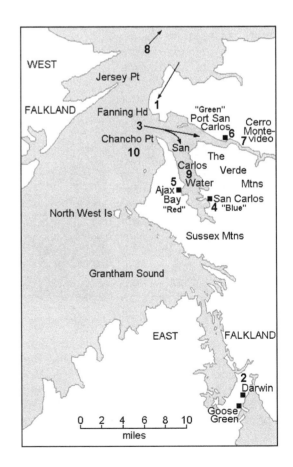

9. AMPHIBIOUS SHIPS IN SAN CARLOS WATER - assault ships Fearless, Intrepid, RFAs Fort Austin, Stromness, LSLs Sir Galahad, Sir Geraint, Sir Lancelot, Sir Percivale, Sir Tristram
10. ESCORTS REMAINING - Antrim (UXB damage), Ardent (SINKING), Argonaut (UXB damage), Brilliant (minor damage), Broadsword (minor damage), Plymouth, Yarmouth

As the **Amphibious Group** sailed in towards Falkland Sound, diversionary raids were mounted starting on Thursday night. Of immediate concern was a half company of infantrymen on the 800 feet high **Fanning Head** overlooking the entrance to San Carlos Water. To deal with these, "Antrim" went ahead with two Wessex, some 25 SBS heavily armed with machine guns, and a naval gunfire observer. The force landed by helicopter to the east of the Argentine positions under covering fire from "Antrim", and the defenders called on to surrender. This they refused to do and the engagement continued with a number of them killed or captured. Others escaped, but Fanning Head was finally under British control and the vulnerable landing craft below saved from attack. Further south, any attempt by the **Darwin** garrison to move towards the beachhead was blocked by the small force of D Sqdn SAS under the command of Major Delves and supported by "Ardent" out in Grantham Sound. Landed by No.846 Sea Kings to the north, the attackers engaged the Argentines with machine guns, anti-tank missiles and mortars to such an extent they were reported to be in battalion strength.

While the diversions took place, the **landings went ahead** admittedly with some delay and confusion, and yet with complete success. With the main body of the Amphibious Group anchored just outside San Carlos Water, the final plan was for 2 Para and 40 Cdo to land at San Carlos first so the Paras could move south to prevent the Argentines at Darwin from occupying the Sussex Mountains. Then 45 Cdo would go ashore at Ajax Bay and 3 Para at Port San Carlos to complete the encirclement of the anchorage. With 42 Cdo remaining on "Canberra" in reserve, Rapier missiles and artillery, ammo, fuel, rations and other stores would then be landed by the few helicopters, landing craft and Mexeflotes. The landing craft carrying the first wave were due to beach at San Carlos at 2.30am on Friday 21st May.

Unfortunately delays built up both in reaching the anchorage and in loading the troops, but eventually they headed in below Fanning Head before turning south towards San Carlos led in by Major Southby-Tailyour RM. The landing craft from "Fearless" including the smaller LCVPs carried 40 Cdo, with two of the LCUs carrying a Scorpion and Scimitar each in the bows (four light tanks in total) ready to provide gunfire support. With them in "Intrepid's" four LCUs was 2 Para from "Norland". "Plymouth" accompanied them in as close escort. Then 3,800 miles from Ascension, the first major British landing since Suez took place around an hour late, but completely unopposed. As soon as 2 Para landed, they moved off the five miles to Sussex Mountains, and 40 Cdo dug in below the western ridge of The Verde Mountains. As dawn broke, the landing craft returned to the ships still outside San Carlos Water to pick up the second wave - most of 45 Cdo from "Stromness" with Z Coy from "Intrepid", and all of 3 Para from "Intrepid". Now in daylight, the Marines went ashore near the disused meat packing plant at Ajax Bay on the western side, and the Paras a mile west of Port San Carlos on the northern side. Before 3 Para could secure the settlement, 3 Cdo Bde suffered its only fatal casualties on D-day.

Argentine Mirage attacking a British frigate in San Carlos Water

With the **three beachheads being secured**, the twelve amphibious ships entered San Carlos Water in broad daylight - "Canberra" and some of the larger ones anchoring in the deeper water to the north, and the smaller LSLs nearer San Carlos. The escorts patrolled nearby in Falkland Sound and took the brunt of the air attacks that followed. Using especially the No.846 Sea Kings, the first priority was to get the T Bty Rapiers ashore, although it took a number of hours to set up the twelve firing posts around the perimeter ready to join in the air defence. Early in this operation, shortly before 9am, one of the Sea Kings flew east of Port San Carlos and within gunfire range of the small Argentine garrison as they withdrew east. It escaped, but the escorting Gazelle of C Flt, 3 CBAS was hit and crashed near the shore, the pilot mortally wounded [b11]. Only minutes later a second C Flt Gazelle shared the same fate, going down on a nearby hillside, and this time both crewmen were killed [b12].

Along with the other tanks of The Blues and Royals, the three 105mm batteries of 29 Cdo Regt RA and the single battery of 4 Field Regt RA also landed. During this time the **air attacks started**, threatening the amphibious ships and their stores, and so every effort was made to unload as much as possible, especially ammo so the merchantmen could leave that night. From "Canberra", reserve 42 Cdo went ashore at Port San Carlos to support 3 Para if any threat there developed, and one of the two Surgical Support Teams landed at Ajax Bay to set up a Field Dressing Station under the command of Surgeon Cdr R T Jolly (awarded OBE) RN, and in the same vicinity as the Brigade Maintenance Area. Because of the air raids, Brigadier Thompson was not flown ashore until late afternoon but immediately started visiting his unit commanders.

At the end of this long and violent day, and with "Canberra" now carrying "Ardent's" survivors, the merchantmen although only partly unloaded and still carrying much of the infantry unit stores, left for the safety of the CVBG. Other amphibious ships and most of the escorts remained. Commodore Clapp and Brigadier Thompson had successfully secured a beachhead on the Falklands - 3 Cdo Bde was ashore with their Rapiers and artillery together with some ammo, a start had been made on bringing a major part of the combat stores ashore, and the Marines and Paras were digging in and actively patrolling. The crucial battle over the next four days would be for air supremacy over the islands.

Part 34. AIR BATTLES of 21st MAY

WEEK EIGHT

Only two days after their arrival, three of the **RAF Harrier GR.3s** started ground attacks by hitting a fuel dump at Fox Bay East with CBUs. Then next morning, Friday the 21st, and after G Sqdn SAS reported Argentine helicopters dispersing at night from Stanley, a number were caught on the ground near Mount Kent and a Chinook and Puma destroyed by 30mm cannon fire [a31, a32]. Later that morning, two more aircraft left "Hermes" but one had to return with under-carriage problems. The lone Harrier carried on and during a photo-reconaissance run over Port Howard was hit by ground-fire and crashed [b13]. The pilot, Flt Lt Glover ejected and was taken prisoner of war.

HMS Ardent mortally damaged with 22 men killed and 30 injured. The frigate standing by is probably HMS Yarmouth which took off "Ardent's" survivors (Courtesy - MOD, Navy)

The first **reaction to the landings** was by Falklands-based aircraft. Grupo 3 Pucaras took off from Goose Green as "Ardent" shelled the airstrip, and one was shot down over Sussex Mountains by a Stinger SAM fired by D Sqdn SAS pulling back from the Darwin raid [a33]. Then a single Aermacchi MB-339A of CANA 1 Esc from Stanley made a cannon and rocket attack on "Argonaut" at 10am causing minor damage and some casualties. Thereafter, mainland-based sorties that day led to heavy losses on both sides with five of the ships on the **defending gunline** lost or hit by bombs or cannon fire, and only "Plymouth" and "Yarmouth" escaping damage. One more Pucara and nine Daggers and Skyhawks were lost to the Sea Harriers on CAP and one to a SAM fired by warships. The fierce AA fire from ship and shore made the Argentine aircraft come in low and fast, and although many of their bombs were on target, they failed to explode. Fortunately, they also failed to hit the transports. The main raids took place around 10.30am, 1.00pm and 3.00pm.

First to arrive were a total of eight Daggers of Grupo 6. Attacking the northern end of the gunline, "Broadsword" was hit by cannon fire and "Antrim" also badly damaged by a UXB with casualties on both ships, but no one killed. One of the Daggers [a34] was brought down probably by a Sea Wolf from "Broadsword". "Antrim" then moved towards San Carlos Water where the bomb was removed, before heading that night for the CVBG. Shortly after midday, the Sea Harriers on CAP had their first success of the day. Two Grupo 3 Pucaras from Goose Green attacked a nearby naval gunfire observer directing "Ardent's" fire from out in Grantham Sound, the three No.801 aircraft closed in, and shot one down with cannon fire [a35].

Summary of Main Events

Attacking and Defending Aircraft
A. FAA Skyhawks of Grupo 4 and 5, FAA Daggers of Grupo 6, CANA Skyhawks of 3 Esc, all from Rio Grande, San Julian and Rio Gallegos
B. Sea Harriers - CAP over Falkland Sound and West Falkland by Nos.800 and 801 NAS from Hermes and Invincible

Aircraft of Both Sides Lost; British Ships Damaged

1. Argentine aircraft lost near Mount Kent - [a31] Chinook), [a32] Puma (both 8am)
2. British aircraft lost in Port Howard area - [b13] Harrier GR.3 (10am)
3. Argentine aircraft lost over Sussex Mountains - [a33] Pucara (10am)
4. Argonaut damaged by cannon fire off entrance to San Carlos Water (10am)
5. Antrim damaged by UXB, Broadsword by cannon fire off entrance to San Carlos Water (10.30am)
6. Argentine aircraft lost off San Carlos Water - [a34] Dagger (10.30am)
7. Argentine aircraft lost near Darwin – [a35] Pucara (12.10pm)
8. Argentine aircraft lost south of Christmas Harbour - [a36, a37] Skyhawks (1.05pm)
9. Argonaut damaged by UXB off entrance to San Carlos Water (2.30pm)
10. Argentine aircraft lost near Teal River Inlet - [a38] Dagger (2.35pm)
11. Ardent damaged by bomb, [b14] Lynx destroyed in Grantham Sound (2.40pm)
12. Brilliant damaged by cannon fire off entrance to San Carlos Water (2.45pm)
13. Argentine aircraft lost north of Port Howard - [a39, a40, a41] Daggers (2.50pm)
14. ARDENT mortally damaged by bombs in Grantham Sound (3.10pm)

15. Argentine aircraft lost near Swan Island - [a42, a43] Skyhawks (3.12pm)
16. Argentine aircraft lost trying to land at Stanley [a44] Skyhawk (3.30pm)

British Escorts at Start Of Day (and summary of damage sustained during day using previous map numbers)

off entrance to San Carlos Water in Falkland Sound
4/9. Argonaut (cannon fire & UXB)
5. Antrim (UXB) and Broadsword (cannon fire)
12. Brilliant (cannon fire) and Yarmouth

in San Carlos Water
Plymouth and Amphibious Ships

in Grantham Sound
11/14. Ardent (bombed and fatally damaged)

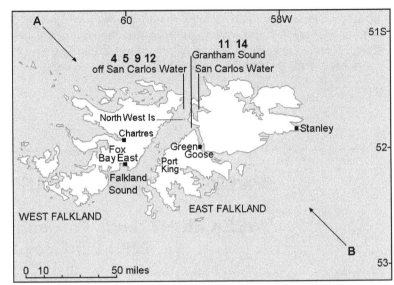

The **next mainland attacks** were due an hour later at 1.00pm by eight Skyhawks. Only two of the four Grupo 5 aircraft reached West Falkland because of fuelling problems, and one of these wasted its bombs on the abandoned "Rio Carcarana" in Port King. The fourth however carried on north up Falkland Sound and near-missed "Ardent" with two bombs. At "Brilliant's" command, two No.800 Sea Harriers chased the returning aircraft without success, but instead spotted the next four incoming Skyhawks from Grupo 4 over Chartres in West Falkland. They tried to escape, but two went down to Sidewinders near Christmas Harbour [a36, a37].

Then the **afternoon sorties** followed, starting at 2.30pm with six Skyhawks of Grupo 5 which nearly put paid to "Argonaut" (some sources put this raid in the morning). Deluged by near misses, two bombs hit without exploding but two men were killed in the Sea Cat magazine. Steaming at high speed and with engine and steering controls damaged, she was anchored by the action of Sub Lt Morgan, but had to stay in the area for a week until the UXBs were removed and the damage temporarily repaired.

Next, twelve Daggers of Grupo 6 were due to arrive. Out of the first group of six from Rio Grande, two aborted and as the remaining four came in over West Falkland, "Brilliant" vectored two No.800 NAS Sea Harriers and one of the Daggers [a38] was shot down near Teal River Inlet by yet another Sidewinder missile. The three surviving aircraft pressed on and caught "Ardent" still in Grantham Sound. Coming in from astern they blanketed her with hits and near-misses destroying her Lynx [b14] and Sea Cat installation and killing a number of men. With only small arms fire left for defence, she headed for the protection of the other escorts off San Carlos Water. As these three Daggers got away, six more from San Julian arrived in two flights of three. The first hit "Brilliant" with cannon fire causing slight damage and some casualties before they safely headed back, but the second flight was wiped out before even reaching the target area. Picked up over West Falkland by "Brilliant" again, two No.801 Sea Harriers shot them down with Sidewinders to the north of Port Howard [a39, a40, a41].

The **last attacks** started some 30 minutes later by two flights of A-4Q Skyhawks of 3 Esc in the only Navy sorties

British Gallantry Awards included:

HMS Antrim - bomb disposal
Fleet CPO (Diver) M G Fellows (DSC) BEM, Fleet Clearance Diving Team 1

HMS Ardent - small arms defense
Lt Cdr J M Sephton (post DSC) RN
PO J S Leake (DSM)
and rescue work
AB (Radar) J E Dillon (GM)
MEA(M)1 K Enticknapp (QGM)

HMS Argonaut - bomb disposal and damage repair
Lt Cdr B F Dutton (DSO) QGM RN, Fleet Clearance Diving Team 1
Sub Lt P T Morgan (DSC) RN
Chief MEM(M) M D Townsend (DSM)

HMS Broadsword - small arms defense
Sgt W J Leslie (DSM) RM

to reach the Falklands that day. The first three aircraft caught poor "ARDENT" off North West Island and again from the stern, bracketed her with hits and near misses. Badly damaged, on fire aft and flooding, with 22 men killed and some 30 injured, Cdr West ordered abandon ship and "Yarmouth" came alongside to pick up the survivors. "Ardent" finally sank the following evening. One of the CANA Skyhawks was damaged by the return small arms fire, and all three were caught by two No.800 Sea Harriers near Swan Island. One was shot down by Sidewinder [a42], cannon fire destroyed a second [a43] and hit the already damaged third. Unable to land at Stanley with undercarriage problems, the pilot of this one ejected [a44]. The second CANA flight ran in fifteen minutes later, but failed to hit any of the ships. The Sea Harriers continued to fly CAP, but there were no more raids that day and the transports continued unloading.

Part 35. INITIAL MOVES OUT OF SAN CARLOS

WEEK EIGHT (end), Falkland Area Operations, 22nd-23rd May 1982

Summary of Main Events

Task Force Ships in and around TEZ (23rd)
Carriers Hermes, Invincible, destroyers Antrim (UXB damage), Coventry, Exeter, Glamorgan, Glasgow, frigates Alacrity, Ambuscade, Argonaut (UXB damage), Arrow (structural damage), Brilliant (cannon damage), Broadsword, Plymouth, Yarmouth, assault ships Fearless, Intrepid, RFAs Fort Austin, Olmeda, Regent, Resource, Stromness, Tidepool, LSLs Sir Bedivere, Sir Galahad, Sir Geraint, Sir Lancelot, Sir Percivale, Sir Tristram, transports Atlantic Conveyor, Canberra, Elk, Europic Ferry, Norland

plus submarine force, hospital ships in RCB, repair ship and tug in TRALA, and some tankers

(Sheffield and Ardent sunk so far)

3 COMMANDO BRIGADE
1. From Port San Carlos, 3 Para out to west and north; 42 Cdo east to Cerro Montevideo
2. 45 Cdo at Ajax Bay
3. 3 Cdo Bde HQ and 40 Cdo at San Carlos
4. 2 Para to Sussex Mtns
5. M&AW Cadre on Bull Hill and Evelyn Hill

AIRCRAFT AND SHIP LOSSES
6. Argentine patrol craft Rio Iguaza damaged and grounded in Choiseul Sound (22nd)
7. Captured Falklands coaster Monsunen driven aground in Lively Sound (23rd)
8. Damaged Argentine cargo ship Rio Carcarana destroyed in Port King (23rd)
9. Argentine aircraft lost near Shag House Cove - [a45, a47] Pumas, [a46] Agusta A-109A (all 23rd)

10. ANTELOPE hit by UXBs in San Carlos Water; Argentine aircraft lost - [a48] Skyhawk (both 23rd)
11. Argentine aircraft lost over Pebble Island - [a49] Dagger (23rd)
12. British aircraft lost 90 miles north east of Stanley - [b15] Sea Harrier (23rd)

On Saturday 22nd, the two assault ships, five LSLs, and RFAs "Fort Austin" and "Stromness" were still in San Carlos Water. Of the original escorts, only "Brilliant", "Plymouth", "Yarmouth" and the damaged "Argonaut" remained in direct support, and "Broadsword" spent some of the time north of Pebble Island with "Coventry" as a **missile trap** for incoming aircraft. "Antrim" had gone, but "Ardent's" place was taken by newly arrived "Antelope", although sadly not for long. Next day, they were joined by LSL "Sir Bedivere" and frigate "Arrow" which had structural damage but could still share in the air defence. Of the merchantmen that left on Friday, "Norland" was back in to disembark her remaining troops and later take on board "Antelope's" survivors, and "Canberra" out in the holding area transferred stores to RFA "Resource" for delivery on Monday.

From now on, only the more important ship movements can be followed. As air supremacy was slowly won, the carriers continued to provide the only fixed wing airpower, the destroyers and frigates escorted the transports into and out of San Carlos Water and protected them there, and also carried out bombardment, special forces insertions and other patrol duties. Meanwhile the merchantmen and RFAs kept the Task Force supplied with fuel, ammo, food and water, and other stores, and played their part in moving the troops towards Stanley. All this took the ships to various parts of the TEZ and around the Falklands, to South Georgia, and when in need of repair, to the TRALA.

Some of the crew on HMS Plymouth's bridge appear to be enjoying "a sail" in more peaceful times. The day before this period in the Falkland's War, she had endured the bombing attacks in San Carlos Water. On the 8th June she was hit by cannon fire and four UXBs. (Courtesy - MOD, Navy)

At the northern end of the beachhead, 3 Para patrolled to the west and north of Port San Carlos, while 42 Cdo followed up the retreating Argentine troops, but only as far as Cerro Montevideo to stay within artillery range. To the west, 45 Cdo was dug in above Ajax Bay and on the east, 40 Cdo above San Carlos, destined to spend a frustrating war mainly defending the area. In the south, 2 Para on Sussex Mountains was about to be the first unit to prepare for action. While waiting for more supplies to be unloaded and for General Moore to arrive, Brigadier Thompson at his mobile HQ at San Carlos made plans to push forward. Apart from the Special Forces patrols scattered about the Falklands, Marines of the Mountain and Arctic Warfare Cadre had been flown to Bull Hill and Evelyn Hill on the way to Stanley. He also decided to launch a battalion raid against the enemy forces at Goose Green, and on Sunday 23rd ordered Lt Col Jones to prepare 2 Para for this task. On the same day, 42 Cdo was ordered back from its exposed position to join in the defence of Port San Carlos, and just to the north, 3 Para suffered wounded casualties when two patrols accidentally clashed.

Meanwhile as General Menendez attempted to supply his outlying forces, more Argentine ships and helicopters were lost. Late on Friday 21st, patrol craft "Rio Iguaza" left Stanley with Pucara spares and 105mm guns for Goose Green, and next morning was found and strafed in Choiseul Sound by two No.800 Sea Harriers on CAP. She ran ashore, but two of the guns were recovered and reached their destination. Then on Saturday evening "Brilliant" and "Yarmouth" searched for the captured coaster "Monsunen" known to be heading for Stanley from Darwin, and early on Sunday, "Brilliant's" Lynx located her off the east coast. A small SBS boarding party tried to capture the ship by helicopter, but gunfire drove them away. The frigates then ran "Monsunen" aground in Lively Sound, but next day she was towed into Darwin by "Forrest". Now into Sunday,

"Yarmouth" returned to San Carlos Water, but "Brilliant" headed for the carriers. Finally the damaged cargo ship "RIO CARCARANA" was finished off in Port King at midday by Sea Skuas fired by "Antelope's" Lynx.

Still on Sunday morning (23rd), three Army Pumas carrying ammo and stores for Port Howard, and escorted by an Agusta, were on the last leg of their dangerous flight from Stanley when they were sighted near Shag House Cove by two No.800 Sea Harriers. One Puma flew into the ground trying to escape [a45], the crew getting clear before it exploded, and cannon fire destroyed the Agusta [a46] and disabled a second Puma. Two No.801 Sea Harriers shortly arrived and finished off this one by strafing [a47]. Just one Puma survived to fly the three crews to Port Howard.

Over the weekend, RAF GR.3s mounted a number of denial attacks against airstrips, and the Sea Harriers continued to fly CAP although bad weather over southern Argentina meant they were hardly needed on Saturday 22nd. The next heavy raids were mounted on Sunday when the FAA also started using Grupo 1 Learjets as pathfinders and decoys. First to arrive in the early afternoon were four A-4B Skyhawks of Grupo 5 which found "ANTELOPE" in San Carlos Water. In a confused

British Gallantry Awards included:

HMS Antelope - defense and rescue
LS (Radar) J D Warren (DSM) rescue alongside with UXB on board
Colour Sgt M J Francis (DSM) RM, coxswain LCU F1, HMS Fearless
Colour Sgt B Johnston (post QGM) RM, coxswain LCU F4, HMS Fearless (killed on 8th June)
Third Offr A Gudgeon (QGM) RFA, ship's boat, also RFA Sir Galahad and bomb disposal

WO2 J H Phillips (DSC), 49 EOD Sqdn RE
Staff Sgt J Prescott (post CGM), 49 EOD Sqdn RE
both involved Argonaut's UXB

action which put two UXBs in her and killed one man, an attacker clipped her mast and another was shot down by possibly a Sea Wolf from "Broadsword" or a Rapier [a48]. That evening as the bombs were being defused, one exploded killing Sgt Prescott RE. Catching fire, she blew up and sank next day with a broken back.

Minutes after the Grupo 5 attack, three Skyhawks of CANA 3 Esc came in but failed to hit any ships, and one crashed on landing back at Rio Grande. Two hours later, two incoming Grupo 6 Daggers were sighted by two No.800 Sea Harriers, and as they tried to escape, one was destroyed over Pebble Island by Sidewinder [a49]. That same afternoon, two CANA Super Etendards flew from Rio Grande on a third Exocet mission, but returned to base without finding any targets. However that evening did see the loss of a fourth Sea Harrier. As four No.800 aircraft took off from "Hermes" to bomb Stanley airfield, one hit the sea and exploded killing Lt Cdr Batt [b15].

Part 36. 5th INFANTRY BRIGADE REACHES SOUTH GEORGIA

WEEK NINE, British Task Force Movements
24th-30th May 1982

Ascension - More ships passed by or called in on their way south including RFAs "Engadine" and "Fort Grange" and mooring vessel "Wimpey Seahorse", but now two tankers headed back for the UK to reload. On Monday 24th it was "British Avon" after picking up POW Lt Cdr Astiz, and then on Wednesday, over-crowded "British Esk" which first got in with more then 260 "Sheffield" survivors who flew on home. Apart from all the usual RAF activity, two Phantom fighters of 29(F) Sqdn flew down on Monday from Coningsby, followed on Wednesday by a third to take over air defence from the three Harriers. These in turn were joined over the weekend by six more GR.3s from Wittering before later continuing south. Then late on Friday in "Black Buck 4", and with the usual Victor support, a Vulcan armed with Shrike anti-radar missiles took off to attack the Stanley command and control radars. Refuelling problems stopped the mission, but late on Sunday, "Black Buck 5" went ahead successfully.

Disposition of British Ships, Aircraft & Land Forces in Summary

UK Departures
Scottish Eagle, Capt A Terras and NP 2040
British Enterprise III, Capt D Grant and NP 2090, Lt Cdr B E M Reynell RN

Ships and Aircraft in Ascension Area
Ships Returning to UK - tankers British Avon, British Esk
RAF Aircraft - Phantoms of No.29(F) Sqdn, Harrier GR.3s, Vulcans, Nimrods, Victors, Hercules, VC.10s, Sea King, Chinook
RAF Harriers on Way South - arriving GR.3s of 1(F) Sqdn
Other Ships at Ascension or Reaching the Area on the Way South - RFAs Engadine, Fort Grange, tankers Alvega (base storage), Balder London, mooring vessels RMAS Goosander, Wimpey Seahorse

Support Tankers in South Atlantic or in Tanker Holding Areas - RFAs Appleleaf, Bayleaf, Pearleaf, Plumleaf, chartered Anco Charger, British Dart, British Tay (sailed for Ascension), British Test, British Trent, British Wye (attacked at 48S, 39W), Eburna, water tanker Fort Toronto

Departing South Atlantic - ? SSN Splendid, destroyer Glasgow

Arriving in South Atlantic - destroyers Bristol, Cardiff, frigates Active, Avenger, Andromeda, Minerva, Penelope, RFA Olna, Tidespring, transport Atlantic Causeway.
5th Infantry Brigade Equipment - transports Baltic Ferry, Nordic Ferry

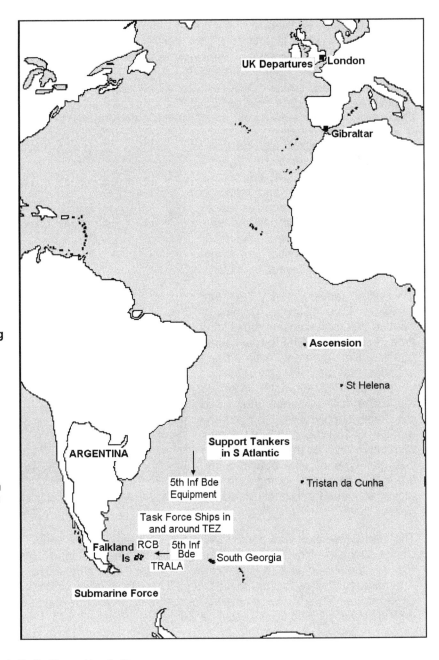

Red Cross Box, RCB - hospital ship Uganda, ambulance ships Hecla (to Montevideo), Herald, Hydra

Tug, Repair & Logistic Area, TRALA - repair ship Stena Seaspread, tugs Irishman, Salvageman, Yorkshireman

SEE FOLLOWING PARTS FOR MAIN TASK FORCE SHIPS DURING THIS PERIOD:
Part 37: 24th-26th May - Falkland Area Operations
Part 39: 27th-30th May - Falkland Area Operations

Submarine Force - SSN Conqueror, Courageous, Spartan, Valiant, SS Onyx

In and Around South Georgia Waters - IPV Endurance, minesweepers Cordella, Farnella, Junella, Northella, Pict, RFA Blue Rover, RMAS Typhoon, transports Saxonia, Lycaon, despatch vessels Iris, Leeds Castle, M Coy 42 Cdo.
At time of transfer of 5th Infantry Brigade - transports Queen Elizabeth 2, Canberra, Norland, RFA Stromness

South Atlantic - By Wednesday morning (26th), the **"Bristol" group** had joined the Task Force to more than make up for the ships lost. With "Bristol" herself were type 42 "Cardiff", type 21 frigates "Active" and "Avenger", and Leander-class "Minerva", "Penelope" and Sea Wolf-armed "Andromeda". Some of them screened the carriers by day, and by night bombarded Argentine positions or escorted transports to and from San Carlos Water. RFA fleet tanker "Olna" arrived with them to start refuelling duties, and she was joined by RFA "Tidespring" at last back from her South Georgia mission. Finally by the end of the week, support ship "Atlantic Causeway" had arrived with her much needed Sea King and Wessex helicopters.

Now the **first warships returned north**. With the arrival of "Cardiff", damaged "Glasgow" was patched up by "Stena Seaspread" and sailed on Thursday 27th with engines under manual control. Also around this time, nuclear submarine "Splendid" presumably left her patrol area to get home by the second week in June.

On Friday, tanker "British Tay" with survivors from "Atlantic Conveyor" headed first for Ascension, but all this time there was still the danger of attack. Not content with flying supplies into Stanley and refuelling air strikes, FAA Grupo 1 Hercules made the only apparent attempt to cut British supply lines. On Saturday a single C-130 dropped eight bombs on "British Wye" to the north of South Georgia. One hit, but bounced into the sea without exploding and the tanker continued her lonely refuelling duties.

Destroyer HMS Glasgow (Courtesy MOD, Navy)

The Red Cross Box was particularly active and early in the week, "Hydra" sailed to the east to pick up San Carlos casualties from "Canberra" for transfer to "Uganda", and "Herald" finally arrived after having diverted to Rio de Janeiro to land a sick crewman. Later, "Hecla" headed for Montevideo with the first British and Argentine casualties for repatriation, and "Uganda" moved closer in to pick up the wounded from the Goose Green battle. The TRALA was also in business, with both "Glasgow" and "Brilliant" there, and the ships in residence were joined from Tristan da Cunha by "Irishman" and "Yorkshireman".

South Georgia - "Endurance" played host to probably the largest tonnage of shipping the island had ever seen, with most there to meet "Queen Elizabeth 2" which could not be risked closer to the Falkland's. Before her arrival, "Canberra" (with "Ardent's survivors), "Norland" (with "Antelope's") and destroyer "Antrim" left the TEZ on Tuesday 25th, followed by RFA "Stromness" (with "Coventry's") from San Carlos Water. On the same day, despatch vessel "Iris" reached Grytviken from Ascension with Lt Mills RM and his men for "Endurance", and loaded scrap steel from the whaling stations for delivery to the TRALA. Other arrivals there to help transfer the troops from "QE2" were despatch vessel "Leeds Castle" from the TEZ and the five minesweeping trawlers of the 11th MCMS.

North east of South Georgia on Thursday 27th, "Antrim" picked up General Moore and Brigadier Wilson before heading back for "Fearless", and "QE2" continued on into Cumberland Bay East. Over the next 24 hours, the Scots and Welsh Guards moved to "Canberra" and the Gurkhas to "Norland", and on Friday, "Stromness" arrived to take on board more troops, together with ammo and Rapiers from the newly-arrived transport "Lycaon". When the transfers were completed, including the two No.825 Sea Kings from "QE2" to "Canberra", the Falkland's bound ships departed. "Queen Elizabeth 2" then headed back north on Saturday with the survivors. "Leeds Castle" followed her but only as far as Ascension to take over as guardship. And in a week that saw 3 Cdo Bde moving out of San Carlos Water, 2 Para's victory at Goose Green and the battle for air supremacy being won, transports "Baltic Ferry" and "Nordic Ferry" approached the Falklands direct with helicopters and equipment for 5th Inf Bde.

Part 37. "COVENTRY" & "ATLANTIC CONVEYOR" SUNK

WEEK NINE (part), Falkland Area Operations
24th-26th MAY 1982

Summary of Main Events

Task Force Ships in and around TEZ (26th)
Carriers Hermes, Invincible, destroyers Bristol, Cardiff, Exeter, Glamorgan, Glasgow, frigates Active, Alacrity, Ambuscade, Andromeda, Arrow, Argonaut (UXB damage), Avenger, Brilliant, Broadsword, Minerva, Penelope, Plymouth, Yarmouth, assault ships Fearless, Intrepid, RFAs Fort Austin, Olmeda, Olna, Regent, Resource, Tidepool, LSLs Sir Bedivere, Sir Galahad, (UXB damage), Sir Geraint, Sir Lancelot (UXB damage), Sir Percivale, Sir Tristram, transports Elk, Europic Ferry

plus submarine force, hospital ships in RCB, repair ship and tugs in TRALA, and some tankers

(Sheffield, Ardent and Antelope lost so far)

3 COMMANDO BRIGADE LOCATIONS & MOVEMENTS
3 Cdo Bde HQ and 40 Cdo at San Carlos
3 Para west and north of Port San Carlos; 42 Cdo returning to Port San Carlos from Cerro Montevideo; 45 Cdo at Ajax Bay
M&AW Cadre on Bull Hill and Evelyn Hill
1. SBS to Port Salvador
2. D Sqdn SAS recon patrol to Mt Kent

AIRCRAFT AND SHIP LOSSES & MOVEMENTS
3. Argentine aircraft lost just north of Pebble Island – [a50, a51, a52] Daggers (24th)
4. LSLs Sir Galahad and Sir Lancelot damaged in San Carlos Water (24th)
5. Argentine aircraft lost in King George Bay, West Falkland - [a53] Skyhawk (24th)
6. Argentine aircraft lost just north of Pebble Island – [a54] Skyhawk (25th)
7. Argentine aircraft lost over San Carlos Water - [a55] Skyhawk (25th)
8. Argentine aircraft lost north east of Pebble Island - [a56] Skyhawk (25th)
9. Broadsword damaged, COVENTRY sunk and Lynx helicopter [b16] lost 10 miles north of Pebble Island (25th)
10. ATLANTIC CONVEYOR sunk 90 miles north east of Stanley; aircraft lost - [b17-22] Wessex, [b23-25] Chinooks, [b26] Lynx (25th)
11. Destroyer Antrim, RFA Stromness, transports Canberra, Norland to South Georgia

3 CDO BDE MOVEMENTS (continued)
12. 2 Para moved from Sussex Mountains half way to Camilla Creek House (26th) on their way to Darwin
13. L Coy 42 Cdo helicoptered from Port San Carlos to Sussex Mountains (26th)

As plans for the Darwin raid went ahead, Brigadier Thompson prepared to move towards Stanley. D Sqdn SAS and then 42 Cdo were to fly to Mount Kent, and when "Atlantic Conveyor" arrived with her Chinooks, more of 3 Cdo Bde would be flown forward. A start was made when an SBS team went ashore in Port Salvador to check Teal Inlet and a D Sqdn patrol landed on Mount Kent, but the weather closed in stopping the rest of D Sqdn joining them. Also 2 Para's artillery could not be flown in, so the raid on Darwin was cancelled. Then on Tuesday 25th, "Atlantic Conveyor" was lost and the planning had to start all over again. By then the battle for control of the air had almost been won, but the losses on both sides were heavy. In this, "Broadsword" and "Coventry" in their missile trap and radar picket role off Pebble Island played a major part.

Monday 24th saw four more Argentine aircraft destroyed. That morning, four Grupo 6 Daggers came in low over Pebble Island, but under "Broadsword's" direction, two No.800 Sea Harriers brought three of them down with Sidewinders [a50, a51, a52]. As this happened, more Daggers and Grupo 4 and 5 Skyhawks reached the anchorage from the south. LSLs "Sir Galahad" and "Sir Lancelot" each received a UXB and "Sir Bedivere" was slightly damaged by a glancing hit, all believed to be from Skyhawks of Grupo 4. The three aircraft in this flight were damaged by the fierce AA, including claims by both "Fearless" and "Argonaut" Sea Cats, and on the way home, one crashed into King George Bay off West Falkland [a53]. Some of the crew of both LSLs was evacuated, but the bombs were later defused, although "Sir Lancelot" was not fully operational for a long time.

Tuesday the 25th May was Argentine National Day and the first target for Grupo 5 Skyhawks that morning was the two missile trap ships, but "Coventry's" Sea Dart brought one of them down at long range north of Pebble Island and the sortie was abandoned [a54]. Then at midday four Grupo 4 aircraft reached San Carlos Water. One was blasted out of the sky by small arms fire and missiles (the claims included "Yarmouth's" Sea Cat), although the pilot ejected safely [a55], and as the three survivors escaped, a second aircraft was destroyed to the north east of Pebble Island by another Sea Dart from "Coventry" [a56]. In the afternoon, the tables were turned, first of all by four Skyhawks of Grupo 5 which reached "Coventry" and "Broadsword". As the first pair approached, the CAP Sea Harriers were warned off, but "Broadsword's" Sea Wolf system broke contact and she was hit by a bomb which bounced up through her stern and out again badly damaging the Lynx on the way. The second pair now went for "Coventry", and just as "Broadsword" prepared to fire Sea Wolf again, the type 42 got in the way and contact was broken for a second time. With little to stop them, the Skyhawks put three bombs into "Coventry" at 3.20pm. Within half an hour she had capsized and been abandoned with 19 men killed and 25 wounded. The survivors were picked up by "Broadsword" and helicopters from San Carlos and she shortly sank with her Lynx [b16]. Of the three Type 42s that first sailed south with the Advanced Group, two were now at the bottom and the third damaged and soon to return.

As "Coventry" went down, and quite separate from the Skyhawk sorties, two Super Etendards of CANA 2 Esc approached the CVBG from the north, after refuelling on the way by Hercules tanker. In their path and close together were the two carriers and transport "Atlantic Conveyor" at this time some 90 miles north east of Stanley and heading in for San Carlos Water. Just after 4.30pm, they launched two Exocets from a range of 30 miles, and in spite of attempts to decoy the missiles away by chaff fired by the warships including "Ambuscade", one of them hit "Atlantic Conveyor" and set her ablaze uncontrollably. Little is known of the fate of the second Exocet. "Alacrity" and "Brilliant" closed in to help, but the order was soon given to abandon ship, and by

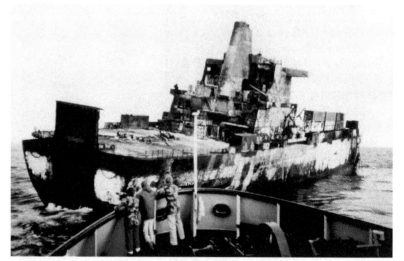

The burnt-out hulk of "Atlantic Conveyor" as a tug (believed to be "Irishman") prepares to take her in tow.

the time the survivors were picked up, a total of twelve men had died including Capt North. Fortunately the Harriers had been flown off before the attack, but all the helicopters apart from an airborne Chinook and thousands of tons of stores including ammunition, Harrier spares and tents, had to be left on the burning ship. Tug "Irishman" went to her aid and on Thursday took the burnt out hulk in tow, but "Atlantic Conveyor" soon sank taking with her six Wessex [b17-22], three Chinooks [b23-25] and a spare Lynx [b26].

Still on Tuesday 25th as "Canberra" and "Norland" made their way to South Georgia, the two remaining merchantmen in the TEZ continued to support the landings. "Europic Ferry" with her 2 Para stores sailed in to complete unloading, while "Elk" prepared to follow her with more vehicles and ammo. Meanwhile to the north, nuclear sub "Conqueror" on patrol had an aerial wrapped around her propeller, and on Tuesday in bad weather and under threat of aircraft attack, PO Libby dived to remove it.

With "Atlantic Conveyor's" loss, and with four Sea Kings already used for night missions and one for Rapier support, Brigadier Thompson had only six more plus five Wessex to move his troops towards Stanley. When his staff met on Wednesday morning (26th), and with new orders from Northwood, fresh plans were made. Goose Green was to be taken and held by 2 Para, and much of the rest of the Brigade would have to walk – "yomp" and "tab"! Late that day, Lt Col Jones led 2 Para south on the path to Darwin, and on Thursday, 45 Cdo and 3 Para started their move overland to Teal Inlet while 42 Cdo waited a later move to Mount Kent. Still on Wednesday, L Coy 42 Cdo flew from Port San Carlos to Sussex Mountains to relieve 2 Para.

British Gallantry Awards included:

HMS Conqueror
PO (Sonar) G J R Libby (DSM)

HMS Coventry - helicopter rescue
CPO Aircrewman M J Tupper (DSM), No.846 NAS

RFA Sir Galahad - bomb disposal
Lt N A Bruen (DSC) RN, CO Fleet Clearance
  Diving Team 3
Chief Eng Offr C K A Adams (QGM) RFA, also
  assisted with Sir Lancelot UXB

RFA Sir Lancelot - bomb disposal
CPO (Diver) G M Trotter (DSM), Fleet Clearance
  Diving Team 3

Merchantman Atlantic Conveyor
Capt I H North (post DSC) MN
  and rescue work
Flt Sgt B W Jopling (QGM), 18 Sqdn RAF
Third Eng B R Williams (QGM), MN

Part 38. 2 PARA'S APPROACH TO and BATTLE FOR DARWIN and GOOSE GREEN

26th-28th May 1982

Summary of Main Events

British Forces
Approx 500 men of **2 Para** including 2x81mm mortars, Milans and GPMGs; 3x105mm artillery, 8 Bty, 29 Cdo
  Regt RA; Blowpipe SAM detachments, Air Defence Troops RM and RA; Recon Troop, 59 Cdo Sqdn RE for
  mine clearance
2xScouts and 2xGazelles, 3 CBAS for forward ammo supply and casevac, joined by 2xScouts, 656 Sqdn AAC
Frigate 'Arrow', 1x4.5in and RAF Harrier GR.3s from 'Hermes' in support
2 Para Commanders:
  Lt Col H Jones, Maj C P B Keeble, second-in-command
  Maj C D Farrar-Hockley A Coy, Maj J H Crosland B Coy, Maj R Jenner C Coy, Maj P Neame D Coy

Argentine Defenders
12th Inf Regt, less one coy, 3 or 4x105mm artillery, elements 601st AA Btn with 20mm and 35mm guns, FAA
  airfield personnel, joined on day of battle by **one Coy, 12th Inf Regt; C Coy 25th Inf Regt**
Total forces - approx 1,000
Commanders:
  Group Capt Pedroza FAA,
  Lt Col Piaggi, 12th Regt, ground forces

1. British aircraft lost west of Goose Green - [b27] Harrier GR.3 (27th)

Early morning.....
2. A Coy 2 Para occupied Burntside House
3. B & D Coys 2 Para moved forward towards Boca House
4. A Coy moved past Coronation Point
5. B & D Coys came up against strongpoint at Boca House
6. A Coy came up against main defences along Darwin Hill
   .... to dawn

By midday - A Coy had taken and held Darwin Hill, and B and D Coys had finally silenced Boca House
7. British aircraft lost west of Camilla Creek House - [b28] Scout (11.55am)
8. Argentine aircraft lost on return to Stanley - [a58] Pucara (c12.00pm)

From midday....
9. D and C Coys fought towards Goose Green airfield
10. B Coy circled around airfield to cut off Goose Green
11. Argentine aircraft lost near Goose Green Schoolhouse - [a59] Aermacchi MB-339A, [a60] Pucara (both 5.00pm)
12. Harrier GR3s hit Argentine AA positions
13. Argentine helicopter-borne reinforcements continued to arrive
    .... to dusk

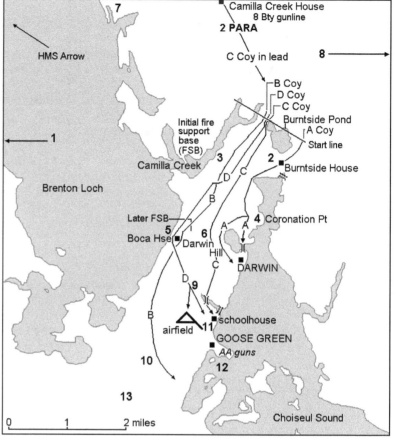

Approach to Darwin - Late on Wednesday 26th as some 500 men of 2 Para moved south towards Darwin, there was much uncertainty about Argentine strength in the area. However by the time of the surrender, and after allowance is made for the nearly 50 killed (not the originally reported 250), there were over 1,000 POWs including the 12th Inf Regt and a Coy from the 25th. With their approaches mined, the infantry were in well-prepared defensive positions, especially between Boca House and Darwin half way down the isthmus, and for support could call on 105mm artillery, AA guns later in the ground defence role, and attack aircraft from Stanley.

By early Thursday morning (27th), 2 Para had marched the eight miles from Sussex Mountains and reached the holding position at Camilla Creek House where most lay up all day. Two patrols from C Coy probed forward towards either side of the isthmus to plot some of the enemy defences, but later pulled back under fire. And then early that afternoon, two Harrier GR.3s attacked Argentine positions with CBUs, and in a subsequent strafing run, one of them was hit probably by 35mm Oerlikon fire and crashed to the west of Goose Green [b27]. Sqdn Ldr Iveson ejected and hid up before being rescued three days later.

That night, the three 105s of 8 Bty RA and their ammo were flown to Camilla Creek House by No.846 Sea Kings, and "Arrow" headed into Grantham Sound, opening fire from there under the control of a naval gunfire observer. A later turret fault was repaired and she remained on station supporting the Paras advance towards Darwin, when with the threat of air attack at dawn, had to return to San Carlos Water. Meanwhile that same evening, 2 Para moved off the two miles to the start line with C (Patrol) Coy leading the way. With D Coy at first in reserve, A and B Coys waited on either side of Burntside Pond, the mortars to their rear, and the fire support company with its Milans initially across Camilla Creek from the forward Argentine positions. Early on Friday the 28th, the men of 2 Para prepared for a night attack against largely unknown forces across the open ground of the Goose Green area, five miles long and over a mile wide.

The Battle for Darwin and Goose Green, Friday 28th May - At 3.30am, A Coy moved off on the left and attacked Burntside House believed to be occupied by an Argentine platoon, but found no-one there other than four unhurt civilians. At 4.10am, B Coy started forward from the other side of Burntside Pond down the right flank with D Coy following them long the middle. With artillery support on both sides, B and D Coys were soon in confused action against a series of enemy trenches, and as they slowly made progress, A Coy moved past unoccupied positions at Coronation Point. Leaving one platoon of A Coy to provide covering fire from the north side of Darwin, the remainder started to circle round the inlet to take the settlement. As dawn broke, the attacks on both flanks bogged down as B Coy came up against the strongpoint of Boca House and A Coy found that a small rise, later known as Darwin Hill, was the key to the Argentine defences.

Not until midday did 2 Para break through. As A Coy was hit and went to ground, Lt Col Jones and his Tac HQ came up, and another attempt to push forward was made which led to two officers and an NCO being killed. Col Jones moved off virtually on his own, and was soon shot and dying in an action which led to the award of a Victoria Cross. Maj Keeble was called up from the rear, and leaving A Coy to slowly wrest Darwin Hill and pulling B Coy slightly back from Boca House, ordered D Coy to move round them on the far right along the edge of the sea. Now in daylight, the battle continued with the Argentines helicoptering in their first reinforcements and flying more support missions. The first attack by Falkland's based aircraft took place earlier when a Grupo 3 Pucara was hit, probably by a Blowpipe SAM, but limped back to Stanley. The next sortie by two more Pucaras caught two Royal Marine Scouts on their way in to casevac Lt Col Jones. Capt Niblett managed to evade them, but Lt Nunn was killed by cannon fire and went down near Camilla Creek House [b28]. One of the Pucaras was later found to have crashed into high ground returning to Stanley [a58].

British Gallantry Awards

Some citations also included the Battle for Wireless Ridge*

2 PARA
Lt Col H Jones (post VC) OBE
Maj C P B Keeble (DSO)
Lt C S Connor (MC), C Coy*
Maj J H Crosland (MC), B Coy*
Maj C D Farrar-Hockley (MC), A Coy*
Pte S Illingsworth (post DCM), B Coy
Cpl D Abols (DCM), A Coy
Sgt J C Meredith (DCM), D Coy*
L/Cpl G D Bingley (post MM), D Coy
L/Cpl S A Bardsley (MM)
Sgt T I Barrett (MM), A Coy*
L/Cpl M W L Bentley (MM), Medic
Cpl T J Camp (MM), A Coy
Pte G S Carter (MM), D Coy
Pte B J Grayling (MM), D Coy
Cpl T W Harley (MM), D Coy
L/Cpl L J L Standish (MM)

3 CBAS RM
Capt J P Niblett (DFC) RM
Lt R J Nunn (post DFC) RM
Sgt W C O'Brien (DFM) RM

656 Sqdn AAC
Capt J G Greenhalgh (DFC) RCT*

David Norris, "Daily Mail", Brigadier J H Thompson RM, 3 Commando Brigade, Colour Sergeant Cotton, 2 Para, Major A Rice RA and Lieutenant Colonel H W Pike, 3 Para waiting to fly to 2 Para memorial service at Goose Green (Courtesy - Airborne Forces Museum)

By midday, A Coy had taken and held Darwin Hill, and B and D Coys had finally silenced Boca House. Still under fire, D and C Coys headed towards the airfield and Goose Green while B Coy circled east to cut off the settlement. During the attack towards the schoolhouse, three men of D Coy were killed in an incident involving a white flag. Now into the late afternoon, aircraft from both sides came on the scene, starting with two MB.339s of CANA 1 Esc and two Pucaras of Grupo 3 which hit the school area. One of the Navy jets was brought down by a Royal Marine Blowpipe [a59], minutes later one of the Pucaras dropped napalm and the other was shot down by small arms fire [a60]. Then three Harrier GR.3s brought much needed relief by hitting the AA guns at Goose Green with CBUs and rockets.

With evening approaching and the Argentines squeezed in towards Goose Green, more reinforcements arrived to the south by helicopter, while to the north, J Coy 42 Cdo was flown in reinforce 2 Para but too late to join in the fighting. Two Argentine POWs were sent in to start negotiations which lasted most of the night, and next morning, Group Capt Pedroza surrendered all his forces to Maj Keeble. British losses were fifteen men from 2 Para, a Royal Engineer and the Marine pilot, and 30 to 40 Paras wounded. Many of the 1,000 Argentine POWs including the FAA men sailed on "Norland" to Montevideo in early June.

Part 39. 3 COMMANDO "YOMPS/TABS" FROM SAN CARLOS

WEEK NINE (end), Falkland Area Operations 27th-30th May 1982

Summary of Main Events

Arriving Helicopters:
First 4 of 10 Sea King HAS.2As of No.825 NAS [Lt Cdr H S Clark (awarded DSC) RN]
1 Chinook of 18 Sqdn RAF [Wing Cdr A J Stables RAF]

Task Force Ships in and around TEZ (30th)
Carriers Hermes, Invincible, destroyers Antrim, Bristol, Cardiff, Exeter, Glamorgan, frigates Active, Alacrity, Ambuscade, Andromeda, Argonaut, Arrow, Avenger, Brilliant, Broadsword, Minerva, Penelope, Plymouth, Yarmouth, assault ships Fearless, Intrepid, RFAs Fort Austin, Olmeda, Olna, Regent, Resource, Tidepool, Tidespring, LSLs Sir Bedivere, Sir Galahad, Sir Geraint, Sir Lancelot, Sir Percivale, Sir Tristram, transports Atlantic Causeway, Elk, Europic Ferry

plus submarine force, hospital ships in RCB, repair ship and tugs in TRALA, and some tankers

(Sheffield, Ardent, Antelope, Coventry and Atlantic Conveyor lost so far)

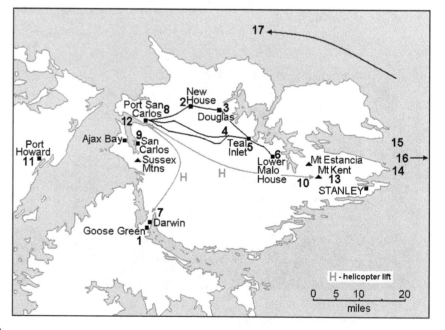

3 COMMANDO BRIGADE
1. 2 Para, 8 Bty RA approach to and battle for Goose Green (26th-28th)
2. 45 Cdo moved from Port San Carlos, first to New House (27th)
3. 45 Cdo reached Douglas (28th) and dug in (29th)
4. 3 Para in two columns moved from Port San Carlos towards Teal Inlet (28th) and stayed there over Saturday (29th)
5. 45 Cdo moved on to Teal Inlet (30th)
6. 3 Para moved on ahead from Teal Inlet to Lower Malo House (30th) on their way to Mount Estancia
7. J Coy 42 Cdo helicoptered from Port San Carlos to Darwin (28th)
8. L Coy 42 Cdo at Port San Carlos
9. 40 Cdo in defence of San Carlos area
10. D Sqdn SAS helicoptered to Mt Kent (28th), followed by K Coy 42 Cdo, 7 Bty RA (part) (30th)
AIRCRAFT LOSSES
11. Argentine aircraft lost near Port Howard [a57] Skyhawk (27th)

12. Argentine aircraft lost over San Carlos Water - [a61] Dagger (29th)
13. Argentine aircraft lost to east of Mount Kent - [a62] Puma (30th)
14. Argentine aircraft lost east of Falklands - [a63, 64] Skyhawks (30th)
15. British aircraft lost east of Falklands at 51.48S, 54.29W - [b29] Sea Harrier (29th)
16. British aircraft lost east of Falklands - [b30] Harrier GR.3 (30th)

5th INFANTRY BRIGADE
17. From South Georgia - Transports Canberra, Norland, RFA Stromness

As 2 Para fought the battle for Goose Green, 45 Cdo 'yomped' and 3 Para 'tabbed' across the rough, boggy ground towards Stanley by the northern route. Often in the dark and wet, and heavily laden, they moved at a fast rate first for Teal Inlet. 3 CBAS helicopters supported 45 Cdo on the way and 3 Para was followed by 4 Troop of The Blues and Royals with two Scimitars and two Scorpions.

Starting on the morning of Thursday 27th, Lt Col Whitehead's 45 Cdo first moved by LCU from Ajax Bay to Port San Carlos before setting out the 12 miles to New House, reaching there late that night. After resting up they completed the eight miles to Douglas on Friday and dug in ready to move to Teal. Lt Col Pike and 3 Para were to follow behind, but instead took a more southerly, direct route in two columns. After marching for 24 hours they met up on Friday a few miles short of Teal Inlet, and when darkness fell, completed the journey late that night and stayed throughout Saturday. On Sunday, 45 Cdo pushed on to join them at Teal Inlet, but 3 Para and the light tanks were ordered to head for Mount Estancia as part of the plan to occupy the heights to the west of Stanley, and by the end of the day had reached Lower Malo House. 45 Cdo stayed put for now.

RAF Harrier GR3s (Courtesy - MOD, RAF). A total of ten aircraft from No 1 (F) Sqn, flew with the Royal Navy and four were lost; two during this period, (b27) during the Battle for Goose Green and (b30) below

On Friday 28th, with J Coy 42 Cdo flying down towards Darwin, the rest of 42 Commando prepared for the Mount Kent operation. K Coy was already at Port San Carlos, and was joined from Sussex Mountains by L Coy, after they in turn had been relieved by B Coy of 40 Cdo which had to stay in defence of the beachhead. That same night, D Sqdn SAS finally completed its helicopter move below Mount Kent, but an attempt to follow them up with 42 Cdo Tac HQ, K Coy and three 105s of 7 Bty over Saturday night was stopped by blizzards. Late on Sunday, No.846 Sea Kings and the lone RAF Chinook managed to get in, in the middle of an SAS fire-fight with Argentine troops, after which K Coy moved on to the summit. The Chinook was slightly damaged on the flight back, but support helicopter strength was increasing. The first No.825 Sea Kings flew ashore from "Atlantic Causeway" on Saturday and joined the other Navy, Marine and Army helicopters as well as the Chinook already flying from the Forward Operating Bases (FOBs) scattered around San Carlos Water.

Although there were few Argentine aircraft attacks between now and the second week in June, they nevertheless chose Thursday afternoon (27th) for their first strike against land targets, when two pairs of Grupo 5 Skyhawks bombed and strafed troop and supply positions. Coming in over the Brigade Maintenance Area at Ajax Bay, one pair killed six men of 45 Cdo and the Cdo Logistics Regt, wounded others and landed UXBs near the Field Dressing Station. This is where Flt Lt Swan later slept beside the bombs to reassure the staff and patients. The second pair hit San Carlos and killed one man each from 40 Cdo and the 59 Ind Cdo Sqdn RE. During the attacks, one of the Skyhawks was hit by 40mm Bofor fire from "Fearless" or "Intrepid" and crashed over West Falkland near Port Howard [a57].

More sorties took place over the weekend. Early Saturday morning (29th), Canberras of Grupo 2 carried out the first of a series of night time harrassing attacks on San Carlos Water, followed in June by raids on the Mount Kent area, and at mid-day when Daggers of Grupo 6 reached the anchorage, one was shot down by the defending Rapiers [a61]. On Sunday morning an Argentine Army Puma was lost near Mount Kent, possibly to its own forces [a62]. And that afternoon, two A-4C Skyhawks were brought down in the first coordinated CANA/FAA mission. The plan was for two Super Etendards to launch the last airborne Exocet at the Task Force carriers, and for four Grupo 4 Skyhawks to finish off the target with bombs. Coming in from the south after tanker refuelling, the aircraft mistakenly released the missile from 20 miles at "Avenger", then east of the Falklands. The Exocet was apparently deflected by chaff, and although the Etendards escaped, two of the Skyhawks were destroyed by Sea Darts from "Exeter" as they went in to attack, although "Avenger's" 4.5 inch may have hit one of them [a63, a64].

British Gallantry Awards included:

Bomb and ordnance disposal - Ajax Bay, and later Goose Green and Darwin
Flt Lt A J Swan (QGM) RAF, CO No.1 EOD RAF

Chinook of 18 Sqdn RAF - 'The Survivor'
Sqdn Ldr R U Langworthy (DFC) AFC RAF

As the Sea Harriers continued to fly CAP and drop bombs on Stanley airfield and the GR.3s flew ground support from the carriers, a total of three were lost over these few days. Apart from the GR.3 near Goose Green on Thursday (see page 88), next to go on Saturday afternoon (29th) was a Sea Harrier of No.801 NAS which slid of "Invincible's" deck as she turned into wind in heavy weather, although fortunately the pilot ejected and was rescued from the sea [b29]. Then at midday on Sunday, the RAF found itself down to just three GR.3s. One of four aircraft over the Stanley area was hit by small arms fire from Argentine troops, and on the way back to "Hermes" ran out of fuel [b30]. Sqdn Ldr Pook parachuted into the sea and was soon rescued by a No.826 Sea King.

Apart from all the shipping activity around South Georgia, Task Force warships continued to bombard Argentine positions and escort supply ships into and out of San Carlos Water, where only now were "Argonaut" and "Sir Lancelot" finally relieved of their UXBs. "Elk" went in Thursday night (27th) to continue unloading her ammo, and over the weekend, "Argonaut" and "Plymouth" finally left, with only "Yarmouth" of the original escorts remaining for a few days more. And now **5th Inf Bde** started to arrive. "Fearless" left San Carlos Water on Thursday, later to meet "Antrim" to the east of the TEZ, and with General Moore on board arrived back early Sunday. When Brigadier Thompson returned to San Carlos from Teal Inlet to find his commander there, final plans were made to receive 5th Inf, put 2 Para under Brigadier Wilson's command, and move 3 Cdo Bde HQ to the Inlet.

Part 40. 5th INFANTRY BRIGADE LANDS AT SAN CARLOS

WEEK TEN, British Task Force Movements, 31st May-6th June 1982

Task Force Arrival and Departure - "British Avon" was the first tanker back to the UK to reload, and arrived at Portsmouth on Saturday 5th with the special prisoner Lt Cdr Astiz who was shortly flown back to Argentina as a POW. Next day, but across the Atlantic, a second repair ship "Stena Inspector" set out from Charleston, South Carolina after a conversion which included the addition of a heavy machine shop.

Ascension - More ships passed by during the week on their way back to Britain including "Queen Elizabeth 2", but aircraft, equipment and supplies were still urgently needed in the south. With a total of nine Harrier GR.3s of 1(F) Sqdn RAF now present, two flew direct to the TEZ on Tuesday 1st and landed on "Hermes", and another four, together with two 3 CBAS Gazelles and the local RAF Chinook sailed on Thursday with the helicopters already on board transport "Contender Bezant". Two more GR.3s flew on south the following week, but the ninth stayed behind with fuel leaks. Then Wednesday night saw the launch of "Black Buck 6", the second successful Shrike raid against the Stanley radars, but this time the Vulcan had to divert to Rio de Janeiro on the way back.

Disposition of British Ships, Aircraft & Land Forces in Summary
(Land Forces now ashore)

United States Departure
Stena Inspector, Capt D Ede and NP 2010, Capt P J Stickland RN

UK Arrival - tanker British Avon

Ships and Aircraft in Ascension Area
Ships Passing Through the Area on the Way North to UK - SSN Splendid, transport Queen Elizabeth 2, tanker British Tay
RAF Aircraft - Phantoms, Harrier GR.3s, Vulcans, Nimrods, Victors, Hercules, VC.10s, Sea King
Other Ships at Ascension or Reaching the Area on the Way South - despatch vessel Leeds Castle, transports Contender Bezant, Geestport, St Edmund, Tor Caledonia, tankers Alvega (base storage), Scottish Eagle, RFA Brambleleaf, mooring vessel RMAS Goosander
Destroyer Glasgow (approaching Ascension)

Support Tankers in South Atlantic or in Tanker Holding Areas - RFAs Appleleaf, Bayleaf, Plumleaf, chartered Anco Charger, Balder London, British Dart, British Tamar, British Test, British Trent, British Wye, Eburna, water tanker Fort Toronto

Departing South Atlantic - frigates Alacrity, Argonaut

Arriving in South Atlantic - RFAs Engadine, Fort Grange

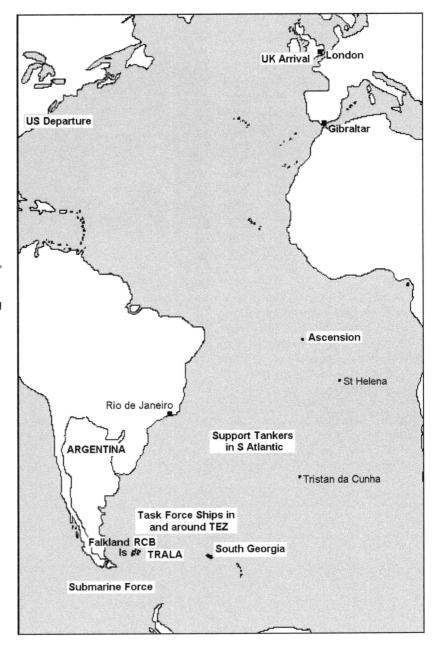

Red Cross Box, RCB - hospital ship Uganda, ambulance ships Hecla (from Montevideo), Herald, Hydra (to Montevideo)

Tug, Repair & Logistic Area, TRALA - repair ship Stena Seaspread, tugs Irishman, Salvageman, Yorkshireman

SEE FOLLOWING PART FOR MAIN TASK FORCE SHIPS DURING THIS PERIOD:
Part 41: 31st May-6th June - Falkland Area Operations

Submarine Force - SSN Conqueror, Courageous, Spartan, Valiant, SS Onyx

South Georgia Waters - destroyer Antrim, IPV Endurance, RFA Pearleaf, RMAS Typhoon, transports Saxonia, Lycaon, M Coy 42 Cdo

---

South Atlantic - During the week, as **5th Inf Bde** was landed at San Carlos, more ships of the original Task Force started to return north. Frigates "Alacrity" and the damaged "Argonaut", after spending a short time in the TRALA with "Stena Seaspread", followed over the weekend in the wake of "Glasgow" bound for the UK. Going in the opposite direction, the three tugs stationed in the area made their way to South Georgia. By then, RFA "Fort Grange" had joined the CVBG to start replenishment operations, and helicopter support ship

"Engadine" was entering the TEZ on her way to San Carlos Water. Earlier in the week, "Iris" also reached the TRALA with the scrap steel from South Georgia and then along with "Dumbarton Castle" continued her despatch duties between the Falklands, South Georgia and Ascension. Carrying casualties of both sides, the Red Cross Box/Montevideo shuttle now started in earnest. On Wednesday 2nd, as "Hydra" followed her north, "Hecla" arrived at the Uruguayan capital and by Sunday was back in the Box. In the meantime, "Herald's" Wasp was used to carry an International Red Cross team over from "Uganda" to inspect the Argentine icebreaker "Bahia Paraiso" now being used in the hospital ship role.

Small Fleet Tanker RFA Blue Rover. During the week she relinquished her role as station tanker at South Georgia (Courtesy - MOD, Navy)

South Georgia - As the only secure base where stores could be transferred between ships with little interference from Argentine aircraft, there were more arrivals from the TEZ. These included RFA "Resource" which called in for replenishment herself, destroyer "Antrim" returning this time as guardship, and RFA "Pearleaf" to take over as station tanker from the departed "Blue Rover".

Approach to and Battle for Stanley
(Parts 41-49)

Part 41. 3 COMMANDO REACHES STANLEY DEFENCES

WEEK TEN, Falkland Area Operations, 31st May-6th June 1982

Summary of Main Events

Task Force Ships in and around TEZ (6th June)
Carriers Hermes, Invincible, destroyers Bristol, Cardiff, Exeter, Glamorgan, frigates Active, Ambuscade, Arrow, Avenger, Andromeda, Brilliant, Broadsword, Minerva, Penelope, Plymouth, Yarmouth, assault ships Fearless, Intrepid, RFAs Blue Rover, Engadine, Fort Austin, Fort Grange, Olmeda, Olna, Regent, Resource, Stromness, Tidepool, Tidespring, LSLs Sir Bedivere, Sir Galahad, Sir Geraint, Sir Lancelot, Sir Percivale, Sir Tristram, transports Atlantic Causeway, Baltic Ferry, Canberra, Elk, Europic Ferry, Nordic Ferry, Norland

  plus submarine force, minesweeping trawlers, hospital ships in RCB, repair ship and tugs in TRALA, and some tankers

  (Sheffield, Ardent, Antelope, Coventry and Atlantic Conveyor now lost)

Arriving Aircraft
HMS Hermes - Further 2 of 4 Harrier GR.3s of 1(F) Sqdn RAF
Remaining 6 Sea King HAS.2As of No.825 NAS
First of 20 Wessex HU.5s of No.847 NAS [Lt Cdr M D Booth (awarded DSC) RN]

3 COMMANDO BRIGADE LOCATIONS & MOVEMENTS
1. 40 Cdo in defence of San Carlos area
2. M & AW Cadre attacked Top Malo House (31st)
3. 42 Cdo K Coy on summit of Mt Kent (by 31st)
4. 42 Cdo L Coy helicoptered from Port San Carlos (31st May), and J Coy from Goose Green (2nd June). Both Coys reached Mount Challenger
5. 3 Para secured Estancia House (31st), then dug in around Mount Estancia (1st June)
6. 45 Cdo completed yomp from Teal Inlet to Mount Kent slopes (4th June)

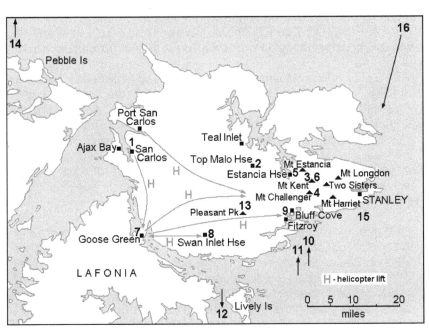

5TH INFANTRY BRIGADE LOCATIONS & MOVEMENTS

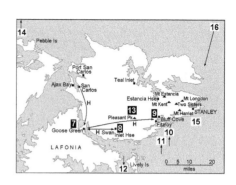

MAIN COMMANDERS
Brigadier M J A Wilson OBE MC
2nd Scots Guards, Lt Col M I E Scott (awarded DSO)
1st Welsh Guards, Lt Col J F Rickett (OBE)
1/7th Gurkha Rifles, Lt Col D P de C Morgan (OBE)
4 Field Regt RA, Lt Col G A Holt RA
36 Eng Regt RE, Lt Col G W Field MBE RE
No.656 AAC Sqdn, Maj C S Sibun (MID) AAC, 6 Gazelles, 3 Scouts

7. 1/7 Gurkhas helicoptered from San Carlos to Goose Green (c 3rd)
8. B Coy 2 Para helicoptered from Goose Green to Swan Inlet House and back (2nd)
9. 2 Para helicoptered from Goose Green to Fitzroy and Bluff Cove (2nd/3rd)
10. 2nd Scots Guards sailed in assault ship Intrepid from San Carlos Water to Lively Island, and on to Bluff Cove by four LCUs (5th/6th)
11. HQ & 2 Coy 1st Welsh Guards in assault ship Fearless from San Carlos Water also to Lively Island, and on to Bluff Cove by two LCUs (6th)
12. Rest of Welsh Guards had to return in Fearless to San Carlos Water (6th/7th)
13. British AAC aircraft lost near Pleasant Peak - [b32] Gazelle (6th)

OTHER AIRCRAFT LOSSES/OPERATIONS
14. Argentine aircraft lost north of Pebble Island - [a65] Hercules (1st)
15. British aircraft lost just south of Stanley - [b31] Sea Harrier (1st)
16. 'Black Buck 5' & '6' - Vulcan Shrike raids on Stanley (31st May & 3rd June)

As General Moore assumed overall command, Brigadier Thompson was freed to concentrate on **3 Cdo Bde**'s move on Stanley by the northern route. But in the process he lost 40 Cdo for base defence, 2 Para, 29 Bty RA and The Blues and Royals to 5th Inf Bde, and the Cdo Logistics Regt now had to support both main units. The newly arriving 5th Infantry would move on Stanley from the south west, by which time Forward Brigade Maintenance Areas would be established both at Teal Inlet and Fitzroy.

During a week when 3 Cdo Bde completed its moves forward, the first action came Monday morning (31st) when a small M & AW Cadre force helicoptered in to attack an Argentine patrol at Top Malo House, and killed or captured all 17 in exchange for three marines wounded. By then, **K Coy 42 Cdo** was on the summit of Mount Kent, and stayed through the week. Not so the rest of 42 Cdo. Over Monday night, L Coy (and the rest of 7 Bty RA) flew in from Port San Carlos, and marched to Mount Challenger, and over Wednesday night, J Coy moved there direct from Goose Green. By then 3 Para had completed its tab; securing Estancia House on Monday, and next day digging in on and around Mount Estancia, before being joined by the six guns of 79 Bty RA. On Friday, 45 Cdo RM finished its yomp from Teal Inlet and reached a position below Mount Kent from where it could reinforce 3 Para or 42 Cdo in their exposed positions within range of the Argentine guns.

With 3 Cdo Bde on Mount's Estancia, Kent and Challenger, preparations were made for the coming Battle for Stanley. In increasingly foul and wintry weather, the three units started patrolling towards their objectives: *3 Para and Mount Longdon, 45 Cdo and Two Sisters, 42 Cdo and Mount Harriet*. To complete 3 Cdo's move, Brigade HQ and the supplies needed converged on Teal Inlet. On Monday, the HQ staff flew in, followed by their Bandwagon snow vehicles and escorting tanks of 3 Troop, although these continued on to join 4 Troop at Estancia House before both moved down to Bluff Cove. To open up Teal as the forward base, "Intrepid" arrived over Monday night with an LCU going in with the first supplies and accompanied by two LCVPs fitted with light minesweeping gear. They were followed on Tuesday night by LSL "Sir Percivale" as she and other LSLs started a delivery service from San Carlos Water.

Welcome reinforcements, especially **5th Inf Bde** now started arriving. The first transports reached San Carlos Water on Tuesday morning (1st) and "Norland" landed the Gurkhas by LCU, "Baltic Ferry" her Scouts, and "Atlantic Causeway" the remaining No.825 Sea Kings and some of the No.847 Wessex. That same day, frigate "Penelope" picked up 2 Para's new CO after he parachuted into the sea from an extended range Hercules, and "Canberra" reached the CVBG. Heading on in, she offloaded the two Guards battalions on Wednesday morning again using the hard-worked LCUs plus her two No.825 Sea Kings. And on Thursday, "Nordic Ferry" arrived with the rest of the Gazelles, while "Canberra" left for the TRALA for the remaining days of the war.

Once they had landed, most of the 1/7th Gurkhas flew in the lone Chinook to Goose Green to relieve 2 Para, and to spend the next week patrolling into Lafonia. Now 5th Inf started its push forward when on Wednesday 2nd, elements of B Coy 2 Para flew to Swan Inlet House in five Army Scouts and Major Crosland made his famous 'phone call to find that Fitzroy and Bluff Cove were clear of the enemy. Later that day and the next, 2 Para was helicoptered the 35 miles from Goose Green to occupy the two settlements.

With 2 Para so far forward, and lacking helicopter lift, General Moore decided to risk the assault ships on night runs from San Carlos Water with the two Guards units. Starting on Saturday night (5th), "Intrepid" carried the 2nd Scots around the south of Lafonia and off Lively Island, transferred them to her four LCUs. After a lengthy and rough passage they arrived at Bluff Cove early on Sunday to stay, while the three coys of 2 Para already there were ferried to Fitzroy by the same LCUs to join the rest of the battalion. That night it was the turn of "Fearless" to bring round the 1st Welsh. Reaching Lively Island, only her two LCUs were available to carry HQ and 2 Coy on to Bluff Cove. The rest had to return to San Carlos Water to try again Monday night. Before then a plan to improve communications links was thwarted. Early on Sunday morning as an AAC Gazelle flew forward with two Royal Signals to set up a relay station, it was accidentally shot down near Pleasant Peak by a Sea Dart fired by "Cardiff", and all four men on board killed [b32].

Back to Tuesday 1st and the Task Force Harriers. Late that morning, a Grupo 1 Hercules on a reconnaissance mission was detected by frigate "Minerva" in San Carlos Water, and a vectored No.801 Sea Harrier brought it down 50 miles north of Pebble Island using Sidewinder and cannon fire [a65]. Then in the afternoon, the last Sea Harrier was lost when another No.801 aircraft on a sortie over Stanley was hit by a Roland SAM [b31]. Flt Lt Mortimer bailed out into the sea just to the south, but it was nine hours before he was found and rescued by a No.820 Sea King. Next day, the first step was taken in extending Harrier operations when the Royal Engineers completed a Forward Operating Base at Port San Carlos, with two No.800 Sea Harriers arriving on Saturday.

Major General J J Moore MC* RM, Commander, Land forces Falkland Islands (Courtesy – Royal Marines Museum)

Earlier in the week on Monday morning, the first Shrike attack had been made on the Stanley radars in "Black Buck 5", but the TPS-43 surveillance radar was only slightly damaged. A repeat "Black Buck 6" raid early on Thursday by the same Vulcan, destroyed a Skyguard AA radar, but on the return flight the bomber had to divert to Rio de Janeiro with refuelling difficulties, but was released a week later.

British Gallantry Awards included:

Vulcan Shrike raids - 'Black Buck 5 & 6'
Sqdn Ldr C N McDougall (DFC) RAF

Part 42. FINAL TASK FORCE MOVES

WEEKS ELEVEN & into TWELVE, British Task Force Movements 7th-15th June 1982

Conclusion & Surrender - In just eight days, the war was brought to a close and the Argentines surrendered their forces on West and East Falkland. But before they did, the FAA, in one last major effort damaged frigate "Plymouth", sank one of "Fearless"' LCUs, mortally damaged LSL "Sir Galahad" inflicting heavy casualties on the 1st Welsh Guards, and nearly put paid to "Sir Tristram". Apart from the later hit on destroyer "Glamorgan" by a land-based Exocet, these were virtually the last losses in ships or aircraft.

But before the war was won, the Argentine troops defending Stanley in the mountains to the west had to be defeated by Marines, Paras and Guardsmen in combat - often man against man, using rifle and bayonet, machine gun and grenade, supported by mortar and artillery, in the dark, in often atrocious weather and over rough, rocky well-defended terrain. Over the night of Friday 11th, the outer ring of defended heights would be taken:

>Mount Longdon by 3 Para, Two Sisters by 45 Cdo, and Mount Harriet by 42 Cdo.

Two nights later, over Sunday 13th, the next line would fall:

>Wireless Ridge to 2 Para so soon after Goose Green,
>and Tumbledown Mountain to the 2nd Scots Guards.

And meanwhile the 1/7th Gurkha Rifles stood by ready to attack Mount William, and a depleted 1st Welsh Guards, reinforced by 40 Cdo, prepared to occupy Sapper Hill. In the event, the surviving Argentine troops streamed back to Stanley where they still outnumbered the British attackers, but throughout Monday 14th, a surrender was negotiated, timed to take place from 9pm local time. But still more ships, aircraft and supplies were needed.

Task Force Departures from Monday 7th June - During the week, four merchantmen headed south. On Tuesday from Plymouth, "Astronomer" set out as a helicopter carrier and repair ship with a variety of helicopters and additionally equipped with 2x20mm Oerlikons, chaff launchers and a Unifoxer acoustic torpedo decoy. Leaving the same day was ammo ship "Laertes", and two days later tanker "G A Walker". Refrigerated stores ship "Avelona Star" sailed at this time from Portsmouth loaded with food. Then on Sunday, cargo vessel "St Helena" sailed from Portland after working up as a minesweeper support ship. Armed with 4x20mm Oerlikons, she accompanied Hunt class mine countermeasures vessels "Brecon" and "Ledbury", the first Navy minesweepers to leave for the Falklands. Next day, the reloaded tanker "British Avon" sailed from Portland for a second voyage south.

Meanwhile more ships arrived back in the UK. By far the most publicised was on Friday 11th when "Queen Elizabeth 2" sailed into Southampton with the survivors from "Ardent", "Antelope" and "Coventry" to be met by Royal Yacht "Britannia" carrying Queen Elizabeth, the Queen Mother. Nuclear submarine "Splendid" got in to Devonport the next day. By then tanker "British Esk" was back to reload, and as the surrender took place, "British Tay" approached British shores.

Ascension - There was no let up at this one and only advanced base (other than South Georgia), especially on the part of the RAF. On Tuesday 8th, the last two Harrier GR.3s flew direct to "Hermes", and on Friday, "Black Buck 7" was launched - the last Vulcan raid on Stanley and again using conventional bombs. The aircraft returned safely next day. Also returning, but to the UK, was destroyer "Glasgow" which passed through the area early in the week, followed by frigates "Alacrity" and "Argonaut" around the time of the surrender.

South Atlantic - Tuesday 8th saw the only non-belligerent casualty when two Grupo 2 Canberras mistakenly bombed the American-registered tanker "Hercules" then on passage to the north east of the TEZ. On putting into Rio de Janeiro, a UXB was found that was too dangerous to disarm, and the ship had to be scuttled off Brazil in late July. Fortunately the FAA's attempts to hit the British lines of communications were unsuccessful as later in the week, tankers "British Test" and "British Trent" sailed north for Ascension respectively carrying the survivors from "Sir Galahad" and "Sir Tristram".

In the Falkland's area itself, the hard-worked transport "Norland" headed out of San Carlos Water on Monday 7th with a thousand Argentine POWs bound for Montevideo, and got in over the weekend. Aircraft and helicopter carrier "Contender Bezant" reached the TEZ on Thursday with her Navy Sea King, Marine Gazelles, and RAF Chinooks and four GR.3s too late to join in the fighting although the helicopters were needed to help in the clearing-up. Over the weekend, transport "Tor Caledonia" reached the TRALA to start offloading stores and just after the surrender, transport "St Edmund" reached the CVBG. On the same day, Tuesday 15th, nuclear sub "Conqueror" left for the UK after her active eight weeks of patrols in the South Atlantic, while frigate "Yarmouth" and RFA "Olmeda" headed in the opposite direction, first for South Georgia on their way to re-occupy Southern Thule. Well before then, on Monday 7th, the first RFA south, "Fort Austin" was returning north for Devonport and England.

South Georgia - This almost Antarctic island, still garrisoned by M Coy 42 Cdo and attended by "Endurance", saw more comings and goings. "Wimpey Seahorse" arrived to lay out moorings at various anchorages, RFA "Regent" got in from the TEZ to replenish from refrigerated stores ships "Saxonia" and the newly arrived "Geestport", and at the time of the surrender, "Scottish Eagle" was heading there as base storage tanker. Well before then, RMAS tug "Typhoon" had left for the TRALA, as had ammo ship "Lycaon", and over the weekend, "Saxonia" sailed for the UK to reload after her three weeks at South Georgia.

RFAs Fort Grange and Fort Austin (Courtesy - MOD, Navy). During this week, "Fort Austin" headed north back to the UK

Disposition of British Ships, Aircraft & Land Forces in Summary

UK Departures
Royal Navy
Brecon, Cdr P A Fish RN
Ledbury, Lt Cdr A Rose RN
Merchant Ships
Astronomer, Capt H S Braden and NP 2140, Lt Cdr R Gainsford RN
Avelona Star, Capt H Dyer
G A Walker, Capt E C Metham
Laertes, Capt H T Reid
St. Helena, Capt M L M Smith and NP 2100, Lt Cdr D N Heelas RN
plus tanker British Avon returning to the South Atlantic
Helicopters Embarked
6 Wessex HU.5s of No.848 NAS, D Flt, 3 Scouts for No.656 AAC Sqdn and 3 Chinooks of 18 Sqdn RAF on Astronomer

UK Arrivals - SSN Splendid, transport Queen Elizabeth 2, tanker British Esk
Tanker British Tay (approaching UK)

Ships and Aircraft in Ascension Area
Ships Passing Through the Area on the Way North to UK - destroyer Glasgow, frigates Alacrity, Argonaut
RAF Aircraft - Phantoms, Vulcans, Nimrods, Victors, Hercules, VC.10s, Sea King
South Atlantic Despatch Vessels - Dumbarton Castle, Leeds Castle, Iris
Other Ships at Ascension - tanker Alvega (base storage), mooring vessel RMAS Goosander

Support Tankers in South Atlantic or in Tanker Holding Areas - RFAs Appleleaf, Bayleaf, Brambleleaf, Plumleaf; chartered British Dart, British Test and British Trent (all three sailing for Ascension), Anco Charger, Balder London, British Tamar, British Wye, Eburna, water tanker Fort Toronto

Departing South Atlantic - SSN Conqueror, RFA Fort Austin both from Falkland's area, transport Saxonia from South Georgia

Arriving in South Atlantic - transports Contender Bezant, St Edmumd, Tor Caledonia, followed by despatch vessel British Enterprise and repair ship Stena Inspector on passage to TEZ

Red Cross Box, RCB - hospital ship Uganda, ambulance ships Herald, Hecla, Hydra (all to Montevideo)

Tug, Repair & Logistic Area, TRALA - repair ship Stena Seaspread

SEE FOLLOWING PART FOR MAIN TASK FORCE SHIPS DURING THIS PERIOD:
Part 43: 7th-13th June - Falkland Area Operations

Main Task Force Ships at Time of Surrender on 14th JUNE:
Carriers Hermes, Invincible, destroyers Bristol, Cardiff, Exeter, Glamorgan (Exocet damage), frigates Active, Ambuscade, Andromeda, Arrow, Avenger, Brilliant, Broadsword, Minerva, Penelope, Plymouth (bomb damage), assault ships Fearless, Intrepid, RFAs Blue Rover, Engadine, Fort Austin, Fort Grange, Olna, Resource, Stromness, Tidepool, Tidespring, LSLs Sir Bedivere, Sir Geraint, Sir Lancelot, Sir Percivale, Sir Tristram (bomb damage), RMAS Typhoon, minesweepers Cordella, Farnella, Junella, Northella, Pict, transports Atlantic Causeway, Baltic Ferry, Canberra, Elk, Europic Ferry, Lycaon, Nordic Ferry, Norland

Submarine Force - SSN Courageous, Spartan, Valiant, SS Onyx

Departing Falkland's Area for Southern Thule - frigate Yarmouth, RFA Olmeda (both via South Georgia)

South Georgia Waters - tanker Scottish Eagle approaching South Georgia, destroyer Antrim, IPV Endurance, RFA Pearleaf, Regent, transport Geestport, tugs Irishman, Salvageman, Yorkshireman, mooring vessel Wimpey Seahorse

Part 43. "SIR GALAHAD" & "SIR TRISTRAM" BOMBED

WEEK ELEVEN, Falkland Area Operations
7th-13th June 1982

Summary of Main Events

Arriving Aircraft:
HMS Hermes - Last 2 of 4 Harrier GR.3s of 1(F) Sqdn RAF
4 Wessex HU.5s of No.847 NAS

Task Force Ships in and around TEZ (at time of surrender on 14th)
Carriers Hermes, Invincible, destroyers Bristol, Cardiff, Exeter, Glamorgan (Exocet damaged), frigates Active, Ambuscade, Andromeda, Arrow, Avenger, Brilliant, Broadsword, Minerva, Penelope, Plymouth (bomb damage), assault ships Fearless, Intrepid, RFAs Blue Rover, Engadine, Fort Austin, Fort Grange, Olna, Resource, Stromness, Tidepool, Tidespring, LSLs Sir Bedivere, Sir Geraint, Sir Lancelot, Sir Percivale, Sir Tristram (bomb damaged), RMAS Typhoon, minesweepers Cordella, Farnella, Junella, Northella, Pict, transports Atlantic Causeway, Baltic Ferry, Canberra, Elk, Europic Ferry, Lycaon, Nordic Ferry, Norland

plus submarine force, hospital ships in RCB, repair ship in TRALA, and some tankers

(Sheffield, Ardent, Antelope, Coventry, Atlantic Conveyor and Sir Galahad lost)

AIRCRAFT AND SHIP LOSSES
1. Plymouth damaged in Falkland Sound off San Carlos Water (8th)
2. SIR GALAHAD mortally hit and Sir Tristram damaged off Fitzroy (8th)
3. Fearless LCU F4 sunk in Choiseul Sound; Argentine aircraft lost - [a67,a68, a69] Skyhawks (8th)

3 COMMANDO BRIGADE LOCATIONS
4. 3 Para on Mount Longdon (12th) – see Part 44
5. 45 Cdo on Two Sisters (12th) – Part 45
6. 42 Cdo on Mount Harriet (12th) – Part 46

SHIP DAMAGED (continued)
7. Glamorgan damaged and helicopter [b34] Wessex destroyed 17 miles south west of Stanley (12th)

5TH INFANTRY BRIGADE LOCATIONS

8. 2 Para on Wireless Ridge (14th) – see Part 47
9. 2nd Scots on Tumbledown Mountain (14th) – Part 48
10. 1/7 Gurkhas behind Tumbledown Mountain – Part 49
11. C Coy 1/7 Gurkhas at Goose Green
12. 1st Welsh Guards and A & C Coys 40 Cdo to the south west of Mount Harriet
13. B Coy 40 Cdo in defence of San Carlos Water

OTHER AIRCRAFT LOSSES AND OPERATIONS

14. Argentine aircraft lost over Pebble Island - [a66] Learjet (7th)
15. British aircraft lost at Port San Carlos - [b33] Harrier GR.3 (8th)
16. 'Black Buck 7' - Vulcan raid on Stanley (12th)
17. Argentine aircraft lost in Mount Kent area? - [a70] Canberra (13th)

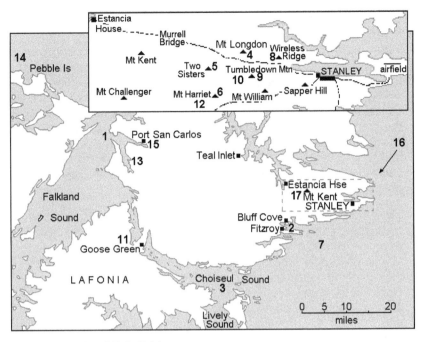

The decision was now taken to use the LSLs to continue **5th Infantry**'s move forward. "Sir Tristram" reached Fitzroy on Monday 7th to start unloading ammo, and in San Carlos Water, "Sir Galahad" took on board the rest of the 1st Welsh from "Fearless" before sailing around Lafonia to arrive on Tuesday morning (8th). By now, only one LCU and a Mexeflote were left to complete offloading "Sir Tristram", and although by early afternoon, Rapier SAMs and 16 Field Ambulance had gone ashore from "Sir Galahad", plans to move the Guards to Bluff Cove to join the rest of the battalion had come to nothing. Worse still, the LSLs had been reported by enemy observers, and around 2.00pm, five Skyhawk's of Grupo 5 and five Daggers of Grupo 6 were coming in over the Falklands.

First to be attacked by the Daggers, but in Falkland Sound was frigate "Plymouth" on her way to bombard an Argentine position on West Falkland. Hit by cannon fire and four UXBs, one of which detonated a depth charge, she was only slightly damaged. Shortly after, the Skyhawks reached Fitzroy. Three of them put two or more bombs into the crowded "SIR GALAHAD", and the other two hit "Sir Tristram" with two UXBs killing two crewmen. The ships caught fire and were soon abandoned, but by then the results for "Sir Galahad" was catastrophic with a total of 48 killed - five RFA crewmen, 32 Welsh Guards and eleven other Army personnel, with many more badly burned and wounded. "Sir Tristram" was later returned to the UK for repairs, but the burnt-out "Sir Galahad" was scuttled at sea as a war grave on the 25th June.

As the FAA's last major effort continued, four Grupo 4 Skyhawks attacked troops in the Fitzroy area later that afternoon, and minutes after, four Skyhawks of Grupo 5 arrived over Choiseul Sound to catch LCU F4 (belonging to "Fearless") sailing from Goose Green to Fitzroy with 5th Infantry HQ vehicles. Hit by one bomb, which killed the coxswain, Colour Sgt Johnston (post QGM) and five of the crew, she shortly sank. Two No.800 Sea Harriers over head on CAP immediately dived to the attack and brought down three of the Skyhawks with Sidewinders [a67, a68, a69].

During the week, both Land Forces and 5th Inf HQs moved to Fitzroy and 3 Cdo Bde's to Mount Kent, and although the "Sir Galahad" disaster caused delays, planning continued for the attack towards Stanley. In the first phase, 3 Cdo Bde would take Mount Longdon, Two Sisters and Mount Harriet, and if possible Tumbledown Mountain and Wireless Ridge. Otherwise these two plus Mount William would be assaulted in phase two, and Sapper Hill and the ground south of Stanley in phase three. As part of the build-up, 3 Cdo continued its reconnaissance patrols, and the Special Forces their covert operations, but with casualties. Only the previous week, an SBS sergeant was killed in an accidental clash with the SAS, and over on West Falkland, as the SAS kept a careful watch on the two large Argentine garrisons there, an observation post near Port Howard was surrounded on Thursday 10th and Capt Hamilton killed as he tried to fight his way out.

With seven of the eight infantry battalions and all five 105mm batteries forward, the first phase started on the night of Friday 11th, and by next morning **3 Cdo Bde** was on Mount Longdon, Two Sisters and Mount Harriet, but during the night there were other losses. The supporting warships shelled Argentine positions in the mountains, and near Stanley, a house in the capital was hit killing two women and mortally wounding a third in the first and only civilian deaths of the war. Then as destroyer "Glamorgan" retired out to sea after 45 Cdo's attack, a land-launched Exocet fired from Stanley hit her in the hangar area, badly damaging that part of the ship, killing thirteen men and destroying her Wessex [b34].

HMS Glamorgan (Courtesy - MOD, Navy)

The second phase was delayed until Sunday night (13th), but by the morning, 2 Para had taken Wireless Ridge and 2nd Scots were on Tumbledown, but too late for the Gurkhas to assault Mount William in the dark. The movements during the week of the attacking battalions, including the Gurkhas (less C Coy at Goose Green) are covered by Parts 44-49. As for 40 Cdo and the 1st Welsh, the badly depleted Guards stayed at Bluff Cove until Friday 11th when they were reinforced by A and C Coys 40 Cdo released from San Carlos defence (B Coy remained), and marched that day to the south west of Mount Harriet to stay in reserve for the next two days. During this time, a battalion dispatch rider was mortally wounded by Argentine shellfire.

Even aside from the Tuesday strikes, there was little let-up in the air-war during the week. On Monday morning (7th), a reconnaissance Learjet of FAA Grupo 1 was shot down over Pebble Island by one of "Exeter's" Sea Darts [a66]. Next day, the last two RAF Harrier GR.3s from Ascension arrived on "Hermes", and earlier, the fourth and last GR.3 lost was damaged beyond repair landing heavily at the Port San Carlos FOB with a partial engine failure [b33]. On Wednesday, RFA "Engadine" flew off her four Wessex HU.5s of No.847 NAS to San Carlos Water to add to the helicopter lift, and early Saturday morning, in "Black Buck 7", Stanley airfield was bombed by a Vulcan for the final time.

Sunday 13th also saw the last Argentine air raids. Late that morning, Skyhawks of FAA Grupo 5 concluded their successful war with an attack on 3 Cdo Bde HQ on Mount Kent and 2 Para on Mount Longdon, but without causing casualties, and that evening, two Grupo 2 Canberras bombed Mount Kent, and as they turned away, one was brought down by a Sea Dart from "Exeter" (or possibly "Cardiff") [a70]. All this time, RAF GR.3s were hitting Argentine positions around Stanley, and still on Sunday, made their first successful laser-guided bomb attacks.

British Gallantry Awards included:

LSL Sir Galahad - rescue work:

on board:
Second Eng Offr P A Henry (post GM) RFA
Third Offr A Gudgeon (QGM) RFA
Gdsm S M Chapman (MM) 1WG
L/Cpl D J Loveridge (MM) 1WG
Sgt P H R Naya (MM) RAMC
WO2 B T Neck (MM) 1WG

by Sea King helicopters of No.825 NAS:
Lt Cdr H S Clark (DSC) RN
Lt J K Boughton (QGM) RN
Lt P J Sheldon (QGM) RN

alongside:
Colour Sgt M J Francis (DSM) RM, coxswain LCU F1, HMS Fearless
Sgt D S Boultby (MM) 17 Port Regt RCT NCO i/c, Mexeflote unit

Additional SAS awards
Capt G J Hamilton (post MC) Green Howards, including South Georgia, Pebble Island and Darwin diversion raids, Mount Kent
Capt T W Burls (MC) Para Regt, South Georgia and Pebble Island

Part 44. 3 PARA'S APPROACH TO and BATTLE FOR MOUNT LONGDON

11th/12th June 1982

British Forces
3 Para, including GPMGs, LAWs, MAWs, Milans and 81mm mortars; in support, 6x105mm artillery of 79 Bty, 29 Cdo Regt RA, frigate "Avenger" with 1x4.5in. In reserve - 2 Para
3 Para Commanders: Lt Col H W R Pike, Maj D A Collett A Coy (1, 2 and 3 Platoons), Maj M H Argue B Coy (4, 5 and 6 Platoons), Maj H M Osborne C Coy, Maj P P Butler D (Patrol) Coy

Argentine Defenders
7th Inf Regt defending Mount Longdon and Wireless Ridge area, supported by snipers, heavy mg's, mortars and artillery.

Approach to Mount Longdon - After tabbing across East Falkland from Port San Carlos, securing Estancia House on Monday 31st, and next day moving Tac HQ and A Coy on to Mount Estancia, B Coy to the south of Mount Vernet and C Coy on to Mount Vernet itself, 3 Para prepared for its attack on **Mount Longdon**.

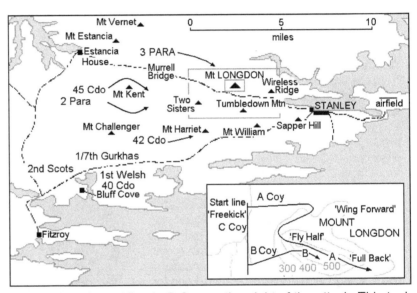

On Thursday 3rd, A and B Coys set up patrol bases near Murrell Bridge, and over the next week, D (Patrol) Coy and the other rifle Coys patrolled intensively towards their objective, at times penetrating Argentine positions and clashing with the enemy. Two members of D Coy were decorated for their reconnaissance patrols as well as for guiding in B Coy on the night of the attack. This took place on Friday 11th, after 3 Para moved from Murrell Bridge to the attack start line.

With minefields to the south, the Argentines on Wireless Ridge to the east, and given the long and narrow summit ridge of **Mount Longdon**, Lt Col Pike decided to launch a silent attack from the west. With **C Coy** in reserve and fire support teams staying on the start line, the plan was for **B Coy** to take the length of the summit ('Fly Half' and 'Full Back') while **A Coy** occupied the northern spur ('Wing Forward') as a fire support base for the B Coy attack. Once Mount Longdon was secured, A and C Coys would, if possible, move on to Wireless Ridge. After a short delay, A and B Coys started off from 'Freekick' at 8.15pm.

In the actual battle, A Coy was unable to reach 'Wing Forward' and took over from B Coy the taking of 'Full Back'. 2 Para had the task of capturing Wireless Ridge two days later.

Battle for Mount Longdon - As **B Coy** (4, 5 and 6 Platoons) approached Mount Longdon in the dark, on the left, one of 4 Platoon's men stepped on a mine and the alerted Argentines opened fire at the start of a battle that stretched through to dawn, ten hours later. On the right, 6 Platoon got on to the western summit with little fighting, but a by-passed bunker fired into them as they pushed through 'Fly Half', and later, when pinned down, they suffered a number of men killed by mainly sniper fire. Meanwhile 4 and 5 Platoons, using anti-armour weapons against enemy bunkers, fought their way on to the western end, but as they attempted to move to the east came under heavy automatic fire. With 4 Platoon's commander wounded, platoon Sgt McKay took over, and collecting some of his men and Cpl Bailey moved in to knock out a heavy machine gun post. In an action which led to the posthumous award of the Victoria Cross, Sgt McKay and one of the men were killed, but the enemy position was silenced. Now a second heavy machine gun held up B Coy HQ and 5 Platoon. Sgt Fuller was put in charge of 4 Platoon and with support from 5, tried to knock out this one, but without success. Maj Argue now pulled back both 4 and 5 Platoons, and called down artillery and naval gunfire on the enemy positions, after which a left flanking attack was put in, making some progress. Before long, they and the rest of B Coy found themselves under fire again, and having taken such heavy casualties, Lt Col Pike brought B Coy to a halt half way along the Longdon summit ridge.

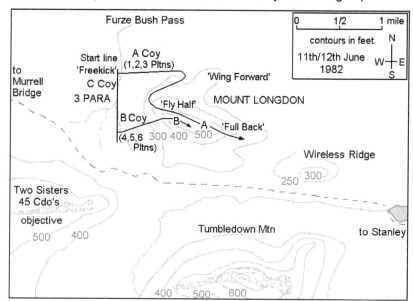

A Coy (1, 2 and 3 Platoons) had meanwhile moved from 'Freekick' towards 'Wing Forward', but taken losses from the fire of the Argentine positions on the eastern end of the summit which were now holding up **B Coy**. With little hope of making progress, A Coy was pulled back to the western end of Longdon, moved through B Coy, and with artillery and GPMG support, 1 and 2 Platoons worked their way along the eastern half of the summit clearing the enemy positions with rifle and bayonet and grenades. Now the Argentines started withdrawing, and as soon as 'Full Back' was secured, 3 Platoon moved down the slope facing Wireless Ridge. As dawn broke, and with no possibility of exploiting forward, 3 Para started digging in on Mount Longdon to spend the next two days under heavy and accurate artillery fire.

Eighteen Paras and an attached Royal Engineer had been killed in the attack with many more wounded, and three more Paras and a REME craftsman were killed in the subsequent shelling.

Men of A Coy, 3 Para after the Battle for Mount Longdon
(Courtesy - Airborne Forces Museum)

British Gallantry Awards
Approach to* and Battle for Mount Longdon by 3 Para

Sgt I J McKay (post VC), B Coy
Lt Col H W R Pike (DSO) MBE
Maj M H Argue (MC), B Coy
Maj D A Collett (MC), A Coy
Staff Sgt B Faulkner (DCM), Regt Aid Post

Sgt J S Pettinger (DCM), D (Patrol) Coy *
Pvt R J de M Absolon (post MM), D (Patrol) Coy *
Cpl I P Bailey (MM), B Coy
Sgt D Fuller (MM), B Coy
Capt W A McCracken (MC) RA, NGFO, 29 Cdo Regt RA (citation also included Wireless Ridge)

Part 45. 45 COMMANDO'S APPROACH TO and BATTLE FOR TWO SISTERS

11th/12th June 1982

British Forces
45 Cdo RM, including GPMGs, LAWs, MAWs, Milans and 81mm mortars, and in support, 6x105mm artillery of 8 Bty, 29 Cdo Regt RA and destroyer "Glamorgan" with 2x4.5in. In reserve - 2 Para.
45 Cdo RM Commanders: Lt Col A F Whitehead RM, CO, Capt I R Gardiner RM, X Coy (1, 2 and 3 Troops), Maj R J Davis RM, Y Coy (4, 5 and 6 Troops), Capt M A F Cole RM, Z Coy (7, 8 and 9 Troops)

Argentine Defenders
4th Inf Regt defending Two Sisters and Mount Harriet area, supported by snipers, heavy mg's, mortars and artillery.

Approach to Two Sisters - **45 Cdo**'s yomp from San Carlos Water via Teal Inlet ended to the west of Mount Kent on Friday 4th, and the next week was spent patrolling towards **Two Sisters**, leading to a number of bloody clashes with the Argentines. On their second patrol, Lt Fox's Recon Troop reached the end of Two Sisters, and when discovered, fought their way out killing up to thirteen of the enemy without loss. Later, Lt Stewart of X Coy broke out in a similar action, and by around Tuesday 8th, 45 Cdo had reconnoitred the main Argentine positions towards the western end.

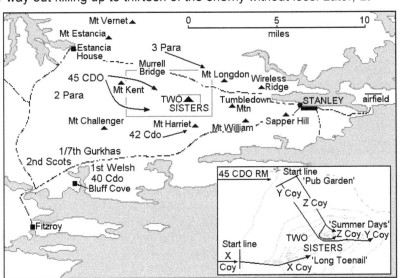

Then over the next two days, Sgt Wassell and other men of the M & AW Cadre completed the picture by covering the eastern end and the ground between Two Sisters, Mount Harriet and Tumbledown Mountain, including Goat Ridge. Sadly these successes did not come without loss. Over Thursday night a Y Coy patrol accidentally fired on a supporting mortar group killing four men.

45 Cdo's night attack would also be silent without any preliminary artillery fire. Lt Col Whitehead's plan was for **X Coy** to leave their start line at 9.00pm, and having taken the south west peak ('Long Toenail') around two hours later, to set up a fire support base that included 40 Cdo's Milan Troop. **Z Coy** would then assault the western part of the north east peak ('Summer Days'), and **Y Coy** the eastern part.

On Friday 11th, 45 Cdo less X Coy left their positions behind Mount Kent and moving around the north side, reached the main start line ('Pub Garden') as planned. Meanwhile X Coy, marching down between Mount's Kent and Challenger and heavily weighed down, especially by the Milans, arrived at the start line over two hours late. After a short rest, they began their move towards 'Long Toenail' at 11.00pm.

Battle for Two Sisters - **X Coy** headed across the open ground towards 'Long Toenail' led by 1 Troop, and less than a mile short of the peak, 3 Troop took over the lead, but half way up was stopped by heavy machine gun fire and temporarily pulled back. The enemy positions were hit by Milans and some mortar fire, and now 2 Troop pushed on to the summit under artillery fire. Reaching there, they were forced back by more shellfire, but shortly returned driving off the Argentine machine gunners. Soon after midnight as X Coy continued its fight for 'Long Toenail', **Z Coy** followed by **Y Coy** to their right, moved off from 'Pub Garden' on their silent uphill approach. As the Argentines were still distracted by X Coy's attack, the other two companies went to ground until a flare near Z Coy led to the right hand 8 Troop opening fire. The return enemy fire including artillery and mortars was so heavy, killing four men, that Lt Dytor led his men of 8 Troop forward in a charge towards the summit, followed by 7 Troop in a firefight that still left them short of their objective.

On their right, **Y Coy** swung further right to come up alongside them, managing to knock out some of the machine guns holding up **Z Coy**. 8 Troop was then able to advance towards the top covered by 7 Troop, and went on to clear the enemy positions on the southern side of their objective, while 7 Troop went on to

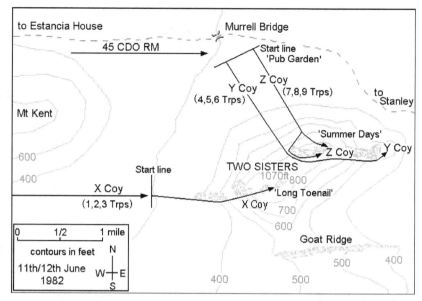

do the same on the northern side. Two and a half hours after crossing the start line, Z Coy had taken the western part of 'Summer Days'. During this time, 9 Troop stayed back in reserve after suffering casualties from the mortars and artillery. Y Coy now moved between the Two Sisters peaks and below Z Coy's 8 Troop, and headed for the eastern part of the north east summit under heavy fire. Pushing on, and again using anti-armour weapons against enemy positions, all of Two Sisters was in 45 Cdo's hands before dawn. As they reorganized and dug in, heavy Argentine shelling started. Lt Col Whitehead prepared to move ahead towards Tumbledown Mountain, but was stopped by Brigadier Thompson. 45 Cdo had now taken one of the main Argentine defenses for the loss of the three Marines and a Sapper of the Royal Engineers killed by shellfire and mortars.

British Gallantry Awards
Approach to* and Battle for Two Sisters by 45 Cdo RM

Lt Col A F Whitehead (DSO) RM
Lt C I Dytor (MC) RM, Z Coy
Lt C Fox (MC) RM, Recon Troop *
Lt D J Stewart (MC) RM, X Coy *
Cpl J Burdett (DCM) RM, Z Coy
Cpl A R Bishop (MM) RM

Cpl D Hunt (MM) RM, Z Coy
Mne G W Marshall (MM) RM *
Cpl H Siddall (MM) RM, Y Coy
Bmdr E M Holt (MM) RA, FOO Party, 29 Cdo Regt RA
Sgt J D Wassell (MM) RM, M&AW Cadre *
   (citation included other patrols)

Part 46. 42 COMMANDO'S APPROACH TO and BATTLE FOR MOUNT HARRIET

11th/12th June 1982

British Forces
42 Cdo RM, including GPMGs, LAWs, MAWs, Milans and 81mm mortars, and in support 6x105mm artillery of 7 Bty, 29 Cdo Regt RA and frigate "Yarmouth" with 2x4.5in. In reserve - 1st Welsh Guards with A and C Coys 40 Cdo.
42 Cdo RM Commanders: Lt Col N F Vaux RM, Maj M J Norman RM, J Coy, Capt P M Babbington RM, K Coy (1, 2 and 3 Troops), Capt D G Wheen RM, L Coy (4, 5 and 6 Troops)

Argentine Defenders
4th Inf Regt defending Two Sisters and Mount Harriet area, supported by snipers, heavy mg's, mortars and artillery.

Approach to Mount Harriet - Following K Coy's helicopter flight forward on to Mount Kent over the night of Sunday 30th May to join D Sqdn SAS, the rest of 42 Cdo moved to Mount Challenger during that week, and were eventually joined by K Coy. From there, they pushed out a troop strength observation post to Wall Mountain, and planned for an attack on the heavily defended Mount Harriet. An advance direct from Wall Mountain across minefields and into Argentine machine guns, was out of the question, and a left flanking move would risk overlapping 45 Cdo's assault on Two Sisters. Lt Col Vaux therefore decided on a right hook taking him well south of the more northerly Fitzroy/Stanley track to come up behind the Argentines from the south east. Finding an approach route through the extensive minefields and pinpointing enemy positions on this side of Mount Harriet called for careful patrolling, and for his part in this, Sgt Collins was decorated. And, as in the other battles and the approaches to them, men of the Royal Engineers played a key role in dealing with the minefields.

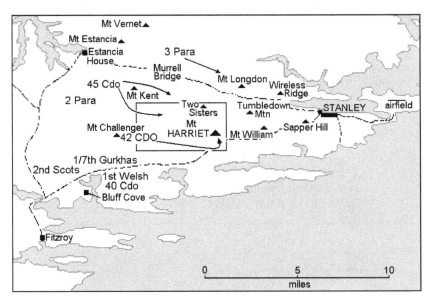

The final plan was to leave **J Coy** on Wall Mountain ('Tara') both as a reserve and to create a diversion, and for K and L Coys to march from the western end of Wall Mountain and across the Fitzroy/Stanley track before swinging east and then up to the start line behind Mount Harriet ('Zoya'). Moving off at 8.30pm, **K Coy** was to attack the eastern end, and an hour later, **L Coy** the western end, after which 42 Cdo would move on to take Goat Ridge ('Katrina'). Unlike the other two attacks, this one was 'noisy' with Mount Harriet receiving a preliminary bombardment as part of the diversion plan. On Friday 11th, as 42 Cdo prepared to move off, Argentine shellfire killed one of the Marines on Wall Mountain. Later, K and L Coys started off from Mount Challenger, with one of J Coy's Troops going ahead to mark the route and drop off Milan sections, including one on the Stanley track in case any of the Argentine Panhard armoured cars should appear. They were also due to meet up with a Welsh Guards patrol assigned to secure 42 Cdo's start line. But there was a delay and H-hour was held up, although J Coy went ahead and opened fire from Wall Mountain to simulate a large scale clash.

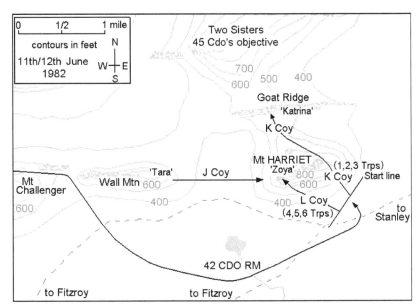

Battle for Mount Harriet - K Coy crossed the start line at 10.00pm, and almost reached the Argentine positions without being spotted. On the left, 1 Troop engaged the first enemy, and 2 Troop to the right went ahead to start clearing their part of K Coy's objective during which time 42 Cdo suffered its only fatal casualty of the night. 3 Troop now passed through 2 Troop on to the summit, and with 1 Troop below them to the

107

south, started to work their way westwards bunker-by-bunker, but were held up by machine gun fire. It was at this time that three K Coy Corporals - Newland of 1 Troop and Eccles and Ward of 3 Troop - won the Military Medal for taking the enemy position.

While K Coy was fighting on the eastern end of the summit and coming under artillery fire, **L Coy** made its way up towards the western end of Mount Harriet under heavy machine gun fire which opened up soon after they crossed the start line. Milans were successful in knocking out these and other enemy sniper positions, but it took a number of hours and casualties from artillery, before L Coy's half of the summit was taken, still in the dark. 5 Troop was then sent forward to the next objective just to the north of the summit, but was initially held up until the enemy resistance crumbled under mortar and artillery fire.

With dawn and **L Coy** still fighting forward, **K Coy** was ordered on to Goat Ridge, by which time **J Coy** had moved directly across from Wall Mountain to join in the final securing of Mount Harriet, running through a minefield on the way. In successfully taking its objective, 42 Cdo had lost just one man killed.

British Gallantry Awards
Approach to* and Battle for Mount Harriet by 42 Cdo RM

Lt Col N F Vaux (DSO) RM
Capt P M Babbington (MC) RM, K Coy
Sgt M Collins (MM) RM, K Coy *

Cpl M Eccles (MM) RM, K Coy
Cpl S C Newland (MM) RM, K Coy
Cpl C N H Ward (MM) RM, K Coy

Part 47. 2 PARA'S APPROACH TO and BATTLE FOR WIRELESS RIDGE

13th/14th June 1982

British Forces
2 Para, including GPMGs, LAWs, MAWs, Milans and 81mm mortars, and in support 3 Troop, The Blues and Royals with 2 Scorpions and 2 Scimitars, two bty's of 6x105mm artillery of 7 and 8 Btys, 29 Cdo Regt RA, mortars of 3 Para and frigate "Ambuscade" with 1x4.5in (and "Yarmouth", 2x4.5in).
2 Para Commanders: Lt Col D R Chaundler, Maj C D Farrar-Hockley, A Coy, Maj J H Crosland, B Coy, Maj R Jenner, C Coy, Maj P Neame, D Coy

Argentine Defenders
7th Inf Regt defending (Mount Longdon and) Wireless Ridge area, supported by snipers, heavy mg's, mortars and artillery

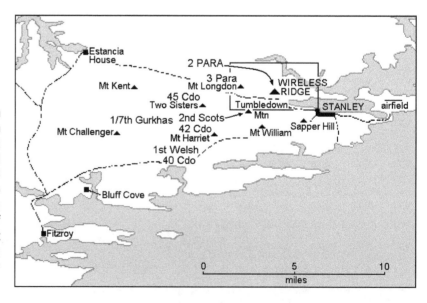

Approach to Wireless Ridge - With 3 Para unable to exploit forward from Mount Longdon over Friday night, 2 Para, now commanded by Lt Col Chaundler and transferred back to 3 Cdo Bde, was given the task two nights later. First helicoptering in from Fitzroy on to the western slopes of Mount Kent on Friday, 2 Para spent the night in reserve for the Longdon and Two Sisters attacks, and early next morning, marched to Furze Bush

Pass and dug in. The battalion was also joined by 3 Troop of The Blues and Royals, themselves back with 3 Cdo Bde.

Lt Col Chaundler's plan was in four 'noisy' phases using opening artillery fire. In phase one, **D Coy** was to attack the occupied feature ('Rough Diamond') north east of Mount Longdon, while in phase two, **A** and **B Coys** would take 'Apple Pie'. From 'Rough Diamond', D Coy would go on in phase three to take the length of Wireless Ridge ('Blueberry Pie') from the west, with fire support from A and B Coys. In phase four, **C** (Patrols) **Coy** would swing to the east to take ring contour 100.

Battle for Wireless Ridge - After 2 Para had finished marching that Sunday evening (13th) from Furze Bush Pass, supporting fire was opened on 'Rough Diamond' at 9.15pm, and 30 minutes later, **D Coy** crossed its start line backed up by the fire of four Scimitars and Scorpions.

D Coy reached 'Rough Diamond' to find the Argentines had withdrawn under the attacking fire, leaving behind a few dead. As the Paras consolidated in the new position, it was their turn to come under defensive fire from the Argentine 155s. Now from behind them to the east, **A** and **B Coys** crossed their start line, but one man was killed by enemy shellfire. Then as the two companies approached 'Apple Pie', the enemy broke and withdrew under the weight of British artillery, mortars and GPMGs, although they themselves were heavily shelled for the rest of the night. With 2 Para moving ahead so quickly, Lt Col Chaundler gave **C Coy** the go ahead to occupy ring contour 100, which it did without opposition.

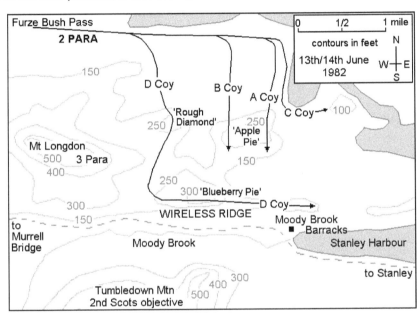

From 'Rough Diamond', **D Coy** moved to the western end of Wireless Ridge and prepared to advance through its length, as the light tanks and supporting Milans and GPMGs joined **A** and **B Coys** on 'Apple Pie' pouring in fire from the left flank. D Coy took the first half of the ridge without trouble, but the Argentines resisted fiercely over the second half, often fighting from bunker to bunker. They eventually broke, and all of Wireless Ridge was in D Coy's hands, although not before one man had been killed by British artillery and another by Argentine small arms. As the men of 2 Para dug in and came under more defensive fire, the Argentines were heard regrouping in the dark in the vicinity of Moody Brook.

With dawn, a small group of Argentines counter-attacked **D Coy**, but were soon driven off with the help of mortars and the Royal Artillery's 105s, by which time 2 Para had taken the whole feature at a cost of three men killed, considerably aided by the fire of the Scorpions and Scimitars and other supporting arms. From their positions, 2 Para watched the Argentines retreating towards Stanley in the morning light and pressed Brigadier Thompson to let them advance.

British Gallantry Awards
Battle for Wireless Ridge by 2 Para (all 2 Para citations included Goose Green)

Lt C S Connor (MC), C Coy
Maj J H Crosland (MC), B Coy
Maj C D Farrar-Hockley (MC), A Coy
Sgt J C Meredith (DCM), D Coy

Sgt T I Barrett (MM), A Coy
Capt W A McCracken (MC) RA, NGFO, 29 Cdo Regt RA (citation also included Mount Longdon)
Capt J G Greenhalgh (DFC) RCT, 656 AAC Sqdn (also included Goose Green)

Part 48. 2nd SCOTS GUARDS APPROACH TO and BATTLE FOR TUMBLEDOWN MOUNTAIN

13th/14th June 1982

British Forces
2nd Scots Guards, including GPMGs, LAWs, MAWs, Milans and 81mm mortars, and in support 4 Troop, The Blues and Royals with 2 Scorpions and 2 Scimitars, up to five bty's each of 6x105mm artillery, mortars of 42 Cdo RM and 1/7th Gurkha Rifles, and frigate "Active" with 1x4.5in (and 'Avenger', 1x4.5in).
2nd Scots Guards Commanders: Lt Col M I E Scott, Maj I E Dalzell-Job, G Coy (7, 8 and 9 Platoons), Maj J P Kiszley, Left Flank Coy (13, 14 and 15 Platoons), Maj S Price, Right Flank Coy (1, 2 and 3 Platoons)

Argentine Defenders
5th Marine Inf Btn defending Tumbledown Mountain, Mount William and Sapper Hill, supported by snipers, heavy mg's, mortars and artillery.

Approach to Tumbledown Mountain - On the same night that 2 Para continued 3 Cdo Bde's advance on Stanley from the west and north, 5th Infantry started its attacks against the main Argentine defences towards the south west of the capital - 2nd Scots aiming for Tumbledown and 1/7th Gurkhas for Mount William. Before then, the Marine's M & AW Cadre had built up a picture of the area to the west of Tumbledown.

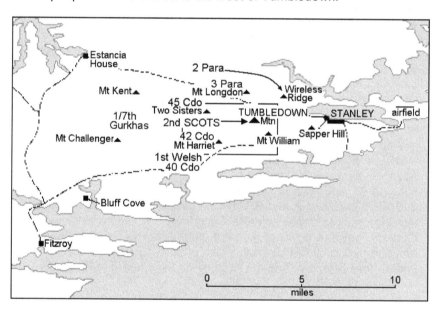

First, the Scots Guards moved by helicopter on the morning of Sunday 13th from their positions at Bluff Cove to the western end of Goat Ridge for a detailed reconnaissance and briefing. By now, Lt Col Scott had decided that an attack across the open southern slopes of Tumbledown would be far too hazardous, and instead opted for a "silent" assault from the west along the line of the summit ridge. Preceded by a diversionary raid along the Fitzroy/Stanley track, in phase one, **G Coy** would take the western end of the mountain. In phase two, Left Flank or **LF Coy** would pass through them before tackling the summit area. And finally, Right Flank or **RF Coy** would move around LF Coy to secure the eastern end. Led in from Goat Ridge by men of the M & AW Cadre, G Coy was followed to the start line by LF and RF Coys. The diversion started on schedule at 8.30pm, and thirty minutes later, G Coy moved forward into the bitterly cold night.

Battle for Tumbledown Mountain - The *diversionary attack* along the Stanley track went in as planned by a small assault group led by the light tanks. Reaching the enemy positions, one of the Guards and a Royal Engineer were killed in a fire-fight that lasted for two hours, and more were wounded withdrawing through a minefield, but the diversion did its job.

By now, in *phase one*, **G Coy** had crossed the start line with 7 Platoon and Coy HQ occupying the first half of their objective and 8 and 9 Platoons the second half. Securing the western end by 10.30pm, the positions were used to support **LF Coy** who came through to face heavy fire from snipers and GPMGs. In this *second phase*, **LF Coy**'s 13 Platoon fought for the high crags on the left and 15 Platoon lower down on the right, while 14 Platoon followed in reserve with Coy HQ. As they pushed forward under increasing mortar and artillery bombardment, two men were killed and a third mortally wounded by snipers. Anti-armour weapons were only partially successful against the Argentine bunkers, but 13 Platoon made some progress with grenades. However, only after three hours, at 2.30am, could artillery fire be brought down on the enemy positions in front of the stalled 15 Platoon, who with Coy HQ were now able to attack forward and up, overcoming the defences often in hand-to-hand fighting. Eventually, and after a seven hour struggle, just a few men of LF Coy reached the summit.

Now in *phase three*, **RF Coy** was able to come up, although the battle was far from over. With 3 Platoon giving covering fire, Number 1 and Lt Lawrence's 3 Platoon continued the assault on the eastern end, again using the MAWs and LAWs, but also moving forward in small groups taking positions with grenades and bayonets. Eventually around 8.15am and well after dawn, Tumbledown was in the Scots Guard's hands after fighting probably the best Argentine unit, and losing eight men killed and the Royal Engineer.

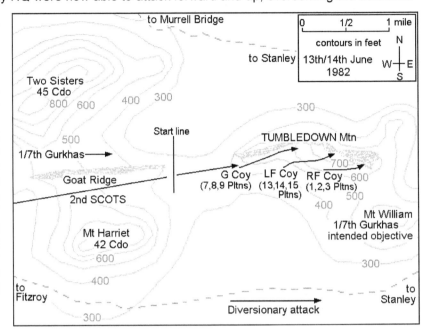

British Gallantry Awards
Battle for Tumbledown Mountain by 2nd Scots Guards

Lt Col M I E Scott (DSO)
Maj J P Kiszely (MC), LF Coy
Lt R A D Lawrence (MC), RF Coy
Gdsmn J B C Reynolds (post DCM), LF Coy
WO2 W Nicol (DCM), LF Coy

Sgt R W Jackson (MM), RF Coy
Gdsmn A S Pengelly (MM), RF Coy
Capt S M Drennan (DFC) AAC, 656 AAC Sqdn
Cpl J A Foran (MM) RE, 9 Para Sqdn RE
Sgt R H Wrega (MM) RE, 9 Para Sqdn RE

Part 49. 1/7th GURKHA'S APPROACH TO and PREPARATION FOR BATTLE OF MOUNT WILLIAM

14th June 1982

Leaving C Coy to garrison Goose Green, the Gurkhas moved towards Stanley. On Monday 7th, D Coy sailed around to the Fitzroy/Bluff Cove area in the Falkland's coaster "Monsunen" now back in British hands after being taken over by the Royal Navy at Darwin. Over the next two days, the rest of the battalion helicoptered in, and then moved to an area south of Mount Challenger in reserve, in time for the 3 Cdo Bde assaults. In preparation for their attack on Mount William, they again helicoptered forward on Sunday 13th to a position just south of Two Sisters. As the Scots Guards battled for Tumbledown, the Gurkhas marched along the line of Goat Ridge, and just to the north of Tumbledown ready for their assault, and on the way suffered casualties from Argentine shellfire. As dawn approached and the Guards had still not secured Tumbledown, it appeared the Gurkhas would have to make a daylight assault on Mount William.

Surrender, Victory and Part of the Price Paid
(Parts 50-55)

Part 50. FALKLANDS, SURRENDER and AFTERMATH

As dawn broke on Monday 14th, and the Scots Guards completed the capture of Tumbledown, 2 Para on Wireless Ridge saw the Argentines streaming back to Stanley as the British artillery shelled their positions at will. The British forces now edged forward.

Under Brigadier Thompson, 2 Para moved off along the Stanley road followed later by 3 Para; 42 Cdo shortly flew forward from Mount Harriet and marched towards Stanley; and 45 Cdo yomped from Two Sisters for Sapper Hill. By nightfall all of **3 Cdo Bde** was close to the capital. With **5th Infantry**, the Gurkhas were ready to make a daylight attack on Mount William, but the Argentines disappeared and D Coy moved onto the summit that morning without any opposition. Meanwhile the Welsh Guards were delayed by minefields on their way to Sapper Hill, but then flew in with A and C Coys 40 Cdo to face slight enemy resistance just as 45 Cdo showed up.

2 Para was the first unit to reach the outskirts, but halted as surrender negotiations got underway. These lasted for much of the day, and as they proceeded, British forces were ordered not to fire on the apparently demoralized enemy. However even now, General Menendez had 8,000 troops in the Stanley area including the largely intact 3rd, 6th and 25th Inf Regts, still well supplied with food and small arms ammo, but with little left for their remaining artillery and with all the high ground taken. Although ordered that morning by Galtieri to continue the fight, Menendez decided to negotiate, and a small British team led by Lt Col Rose of the SAS helicoptered in. A surrender document covering enemy forces both on West and East Falkland was agreed at the end of the afternoon, and that evening, General Moore flew to Stanley for the official signing.

Timed to take effect from 9.00pm local time, the actual signing took place at 9.30pm or half an hour into the 15th, Zulu time. First into Stanley next morning was 2 Para, followed by 3 Para and 42 Cdo, whose men of J Coy, last there with NP 8901, later hoisted the Governor's flag over Government House. With **3 Cdo Bde** staying in the Stanley area, most of **5th Infantry** returned to Fitzroy, although the Gurkhas went to Goose Green where they later lost a man killed on battlefield clearance.

With the surrender of the Argentines around Stanley, and their transfer to the airfield as a POW camp, steps were taken to deal with the forces on West Falkland and far away on Southern Thule. Still on Tuesday 15th, B Coy 40 Cdo crossed over to Port Howard by ship and helicopter to take the surrender of the 5th Inf Regt, and

"Avenger's" Lynx landed a small party at Fox Bay to deal with the 8th Regt, after which all the POWs moved to San Carlos. To re-take Southern Thule in "Operation Keyhole", frigate "Yarmouth" and RFA "Olmeda" reached South Georgia from the TEZ on Thursday 17th to pick up men of M Coy 42 Cdo under the command of Capt Nunn RM, some of whom had already left with "Endurance" and tug "Salvageman". Arriving off the bleak shores on Saturday, "Endurance's" Wasp landed a small group near the Argentine base, and when "Yarmouth" arrived (with "Olmeda") to provide gunfire support on Sunday 20th June, the tiny remaining garrison on Southern Thule surrendered without a shot being fired.

Needing food and shelter for his own men, a priority for General Moore was to ship home the POWs, with the exception of around 500 senior officers and technicians held as a guarantee against the junta fighting on. Both "Canberra" and "Norland" loaded a thousand POWs at San Carlos Water before heading for Stanley. There, "Canberra" took on board a further 3,000, leaving for Argentine on Friday 18th to be escorted into Puerto Madryn next day by destroyers "Santisima Trinidad" and "Comodoro Py". "Norland" sailed from Stanley on Friday with a total of 2,000 POWs to arrive off the same port two days later, and many of the remaining Argentines followed in the icebreaker "Bahia Paraiso". The "specials" returned on "St Edmund" a month later.

Even with their losses during the fighting, the Argentines left behind considerable amounts of war material including artillery and armoured cars, missile and radar systems, and aircraft and helicopters in various states of repair, some of which returned to the UK for evaluation or integration into the Services. And apart from recovering the two Falkland's coasters "Forrest" and "Monsunen" for local duties, the Royal Navy took over two other small craft.

Captured in Stanley Area

Aircraft - 11 FAA Pucaras, 3 CANA Aermacchi MB-339As

Helicopters - 2 FAA Bell 212s, 1 PNA Puma, 1 Army Chinook, 2 Agusta A-109As, and 9 Iroquois UH-1Hs

Ships - small oil rig tender "Yehuin" (renamed "Falkland Sound") and PNA patrol craft "Islas Malvinas" (manned by men of destroyer "Cardiff" and renamed "Tiger Bay")

Sitting, Brigadier J H Thompson RM commanding officer, 3 Commando Brigade and Major General Moore, Commander, Land Forces, Falkland Islands
(Courtesy - Royal Marines Museum)

As the **Task Force** ships started entering Port William and Stanley Harbour, the minesweeping trawlers moved in to successfully sweep a field of contact mines laid off Cape Pembroke. On land, the situation was far worse as apart from the Army having to clear all the battlefield litter and discarded ordnance, the Royal Engineers had to deal with the extensive and mainly unmarked minefields especially around Stanley. (There are doubts if the work will ever be finished.)

As for the Islands themselves, the British Government was committed to their defence in a policy referred to as "Fortress Falklands". If large and continuing expenditure and large, permanent garrisons were to be avoided, rapid reinforcement by air was vital. A first step came on the 24th June when an extended range Hercules landed at Stanley airfield. Then in October, after its lengthening and re-designation as RAF Stanley, the airport could be used by Phantom fighters. But that was still not enough. A major airfield and associated installations were therefore constructed near Pleasant Peak. Completed in 1985, Mount Pleasant airport is able to handle wide-bodied, long-range jet transports capable of reinforcing the Falklands at short notice.

Part 51. MAIN BRITISH TASK FORCE RETURNS HOME

By the time of the surrender, a number of ships were already well on their way north or had reached the UK, including nuclear submarine "Splendid", destroyer "Glasgow", frigates "Alacrity" and "Argonaut", RFA "Fort Austin", some of the BP tankers and the "Queen Elizabeth 2" to her great welcome. Although more ships would soon follow, a first priority was to start getting the land forces home as soon as "Canberra" and "Norland" had played their part in taking the large number of Argentine POWs off Britain's hands and back to their homeland. First to leave were **3 Cdo Bde** and the attached Paras, with **5th Infantry** staying on (most of 2nd Scots Guards moved to West Falkland) until the arrival of the first garrison troops, 1st Battalion, The Queen's Own Highlanders who reached the Falklands in mid-July on "Norland":

3 Commando Brigade

40 Cdo, 42 Cdo and Z Coy 45 Cdo on "Canberra", departed on 25th June from Falklands and arrived Southampton on 11th July

45 Cdo including X and Y Coy on RFA "Stromness", late June from Falklands. Arrived Ascension 7th/8th July and flew home by VC.10, landing near Arbroath on the 8th and 9th July

M Coy 42 Cdo on "Nordic Ferry", 8th July from South Georgia. Arrived Ascension and flew to RAF St Mawgan

2 and 3 Para on "Norland", 25th June from Falklands. Arrived Ascension 5th July and flew by VC.10 to Brize Norton on 6th July

5th Infantry Brigade

2nd Scots and 1st Welsh Guards on "Norland", c19th July from Falklands. Arrived Ascension and flew by VC.10 to Brize Norton on 29th July.

1/7th Gurkha Rifles on "Uganda", 18th July from Falklands and arrived Southampton on 9th August.

Ships and Aircraft - Some ships sadly would not be returning - destroyers "Coventry" and "Sheffield", frigates "Antelope" and "Ardent", LSL "Sir Galahad" and the "Atlantic Conveyor" - but by the end of August, most of the others had left the Falklands area (some later made a second trip) to be replaced by a smaller number of destroyers and frigates and other vessels mostly on their first journey south. Amongst these were four merchantmen, two minesweepers and their support ship "St Helena" all of which which sailed from the UK before the surrender. MCMS "Brecon" and "Ledbury" arrived in early July to relieve the five minesweeping trawlers, and spent the next five weeks hunting for any ground mines laid by the Argentines, none of which were found.

Of the major warships, assault ships "Fearless" and "Intrepid" set sail a week and a half after the surrender, and arrived at Portsmouth on the 14th July after first unloading Marines and Sea Kings of No.846 NAS at Devonport. As for the carriers, until the arrival of the RAF Phantoms at Stanley, only their Harriers could provide much of the air defence still needed by the Falklands. Following the surrender, "Invincible's" first priority was to sail well clear to the north, escorted by frigate "Andromeda" in order to change a main engine. "Hermes" remained behind until "Invincible" was back, and on the 4th July sailed with escort "Broadsword" for Portsmouth, arriving on the 21st to another great welcome. Well before then, on the 2nd July, Admiral Woodward was relieved as Task Group commander by Rear Admiral Reffell flying his flag on destroyer "Bristol".

But there was no relief for "Invincible" which had to await the arrival of newly-commissioned sister ship "Illustrious" carrying a reformed No.809 Sea Harrier squadron and the first early airborne warning Sea Kings. Reaching the Falklands on the 27th August, and after a day's vertrep, "Invincible" was at last able to head north on the 28th accompanied by "Bristol" and later RFA "Olna", arriving at Portsmouth on the 17th September to be met by Her Majesty Queen Elizabeth II. After 166 days at sea, "Invincible" claimed the record for the longest continuous carrier operations ever.

The Sea Harriers and most of the Navy, Marine and Army helicopters went back to the UK with the returning ships. As for the RAF, mainly based at or flying to Ascension, the few Vulcan bombers flew home by the time of the surrender, and the last Nimrod MR.2s continued operating from Ascension until August, but even then, there was little let-up for the other aircraft. VC.10s maintained the air-link between the UK and Ascension, returning with many of the troops from there. Hercules transports flew south regularly, and from late June were landing at Stanley. (By then, two members of 47 Sqdn had earned gallantry awards for their air-drop missions.) And for many more months, Victor tankers and later Hercules conversions refuelled the extended range Nimrods and Hercules deep into the South Atlantic and on to the Falklands. On the island itself, a number of Harrier GR.3s of 1(F) Sqdn once again fitted with Sidewinder for air defence, were based at Stanley, but in October, 29(F) Sqdn Phantoms flew down from Ascension to the newly opened RAF Stanley to start taking over from them.

Finally there was the question of the last resting place for those British dead not buried or lost at sea. The policy had long been for those killed on active service to remain in the country where they fell, but many families chose to bring their men home. In October, LSL "Sir Bedivere" left the Falklands carrying over sixty back to the UK. Another sixteen however, including Lt Col Jones VC, stayed in the Falklands.

RAF Hercules which played such an important part carrying some of the forces into battle, and then home (Courtesy - MOD, RAF)

POST-WAR MOVEMENTS TO AND FROM THE FALKLAND'S AREA & SOUTH ATLANTIC

Period	DEPARTURES FROM SOUTH ATLANTIC	ARRIVALS IN SOUTH ATLANTIC (excluding **new** merchantmen)
15th-20th June 1982, Week Twelve	RN - SSN Conqueror, frigate Arrow	
21st-30th June 1982, end of Month Three	RN - Destroyers Antrim, Glamorgan, frigates Brilliant, Plymouth, assault ships Fearless, Intrepid, ambulance ships Hecla, Herald	MN - Transport Astronomer, Tanker G A Walker
	RFA - Blue Rover, Olmeda, Resource, Stromness, LSLs Sir Geraint, Sir Percivale	
	MN - Transports Canberra, Elk, Europic Ferry	
July 1982, Month Four	RN - SSN Courageous? Spartan, Valiant, SS Onyx, carrier Hermes, destroyers Cardiff, Exeter, frigates Active, Ambuscade, Broadsword, Minerva, Yarmouth, IPV Endurance, despatch vessels Dumbarton Castle, Leeds Castle, minesweepers Cordella, Farnella, Junella, Northella, Pict	RN - Destroyers Birmingham, Southampton, frigates Apollo, Bacchante, Danae, Diomede, MCMS Brecon, Ledbury and support ship St Helena
	RFA - Engadine, Tidespring, LSL Sir Lancelot, support tankers Appleleaf, Pearleaf, Plumleaf (already in Central Atlantic), RMAS Goosander (from Ascension)	RFA - RFA Olwen
		ARMY - RCT landing craft Antwerp, Arromanches

	MN – transports Atlantic Causeway, Contender Bezant (made 2nd trip), Nordic Ferry, hospital ship/transport Uganda, tankers Balder London, Eburna, repair ship Stena Seaspread	MN - Transport Avelona Star, Laertes
August 1982, Month Five	RN - Carrier Invincible, destroyer Bristol, frigates Avenger, Andromeda, Penelope, MCMS Brecon, Ledbury and support ship St Helena, ambulance ship Hydra	RN - Carrier Illustrious, frigates Amazon, Battleaxe, survey ship Hecate as ice patrol vessel
	RFA - Olna, Regent, Tidepool (to Chilean Navy), support tanker Bayleaf	
	MN - Transports Geestport, Laertes, Tor Caledonia, despatch vessel British Enterprise III, mooring vessel Wimpey Seahorse	
September, Month Six	RN - Destroyers Birmingham, Southampton, frigates Apollo, Danae, Diomede	RN - Destroyes Glasgow (2nd visit), Newcastle, frigates Phoebe, Sirius
	RFA - Fort Grange, RMAS tug Typhoon	RFA - Fort Austin, Olmeda (both 2nd visit)
October-December 1982	RN - Carrier Illustrious, destroyers Glasgow (after 2nd visit), Newcastle, frigates Amazon, Bacchante (to Royal New Zealand Navy), Battleaxe, Brazen, Phoebe, Sirius	RN - Destroyers Antrim (2nd visit), Liverpool, frigates Brazen, Ariadne, Charybdis, Minerva (2nd visit)
	RFA - Fort Austin (after 2nd visit), Olmeda (after 2nd visit), Olwen, LSL Sir Bedivere, support tanker Brambleleaf	RFA - Fort Grange, Tidespring (both 2nd visit)
	MN - Transports Astronomer, Avelona Star (made further visits), tanker British Avon, despatch vessel Iris, tug Irishman	
1983 and after - Departures from South Atlantic	RN - Destroyers Antrim (after 2nd visit), Liverpool, frigates Ariadne, Charybdis, Minerva (after 2nd visit), survey ship Hecate	
	RFA - Fort Grange (after 2nd visit), Tidespring (after 2nd visit), LSL Sir Tristram	
	MN - Transports Baltic Ferry, Lycaon, Norland, St Edmund, tankers Anco Charger, British Esk, British Tamar, British Tay, British Trent (all after reloading trips north), Alvega (Ascension base storage), G A Walker and Scottish Eagle (both Stanley base storage), water tanker Fort Toronto, repair ship Stena Inspector, tugs Salvageman, Yorkshireman	

Part 52. BRITISH SHIPS LOST & DAMAGED

1st May - 12th June 1982

Note: If the frequent unexploded bombs (1-13) had detonated on striking some of the ships listed below, the Royal Navy's additional losses might quite possibly have put the eventual success of the British Task Force in doubt.

Saturday 1st May

HMS Alacrity - slightly damaged by bomb near misses

HMS Arrow - slightly damaged by cannon fire

HMS Glamorgan - slightly damaged by bomb near misses, all off Stanley by Daggers of FAA Grupo 6.

HMS Argonaut post-war in Portland harbour, southern England
(Courtesy - MOD, Navy)

Tuesday 4th May

HMS SHEFFIELD - mortally damaged south east of Falklands by Exocet missile fired by Super Etendard of CANA 2 Esc. Burnt out and sank in tow on Monday 10th May.

Wednesday 12th May

HMS Glasgow - moderately damaged off Stanley by unexploded bomb (UXB 1) dropped by A-4B Skyhawks of FAA Grupo 5. Bomb passed through hull but damage took some days to repair and she shortly returned to UK.

Friday 21st May

HMS Antrim - seriously damaged in Falkland Sound outside San Carlos Water by unexploded bomb (2) dropped by Daggers of FAA Grupo 6. UXB removed but damage took some days to repair.

HMS Broadsword - slightly damaged outside San Carlos Water by cannon fire from Daggers of Grupo 6.

HMS Argonaut - slightly damaged outside San Carlos Water by rockets and cannon fire from Aermacchi MB.339A of CANA 1 Esc, and then seriously damaged by two unexploded bombs (3/4) dropped by A-4B Skyhawks of FAA Grupo 5. Removing the UXBs and carrying out repairs took a number of days and although declared operational, she soon sailed for the UK.

HMS Brilliant - slightly damaged outside San Carlos Water by cannon fire from Daggers of Grupo 6. (Different attack from "Broadsword")

HMS ARDENT (right) - badly damaged in Grantham Sound by bombs - hits, UXBs (5+) and near misses - dropped by Daggers of Grupo 6, then mortally damaged by bombs from A-4Q Skyhawks of CANA 3 Esc off North West Island. Sank the following evening.

Note: The Royal Navy has lost three "Ardent's" in three wars - a destroyer each in World War 1 (Battle of Jutland) and 2 (1940 Norwegian Campaign) and now the Falklands

Sunday 23rd May

HMS ANTELOPE - damaged in San Carlos Water by two unexploded bombs (6/7) dropped by A-4B Skyhawks of Grupo 5. One of the bombs exploded that evening while being defused and she caught fire and sank next day.

Monday 24th May

RFA Sir Galahad - damaged by unexploded bomb (8) and out of action for some days.

RFA Sir Lancelot - damaged by unexploded bomb (9) and not fully operational for almost three weeks.

RFA Sir Bedivere - slightly damaged by glancing bomb, all in San Carlos Water probably by A-4C Skyhawks of FAA Grupo 4.

Tuesday 25th May

HMS Broadsword - damaged north of Pebble Island by bomb from A-4B Skyhawk of Grupo 5 bouncing up through her stern and out again to land in the sea.

HMS COVENTRY - sunk north of Pebble Island in same attack by three bombs.

ATLANTIC CONVEYOR - mortally damaged north east of Falklands by Exocet missile fired by Super Etendard of CANA 2 Esc. Burnt out and later sank in tow.

Saturday 29th May

British Wye, tanker - hit north of South Georgia by bomb dropped by C-130 Hercules of FAA Grupo 1 which bounced into the sea without exploding.

Tuesday 8th June

HMS Plymouth - damaged in Falkland Sound off San Carlos Water by four unexploded bombs (10-13) from Daggers of FAA Grupo 6.

RFA SIR GALAHAD - mortally damaged off Fitzroy by bombs from A-4B Skyhawks of Grupo 5 and burnt out. Later in June towed out to sea and sunk as a war grave.

RFA Sir Tristram - badly damaged off Fitzroy in same attack and abandoned, but later returned to UK and repaired. LCU F4, HMS Fearless - sunk in Choiseul Sound by bomb from A-4B Skyhawk of Grupo 5.

Saturday 12th June

HMS Glamorgan - damaged off Stanley by land-based Exocet missile.

Part 53. BRITISH AIRCRAFT LOST

22nd April - 12th June 1982

Note: Reference numbers, e.g. [b1, b2], b for British, are those used in the text

Thursday 22nd April

[b1, b2] - Two Wessex HU.5s of C Flt, No.845 NAS, RFA Tidespring crashed on Fortuna Glacier, South Georgia in bad weather. All crew rescued.

Friday 23rd April

[b3] - Sea King HC.4 of No.846 NAS embarked on HMS Hermes crashed into the Atlantic at night in bad weather south west of Ascension (8.15pm). Pilot rescued but PO Aircrewman Casey lost.

Tuesday 4th May

[b4] - Sea Harrier of No.800 NAS, HMS Hermes shot down over Goose Green by radar-controlled, 35mm Oerlikon fire (1.10pm). Lt Taylor RN killed.

Thursday 6th May

[b5, b6] - Two Sea Harriers of No.801 NAS, HMS Invincible lost in bad weather, presumably by collision, south east of Falklands (9.00am). Lt Curtiss and Lt Cdr Eyton-Jones RN lost.

Wednesday 12th May

[b7] - Sea King HAS.5 of No.826 NAS, HMS Hermes ditched in sea with engine failure east of Falklands (2.35pm). All crew rescued.

Monday 17th May

[b8] - Sea King HAS.5 of No.826 NAS, HMS Hermes, then to the east of Falklands, hit the sea late at night because of altimeter problems (10.30pm). All crew rescued.

?18th/19th May

[b9] - Sea King HC.4 of No.846 NAS deliberately destroyed by its crew near Punta Arenas, southern Chile around this date.

Sea King Mk 5 of 820 NAS on HMS Illustrious
(Courtesy - MOD, Navy)

Wednesday 19th May

[b10] - Sea King HC.4 of No.846 NAS, then embarked on HMS Hermes crashed into sea north east of Falklands, believed at the time due to a bird strike although this is now open to doubt (7.15pm). Of 30 men on board, the aircrewman, 18 men of the SAS, a member of the Royal Signals and the only RAF man killed in the war were all lost. The two pilots were saved.

Friday 21st May

[b11, b12] - Two Gazelles of C Flt, 3 CBAS shot down by small arms fire near Port San Carlos (c8.45am). Pilot Sgt Evans RM killed in the first incident and pilot Lt Francis RM and crewman L/Cpl Griffin RM in the second.

[b13] - Harrier GR.3 of 1(F) Sqdn RAF shot down over Port Howard, West Falkland probably by Blowpipe SAM (9.35am). Flt Lt Glover ejected and injured, taken prisoner-of-war.

[b14] - Lynx HAS.2 of No.815 NAS destroyed in bombing attack on HMS Ardent in Grantham Sound by Daggers of FAA Grupo 6 (2.40pm).

Sunday 23rd May

[b15] - Sea Harrier of No.800 NAS, HMS Hermes crashed into sea north east of Falklands shortly after take-off and exploded (7.55pm). Lt Cdr Batt RN killed.

Tuesday 25th May

[b16] - Lynx HAS.2 of No.815 NAS lost when HMS Coventry sunk north of Pebble Island in bombing attack by A-4B Skyhawks of FAA Grupo 5 (3.20pm).

[b17 - b22] - Six Wessex HU.5s of No.848 NAS D Flt;
[b23 - b25] - Three Chinook HC.1s of 18 Sqdn RAF;
[b26] - Lynx HAS.2 of No.815 NAS, all destroyed by fire when "Atlantic Conveyor" hit to the north east of Falklands by Exocet from Super Etendard of CANA 2 Esc.

Thursday 27th May

[b27] - Harrier GR.3 of 1(F) Sqdn RAF shot down over Goose Green probably by 35mm Oerlikon fire (1.35pm). Sqdn Ldr Iveson ejected to the west, hid up and later rescued.

Friday 28th May

[b28] - Scout of B Flight, 3 CBAS shot down near Camilla Creek House, north of Goose Green by Pucaras of FAA Grupo 3 (11.55am). Pilot Lt Nunn RM was killed.

Saturday 29th May

[b29] - Sea Harrier of No.801 NAS, HMS Invincible ready for take-off, slid off the deck as the carrier turned into wind to the east of Falklands (3.50pm). Lt Cdr Broadwater RN ejected and was safely picked up.

Sunday 30th May

[b30] - Harrier GR.3 of 1(F) Sqdn RAF damaged near Stanley by small arms fire from Argentine troops. Ran out of fuel short of "Hermes" and Sqdn Ldr Pook RAF ejected to be picked up to east of the Falklands (12.20pm).

Torpedo-armed Lynx of No 815 NAS. Aft is a MAD Magnetic Anomaly Detector (Courtesy - MOD, Navy)

Tuesday 1st June

[b31] - Sea Harrier of No.801 NAS, HMS Invincible shot down south of Stanley by Roland SAM (2.40pm). Flt Lt Mortimer RAF ejected and was later rescued from the sea.

Sunday 6th June

[b32] - Gazelle of 656 AAC Sqdn accidentally shot down west of Fitzroy by Sea Dart SAM fired by HMS Cardiff (1.10am). Pilot, Staff Sgt Griffin, crewman L/Cpl Cockton and two Royal Signals passengers killed.

Tuesday 8th June

[b33] - Harrier GR.3 of 1(F) Sqdn RAF landed heavily at Port San Carlos with partial engine failure, and was damaged beyond repair (12.00pm). Wing Cdr Squire escaped unhurt.

Saturday 12th June

[b34] - Wessex HAS.3 of No.737 NAS destroyed when HMS Glamorgan hit by land-based Exocet off Stanley (3.35am).

Part 54. ARGENTINE AIRCRAFT LOST

3rd April - 15th June 1982

Two British-built English Electric Canberras of the FAA were shot down. One [a8] on the first day of the air war around the Falklands. The second [a70] was the last Argentine aircraft lost in combat

Saturday 3rd April

[a1] - Puma SA.330L of CAB 601 shot down at Grytviken, South Georgia by Royal Marine small arms fire.

Saturday 1st May

[a2, a3, a4] - One Pucara of FAA Grupo 3 destroyed and two more damaged and not repaired at Goose Green by CBUs dropped in attack by No.800 Sea Harriers flown by Lt Cdr Frederiksen, Lt Hale and Lt McHarg RN (8.25am). Lt Jukic killed in the destroyed aircraft.

[a5] - Mirage IIIEA of FAA Grupo 8 shot down north of West Falkland by Flt Lt Barton RAF in No.801 Sea Harrier using Sidewinder (4.10pm). Lt Perona ejected safely.

[a6] - Mirage IIIEA of FAA Grupo 8 damaged in same incident north of West Falkland by Lt Thomas RN in No.801 Sea Harrier using Sidewinder. Then shot down over Stanley by own AA defences (4.15pm). and Capt Cuerva killed

[a7] - Dagger A of FAA Grupo 6 shot down over East Falkland by Flt Lt Penfold RAF in No.800 Sea Harrier using Sidewinder (4.40pm). Lt Ardiles killed.

[a8] - Canberra B.62 of FAA Grupo 2 shot down north of Falklands by Lt Curtiss RN in No.801 Sea Harrier using Sidewinder (5.45pm). Lt Ibanez and Gonzalez ejected but were not rescued.

Sunday 2nd May

[a9] - Lynx HAS.23 of CANA 1 Esc embarked on ARA Santisima Trinidad lost in flying accident probably to north of Falklands.

[a10] - Alouette III of CANA 1 Esc lost on board ARA General Belgrano when she was torpedoed and sunk to south west of Falklands.

Monday 3rd May

[a11] - Aermacchi MB-339A of CANA 1 Esc crashed into ground near Stanley approaching airfield in bad weather (4.00pm). Lt Benitez killed.

[a12] - Skyvan of PNA damaged by naval gunfire at Stanley on the night of 3rd/4th and not repaired.

Sunday 9th May

[a13, a14] - Two A-4C Skyhawks of FAA Grupo 4 lost. Possibly damaged by Sea Darts from HMS Coventry or crashed in bad weather, with one aircraft found on South Jason Island. Lt Casco and Lt Farias killed.

[a15] - Puma SA.330L of CAB 601 shot down over Choiseul Sound by Sea Dart fired by HMS Coventry (4.10pm). Crew of three lost.

Wednesday 12th May

[a16, a17, a18] - Two A-4B Skyhawks of FAA Grupo 5 shot down off Stanley by Sea Wolf fired by HMS Brilliant and third aircraft hit sea trying to evade missile (1.45pm). All three pilots, Lt Bustos, Lt Ibarlucea and Lt Nivoli killed.

[a19] - A-4B Skyhawk of FAA Grupo 5 shot down over Goose Green by own AA fire (2.25pm). Lt Gavazzi killed.

Saturday 15th May

[a20-a25] - Six Pucaras of FAA Grupo 3; [a26-a29] - Four T-34C Mentors of CANA 4 Esc; [a30] - Skyvan of PNA, all destroyed or put out of action at Pebble Island in raid by D Sqdn SAS (early morning)

Friday 21st May

[a31] - Chinook CH-47C of CAB 601 destroyed on ground near Mount Kent by Flt Lt Hare RAF in 1(F) Sqdn Harrier GR.3 using 30mm cannon (8.00am).

[a32] - Puma SA.330L of CAB 601 badly damaged on ground near Mount Kent in same attack by Sqdn Ldr Pook and Flt Lt Hare RAF in 1(F) Sqn Harrier GR.3s using 30mm cannon (8.00am). Destroyed on 26th in same position by Sqdn Ldr Pook using CBUs.

[a33] - Pucara of FAA Grupo 3 shot down over Sussex Mountains by Stinger SAM fired by D Sqdn SAS (10.00am). Capt Benitz ejected safely.

[a34] - Dagger A of FAA Grupo 6 shot down near Fanning Head by Sea Cat fired by HMS Argonaut or Plymouth, or more likely Sea Wolf from HMS Broadsword (10.30am). Lt Bean killed.

[a35] - Pucara of FAA Grupo 3 shot down near Darwin by Cdr Ward RN in one of three Sea Harriers of No.801 NAS using 30mm cannon (12.10pm). Major Tomba ejected.

[a36, a37] - Two A-4C Skyhawks of FAA Grupo 4 shot down near Chartres, West Falkland by Lt Cdr Blissett and Lt Cdr Thomas RN in No.800 Sea Harriers using Sidewinders (1.05pm). Lt Lopez and Lt Manzotti killed.

[a38] - Dagger A of FAA Grupo 6 shot down near Teal River Inlet, West Falkland by Lt Cdr Frederiksen RN in No.800 Sea Harrier using Sidewinder (2.35pm). Lt Luna ejected.

[a39, a40, a41] - Two Dagger A's of FAA Grupo 6 shot down north of Port Howard, West Falkland by Lt Thomas and a third by Cdr Ward RN in No.801 Sea Harriers using Sidewinders (2.50pm). Maj Piuma, Capt Donaldille and Lt Senn all ejected.

[a42] - A-4Q Skyhawk of CANA 3 Esc shot down near Swan Island in Falkland Sound by Lt Morrell RN in No.800 Sea Harrier using Sidewinder (3.12pm). Lt Cdr Philippi ejected.

[a43] - A-4Q Skyhawk of CANA 3 Esc also shot down near Swan Island in Falkland Sound in same incident by Flt Lt Leeming RAF in No.800 Sea Harrier using 30mm cannon (3.12pm). Lt Marquez was killed.

[a44] - A-4Q Skyhawk of CANA 3 Esc damaged over Falkland Sound by small arms fire from HMS Ardent and again in same incident as above by Lt Morrell using 30mm cannon ([a42] above). Unable to land at Stanley with undercarriage problems and Lt Arca ejected (3.30pm).

Sunday 23rd May

[a45] - Puma SA.330L of CAB 601 flew into ground near Shag House Cove, West Falkland attempting to evade Flt Lt Morgan RAF in No.800 NAS Sea Harrier (10.30am). All crew escaped.

[a46] - Agusta A-109A of CAB 601 in same incident near Shag House Cove, West Falkland destroyed on ground by Flt Lt Morgan and Flt Lt Leeming RAF in No.800 NAS Sea Harriers using 30mm cannon (10.30am).

[a47] - Puma SA.330L of CAB 601 also in same incident near Shag House Cove, West Falkland damaged on ground by Flt Lt Morgan with 30mm cannon (10.30am). Then believed shortly destroyed by Lt Cdr Gedge and Lt Cdr Braithwaite RN in No.801 Sea Harriers with more cannon fire.

[a48] - A-4B Skyhawk of FAA Grupo 5 shot down over San Carlos Water by unknown SAM (1.50pm). Claims that day included "Broadsword" Sea Wolf, "Antelope" Sea Cat, and land-based Rapiers and Blowpipe. Lt Guadagnini killed.

[a49] - Dagger A of FAA Grupo 6 shot down over Pebble Island by Lt Hale RN in No.800 Sea Harrier using Sidewinder (4.00pm). Lt Volponi killed.

Monday 24th May

[a50, a51, a52] - Two Dagger A's of FAA Grupo 6 shot down north of Pebble Island by Lt Cdr Auld and a third by Lt D Smith in No.800 Sea Harriers using Sidewinder (11.15am). Maj Puga and Capt Diaz ejected, but Lt Castillo killed.

[a53] - A-4C Skyhawk of FAA Grupo 4 damaged over San Carlos Water by ship and ground-based air defences and crashed into King George Bay, West Falkland on flight home (1.30pm). Claims that day included "Argonaut" and "Fearless" Sea Cat, and Rapier and Blowpipe SAMs. Lt Bono lost.

Tuesday 25th May

[a54] - A-4B Skyhawk of FAA Grupo 5 shot down north of Pebble Island by Sea Dart fired by HMS Coventry (9.30am). Lt Palaver killed.

[a55] - A-4C Skyhawk of FAA Grupo 4 destroyed over San Carlos Water by a variety of weapons, claims included small arms fire, "Yarmouth" Sea Cat, and Rapier and Blowpipe SAMs (12.30pm). Lt Lucero ejected.

[a56] - A-4C Skyhawk of FAA Grupo 4 damaged over San Carlos Water in same attack, and then brought down north east of Pebble Island by Sea Dart fired by HMS Coventry (12.45am). Lt Garcia killed.

Thursday 27th May

[a57] - A-4B Skyhawk of FAA Grupo 5 damaged over San Carlos Water by 40mm Bofors from HMS Fearless or Intrepid, and crashed near Port Howard (5.00pm). Lt Velasco ejected.

Friday 28th May

[a58] - Pucara of FAA Grupo 3 crashed into high ground between Goose Green and Stanley returning from attack in Goose Green area (c10.00am). Lt Giminez killed.

[a59] - Aermacchi MB-339A of CANA 1 Esc shot down at Goose Green by Blowpipe SAM fired by Royal Marine Air Defence Troop (5.00pm). Lt Miguel killed.

[a60] - Pucara of FAA Grupo 3 shot down at Goose Green by small arms fire from 2 Para (5.10pm). Lt Cruzado ejected and became POW.

Saturday 29th May

[a61] - Dagger A of FAA Grupo 6 shot down over San Carlos Water by Rapier SAM (12.00pm). Lt Bernhardt killed.

Sunday 30th May

[a62] - Puma SA.330L of CAB 601 lost in the morning in uncertain circumstances near Mount Kent, possibly to own forces fire.

[a63, a64] - Two A-4C Skyhawks of FAA Grupo 4 shot down east of Falklands by Sea Darts fired by HMS Exeter, although 4.5 inch gunfire from HMS Avenger may have hit one (2.35pm). Lt J Vazquez and Lt O Castillo killed.

Tuesday 1st June

[a65] - Hercules C.130E of FAA Transport Grupo 1 shot down 50 miles North of Pebble Island by Cdr Ward RN in No.801 Sea Harrier using Sidewinder and 30mm cannon (10.45am). Crew of seven killed.

Monday 7th June

[a66] - Learjet 35A of FAA Photo-Reconnaissance Grupo 1 shot down over Pebble Island by Sea Dart fired by HMS Exeter (9.05am). Wing Cdr de la Colina and crew of four killed.

Tuesday 8th June

[a67, a68, a69] - Two A-4B Skyhawks of FAA Grupo 5 shot down over Choiseul Sound by Flt Lt Morgan RAF and a third by Lt D Smith in No.800 NAS Sea Harriers using Sidewinders (4.45pm). Lt Arraras, Lt Bolzan and Ensign Vazquez killed.

Sunday 13th June

[a70] - Canberra B.62 of FAA Grupo 2 shot down west of Stanley by Sea Dart fired by HMS Exeter (10.55pm). Pilot, Capt Pastran ejected safely but Capt Casado was killed.

Postwar - Captured at Stanley

[a71-a81] - Eleven Pucaras of FAA Grupo 3
[a82-a83] - Two Bell 212s of FAA Grupo 7
[a84-a86] - Three Aermacchi MB-339As of CANA 1 Esc
[a87] - Puma SA.330L of PNA
[a88] - Chinook CH-47C of CAB 601
[a89-a90] - Two Agusta A-109A Hirundos of CAB 601
[a91-a99] - Nine Iroquois UH-1Hs of CAB 601

Unknown Date

[a100] - Pucara of FAA Grupo 3 reported lost over in the Atlantic on reconnaissance mission from Comodoro Rivadavia.

Note: For Argentine Ships Lost and Damaged – see Part 32

Part 55. BRITISH GALLANTRY AWARDS

VICTORIA CROSS – Posthumous

Lt Col H Jones OBE,
Co, 2nd Battalion The Parachute Regiment

Sgt I J McKay,
3rd Battalion The Parachute Regiment

ROYAL NAVY, ROYAL MARINES, ROYAL FLEET AUXILIARY and MERCHANT NAVY

Distinguished Service Order
Capt M E Barrow RN, co HMS Glamorgan
Capt J J Black MBE RN, co HMS Invincible
Capt W R Canning RN, co HMS Broadsword
Capt J F Coward RN, co HMS Brilliant
Capt P G V Dingemans RN, co HMS Intrepid
Commodore S C Dunlop CBE RFA,
  co RFA Fort Austin
Lt Cdr B F Dutton QGM RN, co Fleet Clearance
  Diving Team 1
Capt E S J Larken RN, co HMS Fearless
Capt C H Layman MVO RN, co HMS Argonaut
Capt L E Middleton ADC RN, co HMS Hermes
Capt D Pentreath RN, co HMS Plymouth
Capt P J G Roberts RFA, co RFA Sir Galahad
Lt Cdr I Stanley RN, Flt Cdr, No.737 NAS,
  HMS Antrim
Lt Col N F Vaux RM, co 42 Cdo RM
Lt Col A F Whitehead RM, co 45 Cdo RM
Cdr C L Wreford-Brown RN, co HMS Conqueror
Capt B G Young RN, co HMS Antrim

Royal Navy, Royal Marines, Royal Fleet Auxiliary and Merchant Navy - continued

Distinguished Service Cross
Lt Cdr A D Auld RN, co No.800 NAS, HMS Hermes
Lt A R C Bennett RN, No.846 NAS
Lt Cdr M D Booth RN, co No.847 NAS
Cdr P J Bootherstone RN, co HMS Arrow
Lt N A Bruen RN, co Fleet Clearance Diving Team 3
Lt Cdr H S Clark RN, co No.825 NAS
Cdr C J S Craig RN, co HMS Alacrity
Lt Cdr J A Ellerbeck RN, Flt Cdr, No.829 NAS, HMS Endurance
Fleet CPO (Diver) M G Fellows BEM, Fleet Clearance Diving Team 1
Capt G R Green RFA, co RFA Sir Tristram
Lt R Hutchings RM, No.846 NAS
Capt D E Lawrence RFA, co RFA Sir Geraint
Lt Cdr H J Lomas RN, No.845 NAS
Lt K P Mills RM, RM Detachment, HMS Endurance
Sub Lt P T Morgan RN, HMS Argonaut
Cdr A Morton RN, co HMS Yarmouth
Lt N J North RN, No.846 NAS
Capt A F Pitt RFA, co RFA Sir Percivale
Lt Cdr N W Thomas RN, Nos.899/800 NAS, HMS Hermes
Lt S R Thomas RN, No.801 NAS, HMS Invincible
Lt Cdr S C Thornewill RN, co No.846 NAS
Cdr N J Tobin RN, co HMS Antelope
Cdr A W J West RN, co HMS Ardent
Cdr N D Ward AFC RN, co No.801 NAS, HMS Invincible
Posthumous
Lt Cdr G W J Batt RN, No.800 NAS, HMS Hermes
Capt I H North Merchant Navy, co Atlantic Conveyor
Lt Cdr J M Sephton RN, HMS Ardent
Lt Cdr J S Woodhead RN, HMS Sheffield

Military Cross
Capt P M Babbington RM, 42 Cdo RM
Maj C P Cameron RM, co 3 CBAS
Lt C I Dytor RM, 45 Cdo RM
Lt C Fox RM, 45 Cdo RM
Lt D J Stewart RM, 45 Cdo RM

Distinguished Flying Cross
Capt J P Niblett RM, 3 CBAS
Posthumous
Lt R J Nunn RM, 3 CBAS

Air Force Cross
Lt Cdr D J S Squier RN, co No.826 NAS, HMS Hermes
Lt Cdr R J S Wykes-Sneyd RN, co No.820 NAS, HMS Invincible

Distinguished Conduct Medal
Cpl J Burdett RM, 45 Cdo RM

George Medal
AB (Radar) J E Dillon, HMS Ardent
Posthumous
Second Eng Offr P A Henry RFA, RFA Sir Galahad

Distinguished Service Medal
Colour Sgt M J Francis RM, coxswain LCU F1, HMS Fearless
Ldg Aircrewman P B Imrie, No.846 NAS
Sgt P J Leach RM, RM Detachment, HMS Endurance
PO J S Leake, HMS Ardent
Sgt W J Leslie RM, HMS Broadsword
PO (Sonar) G J R Libby, HMS Conqueror
Chief MEM(M) M D Townsend, HMS Argonaut
CPO (Diver) G M Trotter, Fleet Clearance Diving Team 3
CPO Aircrewman M J Tupper, No.846 NAS
LS (Radar) J D Warren, HMS Antelope
Posthumous
PO MEM(M) D R Briggs, HMS Sheffield
Cpl Aircrewman M D Love RM, No.846 NAS

Military Medal
Acting Cpl A R Bishop RM, 45 Cdo RM
Sgt T Collings RM
Sgt M Collins RM, 42 Cdo RM
Cpl M Eccles RM, 42 Cdo RM
Cpl D Hunt RM, 45 Cdo RM
Mne G W Marshall RM, 45 Cdo RM
Cpl S C Newland RM, 42 Cdo RM
Cpl H Siddall RM, 45 Cdo RM
Cpl C N H Ward RM, 42 Cdo RM
Sgt J D Wassell RM, M & AW Cadre RM

Distinguished Flying Medal
Sgt W C O'Brien RM, 3 CBAS

Queen's Gallantry Medal
Chief Eng Offr C K A Adams RFA, RFA Sir Galahad
Lt J K Boughton RN, No.825 NAS
MEA(M)1 K Enticknapp, HMS Ardent
Third Offr A Gudgeon RFA, RFA Sir Galahad
PO Medical Asst G A Meager, HMS Sheffield
Lt P J Sheldon RN, No.825 NAS
Third Eng B R Williams Merchant Navy, Atlantic Conveyor
Posthumous
Colour Sgt B Johnston RM, coxswain LCU F4, HMS Fearless

BRITISH ARMY

Distinguished Service Order
Maj C N G Delves, Devonshire and Dorsets,
 co D Sqdn 22 SAS Regt
Maj C P B Keeble, 2 Para
Lt Col H W R Pike MBE, co 3 Para
Lt Col M I E Scott, co 2 Scots Guards

Distinguished Service Cross
WO2 J H Phillips, 49 EOD Sqdn RE

Military Cross
Maj M H Argue, 3 Para
Capt T W Burls, Parachute Regt,
 D Sqdn 22 SAS Regt
Maj D A Collett, 3 Para
Lt C S Connor, 2 Para
Maj J H Crosland, 2 Para
Maj C D Farrar-Hockley, 2 Para
Maj J P Kiszely, 2 Scots Guards
Lt R A D Lawrence, 2 Scots Guards
Capt W A McCracken, 29 Cdo Regt RA
Capt A J G Wight, Welsh Guards
Posthumous
Capt G J Hamilton, Green Howards,
 D Sqdn 22 SAS Regt

Distinguished Flying Cross
Capt S M Drennan AAC, 656 Sqdn AAC
Capt J G Greenhalgh RCT, 656 Sqdn AAC

Distinguished Conduct Medal
Cpl D Abols, 2 Para
Staff Sgt B Faulkner, 3 Para
Sgt J C Meredith, 2 Para
WO2 W Nicol, 2 Scots Guards
Sgt J S Pettinger, 3 Para
Posthumous
Pte S Illingsworth, 2 Para
Gdsmn J B C Reynolds, 2 Scots Guards

Conspicious Gallantry Medal - Posthumous
Staff Sgt J Prescott, 49 EOD Sqdn RE

Military Medal
Cpl I P Bailey, 3 Para
L/Cpl S A Bardsley, 2 Para
Sgt T I Barrett, 2 Para
L/Cpl M W L Bentley, 2 Para
Sgt D S Boultby, 17 Port Regt RCT
Cpl T Brookes Royal Signals
Cpl T J Camp, 2 Para
Pte G S Carter, 2 Para
Gdsmn S M Chapman, 1 Welsh Guards
Cpl J A Foran, 9 Para Sqdn RE
Sgt D Fuller, 3 Para
Pte B J Grayling, 2 Para
Cpl T W Harley, 2 Para
Bdr E M Holt, 29 Cdo Regt RA
Sgt R W Jackson, 2 Scots Guards
L/Cpl D J Loveridge, 1 Welsh Guards
Sgt J G Mather, SAS
Sgt P H R Naya, 16 Field Ambulance RAMC
WO2 B T Neck, 1 Welsh Guards
Gdsmn A S Pengelly, 2 Scots Guards
L/Cpl L J L Standish, 2 Para
Sgt R H Wrega, 9 Para Sqdn RE
Posthumous
Pte R J de M Absolon, 3 Para
L/Cpl G D Bingley, 2 Para

ROYAL AIR FORCE

Distinguished Service Cross
Flt Lt D H S Morgan RAF, Nos.899/800 NAS, HMS Hermes

Distinguished Flying Cross
Wing Cdr P T Squire AFC RAF, co 1(F) Sqdn RAF
Sqdn Ldr R U Langworthy AFC RAF, 18 Sqdn RAF
Sqdn Ldr C N McDougall RAF, Vulcan aircrew
Sqdn Ldr J J Pook RAF, 1(F) Sqdn RAF
Flt Lt W F M Withers RAF, Vulcan aircrew

Air Force Cross
Wing Cdr D Emmerson RAF, Nimrod aircrew
Sqdn Ldr R Tuxford RAF, Victor aircrew
Flt Lt H C Burgoyne RAF, 47 Sqdn RAF
Sqdn Ldr A M Roberts RAF, 47 Sqdn RAF

Queen's Gallantry Medal
Flt Lt A J Swan RAF, co No.1 EOD Unit RAF
Flt Sgt B W Jopling, 18 Sqdn RAF

BIBLIOGRAPHY

GENERAL and POLITICAL

Coll, Alberto R and Anthony C. Arend, editors, "The Falklands War: Lessons for Strategy, Diplomacy and International Law", George Allen and Unwin, 1985

Daynes, John A, "The Forces Postal History of the Falkland Islands and the Task Force", The Forces Postal History Society, 1983

Goebel, Julius, "The Struggle for the Falkland Islands: A Study in Legal and Diplomatic History", Yale University Press, 1982

Hastings, Max and Simon Jenkins, "The Battle for the Falklands", Michael Joseph, 1983

HMSO, "Falkland Islands Review: Report of a Committee of Privy Counsellors (The Franks Report)", 1983

HMSO, "The Falklands Campaign: The Lessons", 1982

HMSO, "The Falkland Islands: The Facts", 1982

HMSO, Foreign and Commonwealth Office, "The Disputed Islands, The Falklands Crisis: A History and Background"

HMSO, House of Commons, "The Falklands Campaign: A Digest of Debates in the House of Commons 2nd April to 15th June 1982", 1982

Middlebrook, Martin, "Task Force: The Falklands War, 1982", Revised edition, Penguin Books, 1987 - as one of the best military authors, one of the best accounts

Sunday Express Magazine Team, "War in the Falklands: The Campaign in Pictures", Weidenfeld and Nicolson, 1982

Sunday Times Insight Team, "The Falklands War: The Full Story", Andre Deutsch, 1982

Way, Peter, editor, "The Falklands War in 14 parts", Marshall Cavendish, 1983

MILITARY and COMBINED OPERATIONS

Arthur, Max, "Above All, Courage: The Falklands Front Line: First-hand Accounts", Sidgwick and Jackson, 1985

Fox, Robert, "Eyewitness Falklands: A Personal Account of the Falklands Campaign", Methuen, 1982

Jolly, Rick, "The Red and Green Life Machine: A Diary of the Falklands Field Hospital", Century, 1983

Kitson, Linda, The Official War Artist, "The Falklands War: A Visual Diary", Michael Beazley, 1982

McGowan, Robert and Jeremy Hands, "Don't Cry for Me Sergeant Major", Futura, 1983

Perrett, Bryan, "Weapons of the Falklands Conflict", Blandford Press, 1982

Supplement to The London Gazette, 8th October 1982 - British gallantry awards

AVIATION, including NAVAL

Braybrook, Roy, "Battle for the Falklands (3), Air Forces", Osprey Men-at-Arm Series, 1982

"British Aerospace: Harrier and Sea Harrier", Osprey Publishing, 1984

Burden, Rodney A., Michael I. Draper, Douglas A. Rough, Colin R. Smith and David L. Wilton, "Falklands: The Air War", British Aviation Research Group, 1986 - quite outstanding scholarship so soon after the conflict

Ethell, Jeffrey and Alfred Price, "Air War: South Atlantic", Sidgwick and Jackson, 1984

LAND FORCES, including MARINES

Fowler, William, "Battle for the Falklands (1), Land Forces", Osprey Men-at-Arm Series, 1982

Frost, John, Major-General, "2 PARA, Falklands: The Battalion at War", Buchan and Enright, 1983

Gander, Terry, "Encyclopaedia of the Modern British Army", Patrick Stephens, 2nd edition, 1982

Geraghty, Tony, "This is the SAS: A Pictorial History of the Special Air Service Regiment", Arms and Armour Press, 1982

HMSO, "The British Army in the Falklands 1982", 1983

Keegan, John, "World Armies", MacMillan, 1983

Ladd, James D, "SBS: The Invisible Raiders: The History of the Special Boat Squadron from World War Two to the Present", Arms and Armour Press, 1983

McManners, Hugh, Captain, Royal Artillery, "Falklands Commando", William Kimber, 1984

Strawson, John, "A History of the S.A.S. Regiment", Secker and Warburg, 1984

Thompson, Julian, "No Picnic: 3 Commando Brigade in the South Atlantic: 1982", Secker and Warburg, 1985

Vaux, Nick, "March to the South Atlantic: 42 Commando Royal Marines in the Falklands War", Buchan and Enright, 1986

Weeks, John, Colonel, "Jane's Pocket Book: Armies of the World", Janes, 1981

NAVAL and MARITIME

Beaver, Paul, "Modern Combat Ships 2, 'Invincible' Class", Ian Allan, 1984

BP Shipping Ltd, "Operation Corporate: BP Shipping Limited's Involvement in the Falkland Island Crisis 1982", 1982

Brown, David, "The Royal Navy and the Falklands War", Leo Cooper, 1987 - thorough coverage of the Royal Navy's part

Director of Naval Air Warfare, "Flight Deck, The Fleet Air Arm Quarterly: Falklands Edition", Journal, Ministry of Defence, 1982

English, Adrian and Anthony Watts, "Battle for the Falklands (2), Naval Forces", Osprey Men-at-Arm Series, 1982

Hill, J.R., Rear Admiral, R.N., "The Royal Navy: Today and Tomorrow", Ian Allan, 1982

Gavshon, Arthur and Desmond Rice, "The Sinking of the 'Belgrano", Secker and Warburg, 1984

"Jane's Fighting Ships, 1981/82"

Koburger Jnr, Charles W, "Sea Power in the Falklands", Praeger, 1983

Lockett, Andrew, Neil Munro and David Wells, editors, "H.M.S. Endurance 1981-82 Deployment: A Season of Conflict", Andrew Lockett, 1983

Marriot, Leo, "Modern Combat Ships 3, Type 42", Ian Allan, 1985

Meyer OBE, R.N., Cdr C. J., "Modern Combat Ships 1, 'Leander' Class", Ian Allan, 1984

P & O Steam Navigation Company, "P & O in the Falklands; A Pictorial Record, 5th April - 25th September 1982", 1982

Preston, Anthony, "Sea Combat off the Falklands", Willow Books, 1982

Reynolds, Clark, "Command of the Sea", 1976

Ross, P.J., editor, "HMS Invincible: The Falklands Deployment 2nd April - 17th September 1982", privately printed, 1983

Royal Fleet Auxiliary Service, "The RFA in the Falklands", (Journal)

Speed, Keith, "Sea Change: The Battle for the Falklands and the Future of Britain's Navy", Ashgrove Press, 1982

Tinker, Hugh, compiled by, "A Message from the Falklands: The Life and Gallant Death of David Tinker, Lieutenant R.N.", Junction Books, 1982

Villar, Roger, Captain, "Merchant Ships at War: The Falklands Experience", Conway Maritime Press, 1984

BACKGROUND

Cawkwell, Mary, "The Falkland Story 1592-1982", Anthony Nelson, 1983

Headland, Robert, "The Island of South Georgia", Cambridge University Press, 1984

Smith, John, "74 Days, An Islander's Diary of the Falklands Occupation", Century Publishing, 1984

Strange, Ian J., "The Falklands Islands", David and Charles, 1983, 3rd edition

INDEX

PEOPLE, PLACES AND EVENTS

Abols, Army, Cpl D 89, 127
Absolon, Army, Pte R J de M 104, 127
Adams RFA, Chief Eng Offr C K A 87, 126
Aircraft and helicopter losses in summary, *Argentine* 23-4, 37, 71-4, *British* 27, 33, 35
Ajax Bay, Falklands 80-1, 85, 91, *landings a* 75-7
Aldershot, Britain 25
Allara, Rear-Adm Jorge 22
Allen MN, Capt W 41
Anaya, Adm Jorge 13, 20
Anson, Adm Lord 13
Arbroath, Britain 25, 114
Arca, CANA, Lt 123
Ardiles, FAA, Lt 122
Argentina
- Geography and history 12-15
- Diplomatic responses 17, 19-20
Argue, Army, Maj M H 103-4, 127
Armoured vehicles, *Argentine Panhard armoured cars* 23, 38, 107
Armoured vehicles, *British Scorpion and Scimitar light tanks* 34, 48, 76, 91, 108-9, 110
Arraras, FAA, Lt 124
Artillery, *Argentine* 23-4, 38, 98, 105, 107, 108, 110, 112-3, *105mm* 23, 38, 81, 87-8, *155mm*, 23, 38
Artillery, *British* 33-4, 76-7, 81, 86, 89, 98, 104-5, 106, 109, 111-2, *105mm* 33-4, 77, 87-8, 91, 102, 103, 105, 106, 108-9, 110
Ascension 41, 52, 57, 94
- Geography and history 43
- Task Force base and staging post 43-4
- Defense of 43, 82
- RAF operations involving 35-7, 43-4, 53, 55-6, 57, 63, 82, 92, 98, 115
- Ships arriving and departing 40-2, 47, 48-9, 53, 58, 63, 66, 82, 92
- Arrival and departure of 3 Commando Bde 47, 58, 114
- Aircraft staging flights to and from 44, 54, 57, 82, 92, 98
Astiz, Lt-Cdr Alfredo 16, 52, 82, 92
Auld, Lt Cdr A D 55, 73, 123, 126
Averill RFA, Capt D G M 62
Azores, Central Atlantic 42
Babbington RM, Capt P M 106, 108, 126
Badcock RN, Capt P 46
Bailey, Army, Cpl I P 104, 127
Bailey RFA, Capt J A 62
Balfour RN, Capt H M 58
Barber MN, Capt G 41
Bardsley, Army, L/Cpl S A 89, 127
Barker, Capt N J 15
Barrett, Army, Sgt T I 89, 109, 127
Barrow RN, Capt M E 39, 125
Barton, Flt Lt P C 73, 122
Bases, *Argentine* 22, 71-72, *British* 24-5, 43-45, 94
Batt, Lt Cdr G W J 73, 82, 120, 126
Baugh, Wing Cdr D L 41

Bean, CANA, Lt 123
Beaumont MN, Capt J C 58
Beetham, Air Chief Marshall Sir Michael 24
Belaunde, Pres Terry 19
Belize, Central America 40
Benitez, CANA, Lt 122
Benitz, FAA, Capt 123
Bennett RN, Lt A R C 69, 126
Bentley, Army, L/Cpl M W L 89, 127
Berkeley Sound 13, 57
Bernhardt, FAA, Lt 124
Best, Cdr R T N 58
Bicain, Lt-Cdr 51
Bingley, Army, L/Cpl G D 89, 127
Bishop RM, Acting Cpl A R 106, 126
Bishop RN, Lt R J 53
Bithell, Lt Cdr J 53
Black RN, Capt J J 41, 125
"Black Buck" Operations 37, 44; *No 1* 54, 55-6, *No 2* 56-7, 60, *No 3* 63, *No 4* 82, *No 5* 82, 96-7, *No 6* 92, 96-7, *No 7* 98, 101-2
Blisset, Lt Cdr M S 73
Boeing 707 incidents, Argentine Air Force 50, 51
Bluff Cove - see Fitzroy
Boca House, Falklands 88-9
Bolzan, FAA, Lt 124
Bono, FAA, Lt 123
Booth, Lt Cdr M D 95, 126
Bootherstone, Cdr P J 39, 126
Boswell RM, Capt R 75
Bougainville, Antoine de 13-14
Boughton RN, Lt J K 102, 126
Boultby, Army, Sgt D S 102, 127
Bourne RFA, Second Off R 67
Bowman, Wing Cdr A W 46
Braithwaite, Lt Cdr 123
Bramall, Gen Sir Edwin 24,
Briggs, PO MEM(M) D R 61, 126
Britain and British Government
- Diplomatic and political responses 13-14, 17-21
- Military response 21, 24-27
- Falklands defence policy 113
British Antarctic Survey 12, 15-16
British Task Force 19-21, 24, 60, 113
- Land, sea and air forces taking part 24-7
- Departures for South Atlantic 21, 40-1, 46, 48, 52-3, 57-8, 66-7, 92, 98-9, 116-7
- Planning and command decisions 47, 53
- Forces returning to UK 51, 63, 65, 82, 84, 92-3, 98, 114-7
- Disposition of forces in summary 42, 47-8, 50, 54, 59, 67-8, 83, 93, 99-100
- Advanced Group of ships 39-40, 42, 47, 50
- Amphibious Task Group (3 Cdo Bde) 40, 44, 47, 49, 52-3, 57-8, 67, 70, 76-7
- Ascension Island, British Forces Support Unit 43-5
- "Bristol" Group of ships 62, 66, 84,

- Carrier Battle Group (CVBG) 40, 47, 49-50, 52, 54, 55, 58, 60-1, 65, 67, 69-70, 77, 82, 84, 85-6, 92, 93, 96, 98
- LSL Group of ships 49, 53, 58, 63
- South Georgia Task Group 42, 47, 50-1, 54
- 5th Infantry Bde and transports 57, 63, 66, 91, 92-3
Brize Norton, Britain 25, 36, 40, 42, 114
Broadwater, Lt Cdr 121
Brookes, Army, Cpl T 57, 127
Bruen RN, Lt N A 87, 126
Buenos Aires, Argentina 12, 14, 19-20
Bull Hill, Falklands 80-1, 85
Bunn, Wing Cdr O G 39
Burdett RM, Cpl J 106, 126
Burdwood Bank, south of Falklands 56
Burgoyne, Flt Lt H C 37, 127
Burls, Army, Capt T W 102, 127
Burne RN, Capt C P O 41
Burntside House and Pond, Falklands 88-9
Busser, Rear-Adm of Marines Carlos 18, 22
Bustos, FAA, Lt 122
Butler, Army, Maj P P 103
Byron, Capt 13
Cameron RM, Maj C P 75, 126
Camilla Creek House, Falklands 85, 88-9
Camp, Army, Cpl T J 89, 127
Campbell, Cdr R J 49
Campbeltown, Britain 41
Canning RN, Capt W R 41, 125
Canter, Cdr P C B 62
Cape Horn, Chile 13
Cape Pembroke, Falklands 113
Carrington, Lord 20
Carter, Army, Pte G S 89, 127
Casco, FAA, Lt 122
Casey, PO Aircrewman 119
Castillo, FAA, Lt 123
Castillo, FAA, Lt O 124
Casualties, *Argentine* 16, 18, 24, 52, 56, 60-1, 65, 76, 84, 88, 96, 105, 109, 122-4, "red-on-red" 56, 65, 92, 122
Casualties, *British* 27, 61, 65, 70, 77, 78, 79-80, 82, 84, 86, 89-90, 91, 96, 101-2, 103-4, 105-6, 107-8, 109, 110-11, 112, 116, 119-21 "blue-on-blue" 81, 97, 101, 105, 121
Cerro Montevideo, Falklands 80-1, 85
Chapman, Gdsmn S M 102, 127
Charleston, USA 92
Chartres, Falklands 79
Chaundler, Lt Col D R 108-9
Chester RM, Maj J 75
Chile 12, 53, *British helicopter incident* 69, 120
Choiseul Sound, Falklands 61, 66, 80-1, 100-1
Christmas Harbour, Falklands 78-9
Church Crookham, Britain 25
Civilians, Falklands 19, 89, 102
Clapp RN, Cdre M C 25, 40, 47, 53, 70, 77
Clark, Lt Cdr H S 90, 102, 126
Clark MN, Capt J G 49,
Clarke MN, Capt W J C 49
Clio, HMS 14
Cockton, Army, L/Cpl 121
Cole RM, Capt M A F 105
Colina, FAA, Wing Cdr de la 124
Collett, Army, Maj D A 103-4, 127
Collings RM, Sgt T 57, 126
Collins RM, Sgt M 107-8, 126

Commanders, *Argentine* 22-3, 37-8; *British* 24-25, 35, 39-40, 41, 45, 46, 49, 50, 53, 55, 58, 62, 67, 68, 75, 83, 87, 92, 93, 96, 99, 103, 105, 106, 108, 110
Commonwealth, British, response to invasion 20
Comodoro Rivadavia, Argentina 72
Coningsby, Britain 25, 36, 82
Connor, Army, Lt C S 89, 109, 127
Coronation Point, Falklands 88-9
Costa Mendez, Nicanor 20
Coward RN, Capt J F 39, 125
Cow Bay, Falklands 57
Craig, Cdr C J S 41, 126
Crosland, Army, Maj J H 87, 89, 97, 108-9, 127
Cruzado, FAA, Lt 124
Cuerva, FAA, Capt 122
Culdrose, Britain 25
Cumberland Bay, and East, South Georgia 16, 51-2, 59, 84
Curacao, West Indies 40, 49, 53
Curtiss, Air Marshall Sir John 24
Curtiss RN, Lt W A 73, 119, 122
Dalzell, Army, Maj I E 110
Darwin, Falklands 85, 87, 88-9, *SAS raid on* 75-6, 78, *Battle for* – see Goose Green
Darwin Hill, Falklands 88-9
Davidoff, Constantino 15
Davis, Capt 13
Davis RM, Maj R J 105
Delves, Army, Maj C N G 50, 52, 76, 127
Devine, Lt Cdr J G 67
Devonport, Britain 25, 40, 48-9, 52-3, 62-3, 66, 98
Diaz, FAA, Capt 123
Dickinson RFA, Capt J B 41
Dillon, AB (Radar) J E 79, 126
Dingemans RN, Capt P G V 53, 125
Diplomatic negotiations 16-17, 19-20
Dixon RM, Maj R C 75
Donaldille, FAA, Capt 123
Douglas, Falklands 90,
Drennan, Army, Capt S M 111, 127
Dunlop RFA, Cdre S C 39, 125
Dutton, Lt Cdr B F 79, 125
Dytor RM, Lt C I 106, 126
Eccles RM, Cpl M 108, 126
EEC – see European Economic Community
Ellerbeck, Lt-Cdr J A 52, 126
Ellerby MN, Capt D A 53
Emmerson, Wing Cdr D 46, 127
Enticknapp, MEA(M)1 K 79, 126
Esplin-Jones, Cdr C J 53
Estancia House, Falklands 103, *secured* 95-6
European Economic Community, response to invasion 19-20
Evans RM, Pilot Sgt 120
Evans MN, Capt H 58
Evelyn Hill, Falklands 80-1, 85
Exocet – see Missiles
Eyton-Jones RN, Lt Cdr 119
Falkland Islands (and TEZ)
- Geography and history 11-14
- Argentine invasion and occupation of 17-19, 22-24
- Argentine defences on 18, 22-4, 37-8, 76, 103, 105, 107, 108, 110, 112
- Argentine supply operations around 24, 61, 64, 81-2
- British ships and aircraft arriving 25-7, 31-2, 37, 47, 55-6, 63, 67, 69-70, 84, 93-4, 96, 98, 116-7

131

- Plans for retaking 47
- British air and sea attacks on 54, 55-6, 60-1, 64-5, 77, 82, 84, 92, 101-2
- Special forces and deception operations on and around 57, 64, 66, 69-70, 81
- 3 Commando Bde's landings 75-6
- 5th Infantry Bde arrives 92, 93
- Surrender of Argentine forces 90, 112
- "Fortress Falklands" 113

Falkland, Lord 13
Falkland Sound 64-5, 70, 76, 101
Fanning Head, SBS raid on 75-6
Farias, FAA, Lt 122
Farley RFA, Capt M S J 41
Farrar-Hockley, Army, Maj C D 87, 89, 108-9, 127
Faslane, Britain 25, 40
Faulkner, Army, Staff Sgt B 104, 127
Fawley, Britain 46, 49
Fellows, Fleet CPO M G 79, 126
Field, Army, Lt Col G W 96
Fieldhouse, Adm Sir John 24, 47
Fitzroy and Bluff Cove, Falklands 57, 96-7, 101, 108, 110-11, 112, *British moves to* 96-7, 101, *air attack on Welsh Guards at* 100-1
Foran, Army, Cpl J A 111, 127
Fortuna Glacier, South Georgia 50, 51
Forward Brigade Maintenance Area 96
Forward Operating Base 91, 97, 102
Foster MN, Capt G F 67
Fox RM, Lt C 105-6, 126
Fox Bay and Fox Bay East, Falklands 24, 38, 57, 65-6, 77, 113
Francis RM, Lt 120
Francis RM, Colour Sgt M J 82, 102, 126
Frederiksen, Lt Cdr R V 73, 122-3
Freeman RFA, Capt D F 62
Fuller, Army, Sgt D 104, 127
Fulton MN, Capt A 53
Furze Bush Pass, Falklands 108
Gaffrey RFA, Capt J W 49,
Gallantry awards, British 125
Galtieri, Gen Leopoldo 13, 20, 112
Garcia, FAA, Lt 124
Garcia, Lt Gen Osvaldo 18
Gardiner RM, Capt I R 105
Garwood, Lt Cdr D G 53
Gavazzi, FAA, Lt 122
Gedge, Lt Cdr 123
Georgetown, Ascension 43
Gibraltar 29, 39-40, 48, 57, 59, 62-4, 66-7
Giminez, FAA, Lt 124
Glover, Flt Lt J W 77, 120
Goat Ridge, Falklands 105, 108, 110-11
Gonzalez, FAA, Lt 122
Goose Green, Falklands 19, 24, 37-8, 56-7, 65, 75, 78, 81, 84, 92, 95-6, 101, 111, 112, *British attacks on* 55, 61, *approach to and Battle for* 85, 87-90, *airfield* 88-9
Gosport, Britain 25, 46, 52
Gough, Cdr A B 49
Government House, Stanley 17, 112
Grant MN, Capt D 83
Grantham Sound, Falklands 75-6, 78-9, 88
Grass Island, South Georgia 51,
Grayling, Army, Pte B J 89, 127
Green RFA, Capt G R 39, 126

Greenhalgh, Army, Capt J G 89, 109, 127
Green Mountain, Ascension 43
Greenop, Lt Cdr J P S 53
Griffin, Army, Staff Sgt 121
Griffin RM, L/Cpl 120
Grose RN, Capt A 62
Grytviken, South Georgia 12, 15-17, 51-2, 84, *Battle for* 16, *Recapture of* 17, 51-2
Guadagnini, FAA, Lt 123
Gudgeon RFA, Third Offr A 82, 102, 126
Guy MN, Capt J W M 53
Haig, Alexander 20, *shuttle mission* 19-20
Hale RN, Lt M 73, 122-3
Halliday, Cdr R I C 49
Hamilton, Lt Cdr C F B 53
Hamilton, Army, Capt G J 65, 101-2, 127
Hare, Flt Lt 122-3
Harley, Army, Cpl T W 89, 127
Harriet, Mount – see Mount Harriet
Harris RN, Capt M G T 62
Harrison MN, Capt E 58
Hart-Dyke RN, Capt D 39
Hatton MN, Capt B 49
Helicopter crash at sea, SAS 70
Hellberg, Army, Lt Col I J 75
Henderson, Sir Nicholas 20
Henry RFA, Second Eng Offr P A 102, 126
Herbert, Vice-Adm P G M 24
Hereford, Britain 25
Hestesletten, South Georgia 51-2
Hoddinott RN, Capt A P 39
Holloway, Lt Cdr M C G 53
Holroyd-Smith, Army, Lt Col M J 75
Holt, Bdr E M 106, 127
Holt, Army, Lt Col G A 96
Hope, Capt G L 49
Hound Bay, South Georgia 51
Hunt RM, Cpl D 106, 126
Hunt RM, Lt Col M P J 75
Hunt, Governor Rex 11, 17-18, 40
Hunter RFA, Capt A E T 53
Hutchings RM, Lt R 69, 126
Ibanez, FAA, Lt 122
Ibarlucea, FAA, Lt 122
Illingsworth, Army, Pte S 89, 127
Imrie, Ldg Aircrewman P B 69, 126
Isle of Grain, Britain 46,
Iveson, Sqn Ldr R D 88, 120
Jackson MN, Capt P 62
Jackson, Army, Sgt R W 111, 127
James RN, Capt N C H 62
Jenkins MN, Capt R 58
Jenner, Army, Maj R 87, 108
Joffre, Maj-Gen Oscar 37-8
Johnston MN, Colour Sgt B 82, 101, 126
Johnston, Cdr S H G 62
Jolly, Surgeon Cdr R T 77
Jones MN, Capt D O W 46
Jones, Lt Col H 75, 81, 87, 89, 116, 125,
Jopling, Flt Sgt B W 87, 127
Jukic, FAA, Lt 122
Keeble, Army, Maj C P B 87, 89-90, 127
Kidney Island, Falklands 56
King Edward Point, South Georgia 12, 15-16, 51
King George Bay, Falklands 85-6

Kinloss, Britain 25, 36, 47
Kinnear MN, Capt R I 49
Kiszely, Army, Maj J P 110-11, 127
Lafonia, East Falklands 57, 97, 101
Lami Dozo, Brig Gen Basilio 13, 20
Lane-Nott, Cdr R C 39
Langworthy, Sqdn Ldr R U 92, 127
Larken RN, Capt E S 41, 125
Lawrence RFA, Capt D E 41, 126
Lawrence, Army, Lt R A D 111, 127
Lawton MN, Capt H R 58
Layard RN, Capt M H G 49
Layman RN, Capt C H 49, 125
Lazenby MN, Capt A 58
Leach, Adm Sir Henry 24
Leach RM, Sgt P J 17, 126
Leake, PO J S 79, 126
Leeming, Flt Lt J 73, 123
Leith, South Georgia 15-17, 51-2
Le Marchand, Cdr T M 58
Leslie RM, Sgt W J 79, 126
Lewin, Adm of the Fleet Sir Terence 24
Lexington, USS 14
Libby, PO (Sonar) G J R 87, 126
Lively Island, Falklands 96-7
Lively Sound, Falklands 80-1
Loch Striven, Britain 49
Logan RFA, Capt J 49
Lomas, Lt Cdr H J 75, 126
Lombardo, Vice-Adm Juan 22
London, Britain 19-20, 25
Longdon, Mount – see Mount Longdon
Lopez, FAA, Lt 123
Love, Cpl Aircrewman M D 57, 70, 126
Loveridge, Army, L/Cpl D J 102, 127
Lower Malo House, Falklands 91
Lucero, FAA, Lt 124
Luna, FAA, Lt 123
Lyneham, Britain 25, 35, 39-40
MacBride, Capt 13
McCarthy RFA, Capt P J 53
McCracken, Army, Capt W A 104, 109, 127
McCulloch RFA, Capt J 41
McDonald, Army, Maj R 75
McDougal, Sqdn Ldr C N 97, 127
McDougall RFA, Capt G P A 39
MacGregor RMAS, Capt A 53
McHarg RN, Lt 122
McKay, Sgt I J 103-4, 125
MacKinnon MN, Capt A 67
McQueen RN, Capt R 45
Magellan, Ferdinand 13
Malouines, Les Iles 13
Malvinas, Islas 13-14
Manzotti, FAA, Lt 123
Marchwood, Britain 25, 40, 52
Marham, Britain 25, 37,
Maritime Exclusion Zone (MEZ) 10, 18, 40, 48
Marquez, CANA, Lt 123
Marshall, Mne G W 106, 126
Mather, Army, Sgt J G 57, 127
Meager, PO Medical Asst G A 61, 126
Mendez, Snr Nicanor Costa 20
Menendez, Maj-Gen Mario 18, 81, 112
Meredith, Army, Sgt J C 89, 109, 127

MEZ – see Maritime Exclusion Zone
Middleton RN, Capt L E 41, 125
Middle Wallop, Britain 25
Miguel, CANA, Lt 124
Milford Haven, Britain 41, 46
Mills RM, Lt K P 16-17, 84, 126
Minefields, *Argentine, land, including clearing* 52, 88, 103, 107-8, 110, 112-3
Minefields, *Argentine, sea, including sweeping* 96, 113
Missiles, *Argentine Exocet* 14, 19, 23, 28, 29, 31, 37, 47, 55-6, 58, 60-1, 71, 82, 86, 92, 97, 102, 118, 119-21
Missiles, *British Exocet* 28, *Rapier* 34, 66, 76-7, 82, 84, 87, 92, 101, 123-4, *Sea Cat* 28, 79, 86, 123-4, *Sea Dart* 28, 61, 64, 86, 92, 97, 102, 121-2, 124, *Sea Skua* 28, 42, 60, 82, *Sea Wolf* 28, 61, 64-5, 70, 78, 82, 84, 86, 122-3, *Shrike* 37, 82, 92, 96-7, *Sidewinder* 28, 37, 44, 56, 72, 79-80, 82, 86, 97, 101, 115, 122-4, *Stinger* 78, 123
Montevideo, Uruguay 17, 36, 40, 48, 84, 94, 98
Montgomery, Sqn Ldr A C 53
Moody Brook, Falklands 17-18, 109
Moore, Maj-Gen J J 24, 34-5, 53, 66, 81, 84, 96-7, 112-3
Moraine Fiord, South Georgia 51
Morgan, Flt Lt D H S 73, 123-4, 127
Morgan, Army, Lt Col D P de C 96
Morgan, Sub-Lt P T 79, 126
Morrell RN, Lt C R W 73, 123
Morris RMAS, Capt J N 39
Morris MN, Capt P T 41
Mortimer, Flt Lt I 97, 121
Morton, Cdr A 41, 126
Morton MN, Capt J P 41
Mosse, Cdr P J 58
Mount Challenger, Falklands 107, 111, *British occupation of* 95-6
Mount Estancia, Falklands 90, 103, *British occupation of* 91, 95-6
Mount Harriet, Falklands 105, 112, *British approach to and Battle for* 96, 100-2, 106-8
Mount Kent, Falklands 77-8, 85, 87, 91-2, 101, 105, 107-8, *British occupation of* 86, 90-1, 95-6, 102
Mount Longdon, Falklands 103, *British approach to and Battle for* 96, 100-2, 103-4, 108
Mount Vernet 103
Mount William, Falklands 110-11, *British approach to and occupation of* 98, 102, 112
Mullet Creek, Falklands 17-18
Murrell Bridge, Falklands 103
NATO – see North Atlantic Treaty Organisation
Naya, Army, Sgt P H R 102, 127
Neame, Army, Maj P 87, 108
Neck, Army, WO2 B T 102, 127
Netheravon, Britain 25
New House, Falklands 90-1
Newland RM, Cpl S C 108, 126
Niblett RM, Capt J P 89, 126
Nicol, Army, WO2 W 111, 127
Nivoli, FAA, Lt 122
Norman RM, Maj M J 17-18, 106,
North MN, Capt I H 49, 86-7, 126
North RN, Lt N J 52, 126
North Atlantic Treaty Organisation, response to invasion 20
Northwood, Britain 16, 24, 47, 70, 87
Nott MP, John 20
Nunn RM, Capt C J 50, 113
Nunn RM, Lt R J 89, 126

133

O'Brien RM, Sgt W C 89, 126
Odiham, Britain 25, 37
Oliphant MN, Capt I A 41
Onslow RN, Capt 14
Operation Corporate – see British Task Force
Operation Keyhole 113
Operation Paraquet - see South Georgia, British recapture
Operation Rosario - see Falkland Islands, Argentine invasion of
Operation Springtrain 40
Operation Sutton - see San Carlos Water, landings at
Organisation of American States (OAS), response to invasion 20
Osborne, Army, Maj H M 103
Overbury RFA, Capt G P 41
Palaver, FAA, Lt 124
Parada, Maj-Gen Omar 37
Paraguayan War 22
Parkinson MP, Cecil 20
Parsons, Sir Anthony 20
Pebble Island 23, 37, 56-7, 81-2, 85-6, 96-7, 101-2, *SAS raid on* 64-5
Pedroza, FAA, Gp Capt 87, 90
Penfold, Flt Lt R 73, 122
Pengelly, Gdsmn A S 111, 127
Pentreath RN, Capt D 39, 125
Perez de Cuellar, Secretary Gen Javier 20
Peron, Evita and Juan 12
Perona, FAA, Lt 122
Peruvian peace proposals 20
Pettinger, Army, Sgt J S 104, 127
Philippi, CANA, Lt Cdr 123
Phillips, Army, WO2 J H 82, 127
Piaggi, Argentine Army, Lt Col 87
Pike, Army, Lt Col H W R 75, 91, 103-4, 127
Pitt RFA, Capt A F 41, 126
Pimua, FAA, Maj 123
Pleasant Peak 96-7, *post-war airfield near* 113
Plymouth, Britain 25, 57, 98
Pook, Sqdn Ldr J J 73, 121, 123, 127
Poole, Britain 25
Port Egmont, Falklands 13-14
Port Howard, Falklands 24, 38, 57, 64, 77-9, 82, 90-1, 112, *SAS action near* 101
Port King, Falklands 65, 79, 80-1
Portland, Britain 25, 40-1, 48-9, 52-3, 63, 66, 98
Port Louis, Falklands 13-14
Port Salvador, Falklands 57, 85-6
Port San Carlos 77, 80-1, 85, 87, 90-1, 95-7, 101-2, 103, *landings at* 75-6
Portsmouth, Britain 25, 40-1, 46, 48, 52-3, 57, 62-3, 66, 92, 98, 115
Port Stanley, Falklands 47
Port William, Falklands 18, 113
Prescott, Army, Staff Sgt J 82, 127
Price, Army, Maj S 110,
Prisoners-of-War, *Argentine* 35, 52, 54, 58, 63, 88, 90, 92, 98, 112-3, 114
Prisoners-of-War, *British* 16, 18, 35, 77
Puerto Deseado, Argentina 60
Puerto Madryn, Argentina 113
Puerto Soledad, Falklands 14
Punta Arenas, Chile 69
Purtcher-Wydenbruck RFA, Capt C A 41

Pym MP, Francis 20
Radar, *Argentine* 18, 37, 61, 65, 82, 92, 97, 113
Radar, *British* 18, 37, 43, 51, 61, 64, 86
Randall, WO1 R G 45
RCB – see Red Cross Box
Reagan, Pres Ronald 19-20
Reconnaissance flights, Argentine 50-1, 97, 102, British 37, 43-4, 47, 51, 63, 66, 77
Red Cross Box (RCB) 26, 48, 63, 67, 84, 94
Redmond RFA, Capt S 39
Reffell, Rear-Adm D 115
Reynell, L Cdr B E M 83
Reynolds RFA, Capt D A 46
Reynolds, Gdsmn J B C 111, 127
Rickard, Cdr P V 62
Rickett, Army, Lt Col J F 96
Rimmer MN, Capt P 46
Rintoul RN, Surgeon Captain A J 49
Rio de Janeiro, Brazil 84, 97, 98
Rio Gallegos, Argentina 71-2, 78
Rio Grande, Argentina 69, 71-2, 78, 82
Ritchie RN, Cdr A S 41
Roberts, Sqdn Ldr A M 37, 127
Roberts RFA, Capt P J G 41, 125
Roca, Snr Eduardo 20
Roe, Lt Cdr C E K 49
Ros, Snr Enrique 20
Rosas, Juan de 12
Rose, Army, Lt Col H M 75, 112
Rosyth, Britain 25, 40, 53, 63
Rowledge, Lt Cdr M 53
Rundle MN, Capt D M 49
St Athan, Britain 25
St Helena, South Atlantic 43
St Malo, France 13
St Mawgan, Britain 25, 36, 42, 57, 114
Salt RN, Capt J F T G 39, 61
Salvesen & Co, Christian 15
San Carlos 67, 80-1, 85, 91, 96, *landings at* 75-6, *defence of* 95
San Carlos Water 26, 53, 57, 81, 84, 94, 96-7, 98, 100-1, 105, 113,
- Preparations for landings at 66, 70,
- Approach to and landings at 69-70, 75-77
- Air battles around and attacks on 77-80, 82, 86, 91
- Defence and supply of 90-2, 96, 101-2
- As Operating base 81, 87, 96
San Julian, Argentina 71-2, 78
San Martin, General Jose de 12
Sapper Hill 18, 110, *British occupation of* 98, 112
Saunders Island, Falklands 13
Scott MN, Capt A 67
Scott, Lt Cdr A M 67
Scott, Army, Lt Col M I E 96, 110-11, 127
Scott-Masson MN, Capt D J 41
Seccombe RM, Col T 75
Senn, FAA, Lt 123
Sennybridge, Britain 25, 34
Sephton, Lt Cdr J M 79, 126
Seymour RFA, Capt B A 41
Seymour, Cdr R P 62
Shag House Cove, Falklands 80, 82
Sheldon RN, Lt P J 102, 126
Sheridan RM, Maj J M G 50, 52

134

Ships, lost or damaged in summary, *Argentine,* 72-3, *British* 27, 71-2, 79, 86,
Sibun, Army, Maj C S 96
Siddall RM, Cpl H 106, 126
Slack MN, Capt M J 62
Smith RN, Lt D A 73, 123-4
Sorling Valley, South Georgia 51
Southampton 41, 49, 57, 63, 66, 98, 114
Southby-Tailyour, Maj S E 47, 76,
Southern Thule 12, *Argentine occupation and British reoccupation* 14, 98, 112-3
South Georgia 12, 35, 40, 63, 84, 87, 94, 98-9, 113
- Argentine landings 15-17
- RAF recce missions to 37, 47, 51
- British recapture of 42, 50-2
- As Task Force base 58-9, 67, 84, 93-4, 99
- Arrival of 5th Infantry Bde 83-4
South Jason Island, Falklands 61
South Sandwich Islands 12
Squier, Lt Cdr D J S 55, 126
Squire, Wing Cdr P T 68, 73, 121, 127
Stables, Wing Cdr A J 90,
Standish, Army, L/Cpl L J L 89, 127
Stanley, Falkland Islands - see also Falkland Islands 11, 14, 56-7, 64, 80, 82
- Government House 18, 112
- Argentine invasion and occupation 17-18, 23-4, 38
- Airfield 17-18, 24, 55, 60, 113, *RAF Stanley* 113
- British land and sea moves towards 81, 85-7, 90-1, 96-7, 101-2, 111, 112
- RAF missions against 36, 44, 54, 57, 60, 82, 92, 96-7, 98, 101-2
- Plans for taking 53, 86-7, 96, 98, 101
- Civilian casualties in 102
- British reoccupation of, and subsequent operations 112-3, 115, 117
Stanley, Lt-Cdr I 51-2, 125
Stewart RN, Lt D J 105-6, 126
Stiles, Lt Cdr D J 58
Stockman MN, Capt M J 67
Stockwell MN, Capt A J 41
Stromness Bay, South Georgia 51
Strong, Capt 13
Submarine operations and alerts, *Argentine* 18, 47, 50-2, 55-6, 60, 64,
Submarine operations, *British* 40, 47, 55-6, 57, 60, 63, 69, 87
Surrender negotiations, British and Argentine, *South Georgia* 16, 52, *Falklands* 18, 90, 112, *Southern Thule* 113
Sussex Mountains, Falklands 66, 75-6, 78, 80-1, 85, 87, 88, 91,
Swan, Flt Lt A J 91-2, 127
Swan Inlet House, Falklands, 2 Paras move to 96-7
Swan island, Falklands 64, 79-80,
"Tabbing" by British Paras 87, 90-1, 95-6
Takacs, Snr Esteban 20
Taylor RN, Lt 119
Taylor MN, Capt J A M 49
Taylor, Cdr J B 39
Teal and Teal River Inlet, Falklands 78-9, 86-7, 90-1, 95-6
Terras MN, Capt A 83
TEZ – see Total Exclusion Zone
Thatcher, Prime Minister Margaret 19-20
Thomas, Lt Cdr N W 73, 123, 126

Thomas RN, Lt S R 73, 122, 126
Thompson, Brig J H 25, 40, 47, 53, 70, 75, 77, 81, 86-7, 92, 96, 106, 109, 112
Thomson RM, Maj J J 75
Thorburn, Lt Cdr M St J D A 58
Thornewill, Lt Cdr S C 126
Time differences (including "Zulu" time) 9
Tobin, Cdr N J 41, 126
Tomba, FAA, Major 123
Top Malo House, attack on 95-6
Total Exclusion Zone (TEZ) 10, 54, 55-6, 57, 60, 64, 67, 81, 84, 85, 90, 92, 94, 98, 113
Townsend, Chief MEM(M) M D 79, 126
TRALA – see Tug, Repair and Logistic Area
Trant, Lieut-Gen Sir Richard 24
Trelew, Argentina 71
Tristan da Cunha, South Atlantic 49, 84
Trombeta, Capt C 14, 16
Trotter, CPO (Diver) G M 87, 126
Tug, Repair and Logistic Area (TRALA) 26, 59, 63, 67, 81, 84, 93-4, 96, 98-9
Tumbledown Mountain, Falklands 111, *British approach to and Battle for* 101-2, 105, 110-11, 112
Tupper, CPO Aircrewman M J 87, 126
Tuxford, Sqdn Ldr R 56-7, 127
Twomey MN, Capt M H C 62
Two Sisters, Falklands 105, 107, 111, 112, *British approach to and Battle for* 96, 100-2, 105-6
Tyne, HMS 14
Unexploded bombs (UXB) 28, 30, 71-2, 76, 78-80, 81-2, 85-7, 91-2, 98, 101, 118
United Nations 19, *Resolution 2065 (1965)* 14, *Resolution 502 (1988)* 19-20
United States and Falklands 14, *and Ascension* 43, *response to invasion* 20, *aid to Britain* 20, 36, 44
Ushuaia, Argentina 56
Utrecht, Treaty of 13
UXB – see Unexploded bombs
Vancouver, Canada 52
Vaux RM, Lt Col N F 75, 106-8, 125
Vazquez, FAA, Ensign 124
Vazquez, FAA, Lt J 124
Velasco, FAA, Lt 124
Vernet, Louis 14
Verde Mountains, The, Falklands 76
Vespucci, Amerigo 13
Videla, Lieut Gen 13
Viola, Gen 13
Volponi, FAA, Lt 123
Waddington, Britain 25, 37, 54
Wallace MN, Capt K J 62
Wallace RFA, Capt R W M 49
Waller MN, Capt P R 46
Wall Mountain, Falklands 107-8
Ward RM, Cpl C N H 108, 126
Ward, Cdr N D 55, 73, 123-4, 126
Warren, LS (Radar) J D 82, 126
Washington DC, USA 19-20
Wassell RM, Sgt J D 105-6, 126
Weatherall RN, Capt J L 62
Webb, Lt Cdr G B 58
Weert, Sebald de 13
Wells-Cole RM, Maj G V J O'N 75
West, Cdr A W J 49, 80, 126
Wheen RM, Capt D G 106,

135

White RN, Capt H M 62
Whitehead RM, Lt Col A F 75, 91, 105-6, 125
Whitelaw MP, William 20,
Wideawake airfield, Ascension 36, 42-4, 54, 57,
Wight, Army, Capt A J G 57, 127
William, Mount – see Mount William
Williams MN, Third Eng B R 87, 126
Williams MN, Capt N 46
Wilson, Brig M J A 25, 92, 96
Wireless Ridge, Falklands 103, *British approach to and Battle for* 101-2, 103-4, 108-9, 112
Withers, Flt Lt W F M 55, 57, 127
Wittering, Britain 25, 37, 57, 82
Wood, Lt Cdr N D 53

Woodhead, Lt Cdr J S 61, 126
Woods, Cdr G A C 45
Woodward, Rear-Adm J F 25, 40, 42, 47, 55, 64, 67, 70, 115
Wreford-Brown, Cdr C L 39, 125
Wrega, Army, Sgt R H 111, 127
Wykes-Sneyd, Lt Cdr R J S 55, 126
Wyton, Britain 25, 37
Yates, Lt Cdr D H N 67
Yeovilton, Britain 25, 54,
York Bay, Falklands 17-18
"Yomping" by Royal Marines 87, 90-1, 95
Young RN, Capt B G 39, 42, 50, 125
"Zulu" time 9, 112

ARGENTINE AND BRITISH AIR, LAND AND SEA FORCES

Argentine Air Force (FAA)
Air Force 22, 24
GROUPS and AIRCRAFT
Grupo 1 (Transport) Hercules (also bombing and refuelling roles) and Boeing 707's (also reconnaissance) 18, 24, 50-1, 61, 71, 84, 86, 96-7, 119, 124
Grupo 1 (Photo-Recce, also used as pathfinders) Learjets 24, 82, 101, 124
Grupo 2 Canberras 24, 55-6, 60, 71, 92, 98, 101-2, 122, 124
Grupo 3 Pucara 24, 37-8, 55-6, 65, 71, 78, 88-9, 113, 121-5
Grupo 4 Skyhawks A-4Cs 24, 56, 61, 71, 78-9, 85-6, 91-2, 101, 118, 122-4
Grupo 5 Skyhawks A-4Bs 24, 56, 64-5, 71, 78-9, 82, 85-6, 91, 101-2, 118-20, 122-4
Grupo 6 Daggers 24, 55-6, 71, 78-9, 85-6, 91-2, 101, 117-20, 122-4
Grupo 7 Bell helicopters 38, 71, 113, 125
Grupo 8 Mirages 24, 55-6, 71, 122

Argentina Army
Army 22-3
BRIGADES
3rd Mechanised Inf 37-8
10th Motorised Inf 37-8
REGIMENTS
3rd Inf Regt 37-8, 112
4th Inf Regt 37-8, 105, 107
5th Inf Regt 37-8, 112
6th Inf Regt 37-8, 112
7th Inf Regt 37-8, 103, 108, 112
8th Inf Regt 37-8, 113
12th Inf Regt 37-8, 87-8
25th Inf Regt 37-8, 87-8, 112
OTHER UNITS
3rd Artillery Btn 38
9th Engineer Coy 38
181st Military Police and Intelligence Coy 38
601st Anti-Aircraft Btn 38, 87
Armoured Car Sqdn 38, 107

Argentine Army Aviation Command
Aviation Command 24

CAB 601 Agusta, Chinook, Iroquois and Puma helicopters 15-17, 24, 38, 61, 72, 77, 80, 82, 91-2, 113, 121-5

Argentine Coastguard (PNA)
Coastguard 23
Puma and Skyvan aircraft 23, 38, 60, 65, 72, 113, 122, 125
SHIPS
Islas Malvinas, patrol craft 18, 113, *attacked* 56
Rio Iguaza, patrol craft 18, *disabled* 73, 80-1

Argentine Marines
Marines 22-24
South Georgia 15-17
UNITS
2nd Marine Inf Btn 18, 23
5th Marine Inf Btn 37-8, 110, 112
Buzo Tactico 17-18, 23

Argentine Naval Aviation Command (CANA)
SQUADRONS and AIRCRAFT
1 Esc Aermacchis MB-339s 23, 60, 71, 78, 88, 113, 118, 122, 124-5
2 Esc Super Etendards 23, 47, 55-6, 60-1, 69, 71, 86, 92, 118-20
3 Esc Skyhawks 23, 71, 78-80, 82, 118, 123
4 Esc Mentors 23, 38, 65, 71, 122
CANA
1 Esc (Helicopters) Alouettes and Lynx 15-16, 23, 55-6, 122
2 Esc (Helicopters) Sea Kings 18, 23
Neptunes 61

Argentine Navy and Merchant Navy (see also Argentine Marines and Argentine Naval Aviation Command)
Argentine Navy 22-3, 47, 55-7, 60
Task Forces, *TF20* 23, *TF40* 18, 23, *TF60* 16, *TF79* 47, 55-6, 60
Task Groups, *TG40.1* 18, *TGs 79.1 & 2* 55, *TG 79.3* 55, *TG 79.4* 55
SHIPS
25 de Mayo, carrier 22-3, 40, 47, 55-6, 60
Alferez Sobral, patrol vessel 60, *damaged* 60, 73
Almirante Irizar, icebreaker 17-18, 22

Bahia Buen Suceso, fleet transport 14, 15, 18, 23, *disabled* 65-6, 73
Bahia Paraiso, icebreaker, later hospital ship 14, 15-16, 22, 94, 113
Cabo San Antonio, LST 17-18, 22
Comodoro Py, destroyer 22, 113
Drummond, frigate 16-17, 22-3
Formosa, merchantman 18
General Belgrano 22, *sunk* 19, 40, 54, 55-6, 72, 122, *survivors* 57, 60
Granville, frigate 16-17, 22-3
Guerrico, frigate 14, 16, 22, *damaged* 15-16
Hercules, destroyer 17, 22, 56
Hipolito Bouchard, destroyer 22, 55-6
Isla de los Estados, transport 17, 22, *sunk* 64-5, 72
Narwhal, trawler 54, *damaged and sunk* 60, 73
Piedra Buena, destroyer 22, 55-6
Punta Medanos, tanker 22
Rio Carcarana, merchantman 18, 79, *disabled* 65-6, *destroyed* 66, 73, 80, 82
Salta, submarine 47
San Luis, submarine 47, 55-6, 60, 64
Santa Fe, submarine 17-18, 22, 50-2, *disabled and captured* 51-2, 73
Santisima Trinidad, destroyer 17-18, 22, 56, 113, 122
Segui, destroyer 22
Yehuin, small oil rig tender 113

Army Air Corps, British
No 656 Sqn Gazelles and Scouts 34-5, 49, 58, 87, 96, 99, 121

British Army (see also Army Air Corps)
Ascension 43-4
BRIGADE
5th Infantry Bde 26, 33-4, 57, 63, 66, 82, 84, 92, 93, 96-7, 101, 112, 114
Brigade HQ 35, 101
INFANTRY BATTALIONS
1st Welsh Guards 26, 34, 84, 96-7, 98, 101-2, 107, 112, 114, *HQ Coy* 96-7, *2 Coy* 96-7
2nd Scots Guards 26, 34, 84, 96-7, 101-2, 110-11, 112, 114, *G Coy* 110, *Left Flank Coy* 110-11, *Right Flank Coy* 110-11
2nd Battalion The Parachute Regiment (2 Para) 26, 34, 49, 52, 58, 70, 74, 75-6, 80-1, 85, 87-90, 90, 92, 96-7, 101-2, 103, 105, 108-9, 110, 112, 114, 124, *Tac HQ* 89, *A Coy* 87-9, 108-9, *B Coy* 87-9, 96-7, 108-9, *C (Patrols) Coy* 87-9, 108-9, *D Coy* 87-9, 108-9
3rd Battalion The Parachute Regiment (3 Para) 26, 33-4, 41, 57, 70, 75-6, 80-1, 85, 87, 91, 95-6, 100, 103-4, 108, 112, 114, *Tac HQ* 103, *A Coy* 103-4, *B Coy* 103-4, *C Coy* 103, *D (Patrol) Coy* 103
1st Battalion, 7th Duke of Edinburgh's Own Gurkha Rifles 26, 34, 84, 96-7, 101-2, 110-11, 112, 114, *C Coy* 101-2, 111, *D Coy* 111, 112
1st Battalion, The Queen's Own Highlanders 114
ROYAL ARTILLERY
HQ 34
4 Field Regt 77, 96, *No 29 Bty* 34, 96, *No 97 Bty* 34
12 Air Defence Regt, T Bty 34, 74
29 Cdo Regt 33, 77, *No 7 Bty* 33, 90-1, 96, 106, 108, *No 8 Bty* 33, 87-8, 105, 108, *No 79 Bty* 33, 96, 103, *No 148 Bty* 50
32 Guided Weapons Regt 34

43 Air Defence Bty 34
148 Cdo Forward Observation Bty 33
ROYAL ENGINEERS
Ascension 43
Falklands 97
9 Para Sqdn 34-5
36 Engineer Regt 35, 96
49 EOD Sqdn 34
59 Independent Cdo Sqn 33, 87, 91,
Postal and Courier Regt 34, 45
SPECIAL AIR SERVICE
22 SAS Regt 34, 51, 60, 91, *D Sqn* 26, 34, 42, 47, 50, 54, 64-5, 70, 73, 74, 75-6, 78, 85-6, 90-1, 107, 122-3, *Boat Troop* 51, 65, *Mountain Troop* 51, *G Sqn* 26, 34, 47, 57, 70, 77
OTHER UNITS
B Sqn, The Blues and Royals 34, 76-7, 91, 96, *No 3 Troop* 96, 108-9, *No 4 Troop* 96, 110
Royal Army Medical Corps, 16 Field Ambulance 34-5, 101
Royal Army Ordnance Corps 34, 44
Royal Corps of Signals 34-5, 43, 97
Royal Corps of Transport 34-5, 44, *landing craft Antwerp and Arromanches* 116
Royal Electrical and Mechanical Engineers 35
Royal Military Police 35
Tactical Air Control parties 34

Commando Brigade Air Squadron, British
3 CBAS Gazelles and Scouts 26, 33, 41, 71, 75, 77, 87, 89, 91, 92, 98, 120-121

Fleet Air Arm, Royal Navy
Role 28
Ascension 44
Sea Harrier FRS.1 28
NAVAL AIR SQUADRONS and AIRCRAFT
No 737 Wessex 26, 29, 73, 121
No 800 Sea Harrier 26, 28, 41, 55-6, 61, 66, 68, 73, 78-80, 81-2, 86, 97, 101, 119-20, 122-4
No 801 Sea Harrier 26, 28, 41, 55-6, 61, 68, 73, 78, 82, 92, 97, 119, 121-124
No 809 Sea Harrier 26, 28, 53-4, 58, 68-9, 115
No 815 Lynx 26, 29, 42, 47, 51-2, 56, 60-1, 65-6, 73, 81-2, 85-6, 113, 120
No 820 Sea King 26, 29, 41, 55, 61, 97
No 824 Sea King 26, 29, 39-41, 62
No 825 Sea King 27, 29, 62, 84, 90-1, 95-6
No 826 Sea King 26, 29, 41, 55, 60, 65, 69, 92, 120
No 829 Wasp 16, 26, 29, 51-2, 67, 73, 94, 113
No 845 Wessex 26, 29, 41-2, 46-7, 49, 53, 57-8, 62, 75, 119
No 846 Sea King 26, 29, 40-1, 47, 50, 53, 57, 58, 61, 65, 67, 69-70, 75-7, 88, 91, 115, 119-20
No 847 Wessex 27, 29, 62, 95-6, 100, 102
No 848 Wessex 26, 29, 49, 58, 62, 120
No 899 Sea Harrier 28

Merchant Navy, British Ships Taken Up From Trade
Role 31
Conversions 31
SHIPS
Alvega, tanker 26, 32, 57-8, 117
Anco Charger, tanker 26, 32, 49, 117
Astronomer, helicopter carrier and repair ship 32, 98, 116-7
Atlantic Causeway, helicopter support ship 27, 32, 62, 66,

137

84, 91, 95-6, 117
Atlantic Conveyor, aircraft and helicopter support ship 26, 29, 31, 37, 49, 54, 57-8, 69-70, 86, 114, *lost* 71, 85-7, 119-20, *survivors* 84
Avelona Star, refrigerated stores ship 32, 98, 117
Balder London, tanker 27, 32, 62-3, 117
Baltic Ferry, transport 26, 32, 35, 57-8, 66, 84, 95-6, 117
British Avon, tanker 32, 52-3, 82, 92, 98, 117
British Dart, tanker 32, 49, 99
British Enterprise III, dispatch vessel 32, 83, 117
British Esk, tanker 32, 41, 61, 82, 98, 117
British Tamar, tanker 32, 46, 63, 66, 117
British Tay, tanker 32, 41, 84, 98, 117
British Test, tanker 32, 41, 98-9
British Trent, tanker 32, 46, 98, 117
British Wye, tanker 32, 49, *attacked* 84, 119
Canberra, transport/troopship 26, 31, 41, 57-8, 69-70, 75, 77, 81, 84, 85, 87, 91, 95-6, 113, 114, 116
Contender Bezant, aircraft and helicopter carrier 27, 32, 37, 66-7, 92, 98, 117
Cordella, trawler as minesweepers 26, 32, 53, 116
Eburna, tanker 26, 32, 57-8, 117
Elk, transport 26, 31, 41, 49, 57-8, 69-70, 87, 92, 95, 116
Europic Ferry, transport 26, 31, 49, 69-70, 75, 87, 95, 116
Farnella, trawler as minesweepers 26, 32, 53, 116
Fort Toronto, water tanker 26, 32, 49, 117
G A Walker, tanker 32, 98, 116-7
Geestport, refrigerated stores ship 27, 32, 66-7, 99, 117
Iris, cable ship as despatch vessel 26, 32, 53, 84, 94, 117
Irishman, ocean tug 26, 32, 41, 49, 84, 86, 117
Junella, trawler as minesweepers 26, 32, 53, 116
Laertes, ammunition ship 32, 98, 117
Lycaon, ammunition ship 26, 32, 57-8, 84, 99, 117
Nordic Ferry, transport 26, 32, 35, 57-8, 66, 84, 95-6, 114, 117
Norland, transport 26, 31, 52-3, 58, 69-70, 75-6, 81, 84, 85, 87, 90-1, 95-6, 98, 113, 114, 117
Northella, trawler as minesweepers 26, 32, 53, 116
Pict, trawler as minesweepers 26, 32, 53, 116
Queen Elizabeth 2, transport/troopship 26, 31, 35, 62-3, 66, 84, 92, 98, 114
St Edmund, transport/troopship 27, 32, 66-7, 98, 113, 117
St Helena, cargo vessel as minesweeper support ship 32, 98, 114, 116
Salvageman, ocean tug 26, 32, 41, 49, 58, 63, 113, 117
Saxonia, refrigerated stores ship 26, 32, 57-8, 67, 99
Scottish Eagle, tanker 32, 83, 99, 117
Stena Inspector repair ship 32, 92-3, 117
Stena Seaspread, repair ship 26, 32, 46, 63, 67, 84, 93, 117
Tor Caledonia, transport 27, 32, 66-7, 98, 117
Uganda, hospital ship 26, 32, 48-9, 63, 67, 84, 114, 117
Wimpey Seahorse, mooring vessel 27, 32, 62-3, 82, 99, 117
Yorkshireman, ocean tug 26, 32, 46, 84, 117

Royal Air Force
Role 35-7
Ascension 43
RAF Regiment 26, 36, *HQ Unit 3 Wing* 36, 43, *Field Flight 15 Sqn* 36, 43
SQUADRONS and AIRCRAFT
No 1(F) Harrier 26, 36-7, 43, 54, 57-8, 68-9, 74, 77-8, 82, 87-9, 91, 92, 95, 98, 100, 102, 115, 120-2
No 10 VC10 25, 35-36, 39-40, 44, 114-5

No 18 Chinook 25-6, 36-7, 43, 49, 57, 67, 85-6, 91, 92, 97, 98, 120
Nos 24, 30, 47 and 70 Hercules 25, 35, 37, 39-40, 44, 115
No 29(F) Phantom 25-6, 36, 43, 82, 115
No 42(TB) Nimrod 25, 36, 41-2
Nos 44, 50 and 101 Vulcan 25-6, 37, 44, 53, 55, 57, 63, 82, 92, 96-7, 98, 101-2, 115
No 51 Nimrod 37
Nos 55 and 57 Victor 25-6, 36-7, 44, 46-7, 51, 54, 55, 57, 82, 115
Nos 120, 201 and 206 Nimrod 25, 36-7, 43-4, 46-7, 63, 66, 115
No 202 Sea King 26, 36, 43, 57
OTHER AIRCRAFT
Belfast freighters 36
Boeing 707 36
Other chartered 44

Royal Fleet Auxiliary
Role 29, 81
Replenishment at sea 29
SHIPS
Appleleaf, support tanker 26, 30, 39-40, 116
Bayleaf, support tanker 26, 30, 52-3, 117
Blue Rover, small fleet tanker 26, 30, 46, 59, 94, 95, 116
Brambleleaf, support tanker 26, 30, 41-2, 51, 63, 66, 117
Engadine, helicopter support ship 27, 30, 62, 82, 94, 95, 102, 116,
Fort Austin, fleet replenishment ship 26, 29, 39-40, 42, 47, 49, 60, 65, 69-70, 75-6, 81, 95, 98, 114, 117
Fort Grange, fleet replenishment ship 27, 29, 62-3, 82, 93, 95, 117
Olmeda, fleet tanker 26, 30, 40-1, 60, 65, 69, 95, 98, 113, 116-7
Olna, fleet tanker 26, 30, 62, 84, 95, 115, 117
Olwen, fleet tanker 30, 116-7
Pearleaf, support tanker 26, 30, 40-1, 94, 116
Plumleaf, support tanker 26, 30, 48-9, 116
Regent, fleet replenishment ship 26, 29, 48-9, 63, 69, 95, 99, 117
Resource, fleet replenishment ship 26, 29, 40-1, 47, 60, 65, 69, 75, 81, 94, 95, 116
Sir Bedivere, LSL 26, 30, 52-3, 67, 81, 95, 116-7, *damaged* 71, 86, 118
Sir Galahad, LSL 26, 30, 40-1, 69, 75-6, 95, 101, 114, *damaged, later* lost 71-2, 85-6, 100-1, 118-9, *survivors* 98
Sir Geraint, LSL 26, 30, 40-1, 69, 75-6, 95, 116
Sir Lancelot, LSL 26, 30, 40-1, 69, 75-6, 95, 116, *damaged* 71, 85-6, 92, 118
Sir Percivale, LSL 26, 30, 40-1, 69, 75-6, 95-6, 116
Sir Tristram, LSL 26, 30, 39-40, 47, 69, 75-6, 95, 101, 117, *disabled* 72, 100-1, 119, *survivors* 98
Stromness, stores support ship 26, 29, 40-1, 57, 69-70, 75-6, 81, 84, 85, 91, 95, 114, 116
Tidepool, fleet tanker 26, 30, 49, 52, 57, 69, 95, 117
Tidespring, fleet tanker 26, 30, 39-40, 47, 50-2, 54, 58, 62-3, 67, 84, 95, 116-7, 119

Royal Marines (see also Commando Brigade Air Squadron)
Role and equipment 33
Naval Party 8901 16-17, 40, 47, 112
South Georgia 15-17
Falklands and Stanley 17-18

BRIGADE
Role 33
3 Commando Bde 26, 40, 44, 53, 57, 67, 70, 75, 80-1,
  85-6, 90, 95-6, 102, 110, 112, 114
Brigade HQ 33, 41, 48, 75, 81, 85, 92, 96, 101-2
Brigade Maintenance Area 75, 77, 91,
COMMANDOS
40 Commando 26, 33, 41, 57, 70, 75-6, 80-1, 85, 90-1,
  95-6, 98, 102, 114, *A Coy* 101-2, 106, 112, *B Coy* 48, 91,
  101-2, 112, *C Coy* 48, 101-2, 106, 112
42 Commando 26, 33, 41, 57, 70, 75-7, 80-1, 85-6, 87, 91,
  96, 100, 106-8, 110, 112, 114, *Tac HQ* 91, *J Coy* 18, 33,
  89, 90-1, 95-6, 106-7, 112, *K Coy* 48, 90-1, 95-6, 106-8,
  L Coy 48, 85, 87, 90-1, 95-6, 106-8, *M Coy* 26, 42, 47,
  50-2, 99, 113, 114
45 Commando 26, 33, 40, 48, 58, 70, 75-6, 80-1, 85, 87,
  90-1, 95-6, 100, 105-6, 112, 114, *X Coy* 105, 114, *Y Coy*
  105-6, 114, *Z Coy* 70, 76, 105-6
OTHER UNITS
1st Raiding Sqdn 33
Air Defence Troop 33, 87, 124
Cdo Logistics Regt 33, 75, 91, 96
Commando Forces Band 33
Mountain and Arctic Warfare Cadre 33, 80-1, 85, 95-6, 105,
  110
Signal Sqdn 33
Special Boat Squadron (SBS) 25-6, 33, 40-1, 47, 51, 57,
  60-1, 66, 69, 75-6, 81, 85-6, *No 2 Section* 33, 50, 54
Tactical Air Control Parties 33
Y Signals Troop 33

Royal Maritime Auxiliary Service
SHIPS
Goosander, mooring, salvage and boom vessel 26, 31, 53,
  66, 116
Typhoon, ocean tug 26, 31, 39-40, 49, 58, 99, 117

Royal Navy
Role 27, 81
Ascension 44
Nuclear submarines 36, 42
LCUs 53, 70, 72, 75-6, 91, 96-7, 100-1
LCVPs 76, 96
UNITS
1st Flotilla 40
11th MCMS 53, 84
Royal Navy Surgical Support Teams 33, 77
NAVAL PARTIES
1222, Ascension Island 44
1710, Canberra 41
1720, Elk 41
1730, British Tamar 46
1740, British Esk 41
1750, Fort Toronto 49
1760, Salvageman 41
1770, Irishman 41
1780, Yorkshireman 46
1790, British Test 41
1800, British Dart 49
1810, Stena Seaspread 46
1820, RMAS Typhoon 39
1830, Uganda 49
1840, Atlantic Conveyor 49
1850, Norland 53
1860, Europic Ferry 49
1870, Iris 53
1900, Lycaon 58
1910, Saxonia 58
1920, Geestport 67
1930, Goosander 53
1950, Nordic Ferry 58
1960, Baltic Ferry 58
1980, Queen Elizabeth 2 62
1990, Atlantic Causeway 62
2000, Wimpey Seahorse 62
2020, Tor Caledonia 67
2040, Scottish Eagle 83
2050, Contender Bezant 67
2060, St. Edmund 67
2090, British Enterprise III 83
9801 – see Royal Marines
SHIPS
Active, frigate 26, 28, 62, 66, 84, 95, 110, 116
Alacrity, frigate 26, 28, 40-1, 55-6, 60-1, 64-6, 69, 86, 93,
  98, 114, *damaged* 55-6, 72, 117
Amazon, frigate 117
Ambuscade, frigate 26, 28, 57-8, 67, 86, 95, 108, 116
Andromeda, frigate 26, 28, 62, 84, 95, 115, 117
Antelope, frigate 26, 28, 40-1, 53, 58, 63, 66, 67, 73, 81-2,
  114, 123, *damaged and sunk* 72, 81-2, 118, *survivors* 81,
  84, 98
Antrim, destroyer 26, 28, 39-40, 42, 47, 50-2, 54, 58,
  69-70, 73, 75, 78, 81, 84, 85, 92, 94, 116-7, *damaged* 72,
  76, 78-9, 118
Apollo, frigate 116-7
Ardent, frigate 26, 28, 48-9, 67, 69-70, 73, 75-6, 78, 81,
  114, 123, *lost* 71-2, 76, 78-80, 118, *survivors* 77, 84, 98
Argonaut, frigate 26, 28, 48-9, 69-70, 81, 86, 93, 98, 114,
  123, *damaged* 71-2, 76, 78-9, 92, 118
Ariadne, frigate 117
Arrow, frigate 26, 28, 39-40, 56, 60-1, 64-5, 69, 81, 87-8,
  95, 116, *damaged* 55-6, 72, 117
Avenger, frigate 26, 28, 62, 84, 92, 95, 103, 110, 113, 117,
  124
Bacchante, frigate 116-7
Battleaxe, frigate 117
Birmingham, destroyer 116-7
Brazen, frigate 117
Brecon, MCMS 98, 115
Brilliant, frigate 26, 28, 39-40, 50-2, 54, 55-6, 60-1, 64-5,
  69-70, 73, 81-2, 84, 86, 95, 116, 122, *slightly damaged*
  72, 76, 79, 118
Bristol, destroyer 26, 28, 62, 84, 95, 115, 117
Britannia, Royal Yacht 98
Broadsword, frigate 26, 28, 40-1, 55, 60-1, 64-5, 69-70, 73,
  78, 81-2, 86, 95, 115-6, 123, *damaged* 72, 76, 78-9, 118-9
Cardiff, destroyer 26, 28, 62, 84, 95, 97, 102, 113, 116, 121
Charybdis, frigate 117
Conqueror, nuclear submarine 25, 27, 39-40, 51, 54, 55,
  72, 87, 98, 116
Courageous, nuclear submarine 25, 27, 57-8, 63, 116
Coventry, destroyer 26, 28, 39-40, 55, 60-1, 64-5, 69, 73,
  81, 85-6, 114, 122, 124, *sunk* 72, 85-6, 119-20, *survivors*
  84, 98
Danae, frigate 116-7
Diomede, frigate 116-7
Dumbarton Castle, fishery protection vessel as dispatch
  vessel 26, 28, 53, 63, 94, 116
Endurance, ice patrol vessel 15-17, 26, 28, 39-40, 47,

139

49-51, 52, 58, 67, 73, 84, 99, 113, 116
Exeter, destroyer 26, 28, 57-8, 67, 73, 92, 95, 102, 116, 124
Fearless, assault ship 26, 27, 40-1, 47, 57-8, 69-70, 73, 75-6, 84, 86, 91-2, 95-7, 101, 115-6, 123-4; *LCU F4 lost* 72, 100-1, 119
Glamorgan, destroyer 26, 28, 39-40, 42, 47, 56, 60-1, 65, 69, 95, 105, 116, *damaged* 55-6, 72, 100, 102, 117, 119, 121
Glasgow, destroyer 26, 28, 39-40, 55, 60, 64-5, 69, 84, 93, 98, 117, *damaged* 64-5, 72, 114, 118
Hecate, survey ship as ice patrol vessel 117
Hecla, survey ship as ambulance ship 26, 28, 48-9, 63, 67, 84, 94, 116
Herald, survey ship as ambulance ship 26, 28, 48-9, 84, 94, 116
Hermes, carrier 26, 27-8, 37, 40-1, 47, 55-7, 60-1, 65, 68-9, 73, 77-8, 87, 92, 95, 98, 100, 102, 115-6, 119-21
Hydra, survey ship as ambulance ship 26, 28, 48-9, 67, 84, 94, 117
Illustrious, carrier 115, 117
Intrepid, assault ship 26, 27, 52-3, 58, 69-70, 73, 75-6, 91, 95-7, 115-6, 124
Invincible, carrier 26, 27-8, 40-1, 55-6, 60, 65, 68-9, 73, 78, 92, 95, 115, 117, 119, 121
Ledbury, MCMS 98-9, 115-7
Leeds Castle, fishery protection vessel as dispatch vessel 26, 28, 53, 63, 67, 84, 116

Liverpool, destroyer 117
Minerva, frigate 26, 28, 62, 84, 95, 97, 116-7
Newcastle, destroyer 117
Onyx, submarine 25, 27, 52-3, 69, 116
Penelope, frigate 26, 28, 62, 84, 95-6, 117
Phoebe, frigate 117
Plymouth, frigate 26, 28, 39-40, 50-2, 54, 55, 58, 69-70, 73, 76, 78-9, 81, 92, 95, 116, 123, *damaged* 72, 100-1, 119
Sheffield, destroyer 26, 28, 39-40, 55, 57-8, 61, 114, *hit and lost* 19, 60-1, 64-5, 71, 118, *survivors* 61, 82
Sirius, frigate 117
Southampton, destroyer 116-7
Spartan, nuclear submarine 25, 27, 39-40, 47, 55, 116
Splendid, nuclear submarine 25, 27, 39-40, 55, 84, 98, 114
Tiger Bay, ex-PNA patrol craft 113
Valiant, nuclear submarine 25, 27, 57-8, 63, 116
Yarmouth, frigate 26, 28, 40-1, 55-6, 60-1, 64-5, 69-70, 72, 76, 78-80, 81-2, 86, 92, 95, 98, 106, 108, 113, 116, 124

Ships and Aircraft, Falkland Islands and neutral
Falkland Sound, ex-Argentine small oil rig tender 113
Forrest, coaster 18-19, 81, 113
Hercules, US-registered tanker 98
Islander, light aircraft, *damaged* 56
Monsunen, coaster 19, 111, 113, *damaged* 72, 80-1

CPSIA information can be obtained
at www.ICGtesting.com
Printed in the USA
BVHW08s1734080718
521074BV00001B/3/P